PROVERBS

Readings: A New Biblical Commentary

General Editor
John Jarick

PROVERBS

Alan Moss

SHEFFIELD PHOENIX PRESS
2015

Copyright © 2015 Sheffield Phoenix Press

Published by Sheffield Phoenix Press
Department of Biblical Studies, University of Sheffield
Sheffield S3 7QB

www.sheffieldphoenix.com

A CIP catalogue record for this book
is available from the British Library

Typeset by CA Typesetting Ltd
Printed on acid-free paper by Lightning Source

ISBN-13 978-1-909697-45-4 (hardback)
ISBN-13 978-1-909697-46-1 (paperback)

Contents

Preface

Having now written this commentary on the book of Proverbs, I am aware that I have been given the opportunity to examine how the perennial task of educating the next generation might have been understood in the Bible itself. The book stems from my interest in Proverbs going back many years. While studying at the Gregorian University in the 1980s, I was able to take the semester course on the book of Proverbs given by the late Fr Alonso Schökel SJ in the Pontifical Biblical Institute. On returning to Australia, I completed my doctoral thesis on Proverbs' Personified Wisdom texts at the University of Queensland. For the opportunity to write on Proverbs for the Readings series, I wish to thank first of all John Jarick, the series editor, for accepting my proposal. I am particularly grateful to him for his trust, patience, and ever gracious encouragement, and to Sheffield Phoenix Press, for allowing me the time I needed, quite unusual, I am sure, to complete the undertaking. I began to write the commentary while still a full-time staff member of the School of Theology of the Australian Catholic University, and my colleagues and former colleagues, and I include the librarians of the University's Brisbane campus, have provided the supportive context and practical help such a writing project requires. I wish to gratefully acknowledge that Professor Pauline Allen, of the University's Centre for Early Christian Studies, encouraged me to offer to write for the Readings series, and she has given generous assistance and wise counsel throughout the entire process. I am grateful to the University for providing a semester study leave though my secondment to the Institute for Advanced Research in semester two 2005, and I thank Dinah Joesoef and Cara Powdrell for assistance in formatting and editing. Finally, I thank my religious Brothers of the now Oceania Province of the Christian Brothers for their unfailing support in this, as in all my other endeavours in biblical scholarship.

Alan Moss CFC
October 2013

Abbreviations

AB	Anchor Bible
ABD	David Noel Freedman (ed.), *The Anchor Bible Dictionary* (New York: Doubleday, 1992)
Bib	*Biblica*
BZAW	Beihefte zur *ZAW*
CCC	Crossway Classic Commentaries
DBI	Leland Ryken, James C. Wilhoit, and Tremper Longman III (eds.), *Dictionary of Biblical Imagery* (Downers Grove, IL: InterVarsity Press, 1998)
EDB	David Noel Freedman, Allen C. Myers and Astrid B. Beck (eds.), *Eerdmans Dictionary of the Bible* (Grand Rapids, MI: Eerdmans, 2000)
HeyJ	*Heythrop Journal*
ICC	International Critical Commentary
IDB	George Arthur Buttrick (ed.), *The Interpreter's Dictionary of the Bible* (4 vols.; Nashville: Abingdon Press, 1962).
Int	*Interpretation*
JBL	*Journal of Biblical Literature*
JSOT	*Journal for the Study of the Old Testament*
JSOTSup	*Journal for the Study of the Old Testament, Supplement Series*
NAB	New American Bible
NCB	New Century Bible
NICOT	New International Commentary on the Old Testament
NJB	New Jerusalem Bible
NRSV	New Revised Standard Version
OTL	Old Testament Library
OTM	Old Testament Message
RB	*Revue biblique*
RivB	*Rivista biblica*
RSV	Revised Standard Version
Sanh.	*Sanhedrin*
SB	Sources bibliques
VT	*Vetus Testamentum*

Introduction

'The proverbs of Solomon son of David, king of Israel' (1.1) is presented as an educational text, written in figurative language, with the purpose of instructing the youth of Israel in wisdom and the fear of Yahweh (1.2-7). This commentary represents an attempt to understand Proverbs, in its final form, as such a text. As acquiring an understanding of the imagery is the intended method of instruction, the commentary will be mainly concerned with discussing the book's educational impact through an examination of the imagery. Rhetorically and topically, the book comprises five sections. The longer poems that make up the first nine chapters are in the form of second-person instructions delivered by a father, sometimes referred to in the commentary as the parent, and there are occasional references in the instructions to the mother's teaching as well, to a son or sons (child or children, NRSV).[1] The book title, 'the proverbs of Solomon' (1.1), is resumed in 10.1 as the title of the second section of the book (10.1–22.16). Here the proverb has the form of the antithetical bi-colon, a saying comprising two parallel half-verses, normally in the third person, though occasionally the bi-colon has the form of second-person address to an audience. The third section (22.17–24.34) comprises 'the words of the wise' (22.17–24.22), and additional sayings attributed to the wise (24.23-34), and in the commentary the section as a whole will be named 'the words of the wise'. Here the parental instructions resume, though in smaller units than in chs. 1–9. Both topically and rhetorically, the second collection of Solomon's proverbs (25.1–29.27), those transmitted by King Hezekiah's officials (25.1), fall into two parts. In the first part (chs. 25–27), synthetic parallelism is normal, and the use of figurative language more pronounced. Antithetical parallelism resumes in chs. 28–29, where many proverbs are reflections on the challenge of maintaining wisdom and righteousness in a society where oppression and injustice most often prevail. Finally the longer poems resume in chs. 30–31, which, as I will suggest, comprise firstly Agur's extended reflection on his experience in maintaining faith in Yahweh's just ordering of a world where greed and

---

1. The NRSV is cited throughout, unless otherwise indicated.

injustice are evident (30.1-33). Then a queen-mother instructs her son on his royal duty to defend the powerless of society (31.1-9), and the book and the last section conclude with an enthusiastic portrait of a model wife and mother (31.10-31).

Most attention is given in this volume to the context of the passages within the book sections, and within the whole unfolding educational text. Proverbs has a canonical context as well, which I have endeavoured to illustrate in my discussion of the Proverbs imagery, where comparisons with Torah, prophets and other writings are often drawn. A particular canonical comparison can be made in regard to some of the instructional imagery in the parental instructions in chs. 1–9, for example, which evokes the language of Deuteronomy's injunction on Israelite parents to train their children diligently in the divine commands (Deut. 6.4-9). The many similarities between Proverbs and Deuteronomy as educational texts have been demonstrated by Weinfeld (Weinfeld 1972: 228-306). In this commentary such comparisons are made only in view of illustrating where Proverbs may be compared with the other canonical literature. The view taken is that the worldview of Proverbs, with its attention to human experience, and the minimal imagery of a special revelation to the people of Israel, is complementary to much of the other biblical literature, while being integral to, and at home within the canon. (For a record of the scholarly discussion of the relation of the worldview of Proverbs to 'covenantal Yahwism', see Adams 2008: 77-83.) In the following commentary on the completed text, there is little attempt to situate Proverbs' texts in their ancient Near Eastern context, although an exception is made in the case of the sayings in 'the words of the wise' that are similar to the Egyptian *Instruction of Amenemope*. A reference to that work often sheds light on the imagery peculiar to this part of Proverbs, which is commonly considered to derive from the Egyptian instruction.

The conspicuous imagery relating to both father and mother in the educational enterprise is noted throughout this book, and the terms 'father-son' are consistently referred to the household father, the family head, who, along with the mother, are educating their son. While the expression 'my child' is reproduced in the citations of the NRSV, the implied audience is often a youth about to assume adult responsibilities. The scope and audience of Proverbs have been extended beyond the family and household setting, however, through the identification, throughout Proverbs, of the parental teaching with wisdom teaching, and the introduction of a personified Woman Wisdom, who on one level represents the parental teaching. Both parents and personified Wisdom, through the 'son', exhort all who would succeed in life to seek wisdom beyond all other desirable goals. In the parental instructions in chs. 1–9, but also in 'the words of the wise', the attainment of wisdom is associated with a fully human life, in terms of living in the fear of Yahweh and moral rectitude, and the attendant benefits of health, longevity, wealth, and social renown. These benefits are promised to youths who have learned to find the appropriate expression of their sexuality, to live temperately, spend prudently, and to value the long-term outcome of living wisely above the attraction of quick and easy wealth. In both sections of 'the proverbs of Solomon' (10.1–22.16; 25.1–29.27), where the scenario broadens beyond the household setting to society at large, including the royal court, the continuation of father-son and mother-son images in relation to education to wisdom allows us to understand the wise ones who composed and gathered this material to be again promoters of, and mouthpieces for parental education. In the words of Michael V. Fox, 'Prov. 1–9 introduces and tells us how to read the rest of the book' (Fox 2000: 6). In the sections of proverbs (10.1–22.16; 25.1–29.27), it is reiterated that, despite the present evident prosperity of deceivers and unscrupulous oppressors, a youth, and indeed all who would succeed in life, need to be convinced that in the end justice will prevail, and that choices of righteousness, generosity, and care of the poor will be vindicated. Finally, it is not a courtier or schoolmaster who instructs a prince on the duties of kingship, but a queen-mother (31.1).

Reading Proverbs as an educational text expressed in figurative language raises the question of the relationship of such a reading to the text's original date, authorship and addressees, and social setting. Much of the material in Proverbs may have been composed and catalogued into collections before the exile. A plausible chronology is sketched by Clifford, who writes that 25.1 states that officials of King Hezekiah (715–687 BCE) added to an already existing collection under King Solomon's name, that is to all or part of the proverbs in 10.1–22.16. The dependence of 'the words of the wise' on an Egyptian instruction also suggests a date during the monarchy for the composition of this central section of Proverbs. At some stage difficult to define, chs. 1–9 were written and prefaced to the anthology. Adams notes that both chs. 1–9 and 31 may have been added to previous collections as a framing device (Adams 2008: 66). Having carefully surveyed the evidence, Clifford concludes that the final editing of the book took place in the Second Temple period, along with other works of Israel's sacred literature, between the sixth and fourth centuries BCE (Clifford 1999: 3-6).

The book in its entirety, including the parental instructions, is in this commentary attributed to the wise men of Israel. Historically speaking, Fox suggests that chs. 10–29 represent the work of 'learned clerks', who collected, created, and reshaped these sayings. They would have been engaged in the royal administration, and after that, in the postexilic provincial administration. The longer poems in chs. 1–9 and 30–31 were the work of later authors (Fox 2000: 11). On the question of schools in Israel, Adams finds compelling reasons for the existence of schools as early as the era of the monarchy, that is, 'royal and priestly authorities set up institutions or programmes for the mastery of scribal and other tasks, and Hebrew' (Adams 2008: 72). Nonetheless, there is no clear evidence for the use of Proverbs in such schools. As Clifford points out, the teacher in Proverbs is not a school teacher but a father (mother also in 1.8 and 6.20), an identity that is especially evident in 4.3-4 (Clifford 1999: 7), and that the final form of the text does not read as a manual for aspiring officials. Proverbs then will be considered to be a book of parental wisdom teaching, composed for the education of selected youths in Israel. Through the parental and wisdom imagery, however, the book's audience has been enlarged, and may be presented for the consideration of all who would be wise in any generation.

Proverbs 1.1–9.18: Title and Preface, Parental Instructions, and Discourses of Personified Wisdom

Title and Preface (1.1-7)

> The proverbs of Solomon son of David, king of Israel. (1.1)

> He also uttered three thousand proverbs; and his songs were a thousand and five. He spoke of trees, from the cedar that is in Lebanon to the hyssop that grows out of the wall; he spoke also of beasts, and of birds, and of reptiles, and of fish. And men came from all peoples to hear the wisdom of Solomon, and from all the kings of the earth, who had heard of his wisdom (1 Kgs 4.32-34).

'The proverbs of Solomon' is an attribution of the book of Proverbs to the king of Israel renowned both for his wisdom and for his proverbs. In Proverbs, however, the notion of Solomon's authorship and the addressees differ from those in 1 Kings. There the proverbs were an expression of one man's unique, Yahweh-given wisdom (1 Kgs 3.12). In Proverbs, notwithstanding the title's attribution to Solomon, numerous other wise ones have contributed to the book. Two sections are referred to a group of wise ones (22.17; 24.23), and the wisdom of Agur (30.1-9) and Lemuel (31.1-9) are included. In 1 Kings, Solomon's wisdom was admired, but not equalled, by all the kings and peoples of the earth, while in Proverbs wisdom can and must be communicated to others, namely the next generation, the youth of Israel (1.4). In 1 Kings, Solomon's sayings refer to plants and animals (1 Kgs 4.33). While Proverbs contains some plant and animal imagery (5.19; 6.6-8; 23.5; 30.24-31), such expressions are intended to illustrate human behaviour. Finally, unlike the above description of Solomon's wisdom, wisdom in Proverbs is religious, being linked to an attitude of the fear of Yahweh (1.7). In short, 'Solomon's proverbs' in the title serves to link a book offering a training in wisdom (1.2) with the figure of Solomon in 1 Kings 3–5, with his proverbs, and his reputation for wisdom. The title 'the proverbs of Solomon' also heads two sections within the book (10.1–22.16;

25.1–29.27), comprising mostly third-person sayings, structured as two half-verses in parallel. These two sections make up more than half the book's contents. The rest of the book, chs. 1–9; 22.17–24.34; 30.1-33; 31.1-31, comprises longer poems. The word 'proverbs' in the title includes these longer poems as well as the two sections of 'the proverbs of Solomon'.

The preface (1.2-7) as a whole declares that the book has an educational aim. Its audience are principally the young, but the mature may also learn from it. It offers training in wisdom, which is then defined in its intellectual, ethical, and religious dimensions, while an understanding of the book's poetic expression will also be imparted.

> For learning about wisdom and instruction,
> for understanding words of insight,
> for gaining instruction in wise dealing,
> righteousness, justice, and equity;
> to teach shrewdness to the simple,
> knowledge and prudence to the young—
> let the wise also hear and gain in learning,
> and the discerning acquire skill,
> to understand a proverb and a figure,
> the words of the wise and their riddles.
> The fear of the LORD is the beginning of knowledge;
> fools despise wisdom and instruction (1.2-7).

First, the subject-matter is mentioned. Wisdom (1.2), that is, the knowledge of what is wise, and the ability to put that knowledge into practice, is a major concept in the book's thematic organization. In the first section, chs. 1–9, a series of twelve parental instructions exhort a youth, the son in the family, occasionally the sons (5.7; 7.24), to become wise, and so be protected from the enticements of greed for gain and sexual intemperance (e.g. 1.8-19; 5.1-23). These chapters also include a beatitude, extolling the one who attains the fullness of life through wisdom (3.13-20), and two discourses in which personified Lady Wisdom sings her own praises (8.1-36) and summons the simple to her life-giving banquet (9.1-6). Lady Wisdom also delivers a threatening discourse to those who have disregarded her call (1.20-33). Wisdom is the topic of numerous third-person couplets in 'the proverbs of Solomon' (e.g., 10.1, 8, 14). 'The words of the wise' (22.17–24.34) include a father's wisdom instructions (e.g. 23.15, 19, 22-25), and a poem illustrating what wise ones can achieve (24.3-7). In the second section of 'the proverbs of Solomon' (25.1–29.27), the exhortation of a wise father to his son, found at the centre of this section (27.11), provides rhetorical and thematic continuity with the previous sections. The book concludes with the praises of a woman who may be regarded as a paragon of the wisdom the book extols (31.10-31). The term 'instruction' (*mûsār*, 1.2) may refer to the content of the teaching (1.8), but instruction may also suggest the process of education (15.33), which includes discipline and reproof (13.1). The preface makes it clear that wisdom has a practical, ethical dimension, defined in terms of wise dealing, righteousness, justice and equity (1.3). Wise dealing is practical understanding, or prudence, and may refer to a whole way of life (21.16). The three abstract terms righteousness, justice, and equity recur in 2.9, and together they suggest the strong ethical character of Hebrew wisdom. In practice, righteousness is a quality of a judge's ruling (31.9), or of any witness' testimony (12.17). Justice is the particular act or decision made in righteousness (13.23), while equity or rectitude suggests in broadest terms a respect for a created order, which tempers self-interest.

The principal addressees are the inexperienced 'simple' ones (1.4), that is, youths as yet uncommitted to the pursuit of wisdom. They are gullible (14.15), yet able to be educated (19.25). They are just as likely to choose folly as wisdom (7.7; 27.12), and so they are in a perilous state, and they need to choose wisdom urgently (1.32; 8.5). The preface also gently invites the wise, that is, other teachers to profit from reading this book.

Next are named the literary forms in which the wise teaching will be expressed. Proverbs, figures, riddles are difficult to define separately. In Hab. 2.6, the terms, at the least, designate the poetry of the following oracle, so that proverb, figure, and riddles taken together indicate that wisdom teaching will be expressed in various kinds of figurative language, which requires intelligent interpretation.

Finally, the wisdom offered to Israel's youth, besides being ethical, will be essentially religious, being inseparable from the attitude of the fear of Yahweh (1.7a). There is no wisdom without a realistic appraisal of one's place in the world of Yahweh's creation (8.22-31), so that wisdom is linked with humility (8.13), and a healthy respect for the established authority (24.21). The preface concludes (1.7b) with an antithesis that pervades the book, referring to a tension between those who choose to live by wisdom and those who reject it. The latter are designated as fools, and so the audience is presented with the need to choose. The first nine chapters lay down the terms of that choice, and provide earnest encouragement to make it.

First Parental Instruction: On Life-Threatening Greed for Wealth (1.8-19)

The first of the twelve instructions in chs.1–9 is presented as the advice of both parents to their son (child, NRSV). Throughout Proverbs, even though but one parent speaks the words of advice (1.8), both the father and mother are concerned with the upbringing and education of the children. The mother is engaged with the younger children (4.3), and, while the father alone is occasionally specified as the teacher (4.1), the mother's teaching role is also recalled (6.20; 31.1, 26). It will appear that the parents' involvement in their children's education is on a deeply personal level, and they are both affected by the outcome, for good or ill (10.1; 23.22; 31.28). The simple one, referred to in the preface as the book's principle audience (1.4), is, in the parental instructions of chs. 1–9, a son, one still within his parents' household. In the introductory claim for the child's attention, parental advice is presented as very attractive, being compared to the personal adornments which would enhance any youth's appearance.

> Hear, my child, your father's instruction,
> and do not reject your mother's teaching;
> for they are a fair garland for your head,
> and pendants for your neck (1.8-9).

Having gained the youth's attention and interest, the teacher comes to the point of the address, repeating 'my son' (1.10), and warning an apparently naïve and gullible young person about a seductive, ultimately fatal invitation, seeming to come from a band of violent men.

> My child, if sinners entice you,
> do not consent.
> If they say, 'Come with us, let us lie in wait for blood;
> let us wantonly ambush the innocent;
> like Sheol let us swallow them alive
> and whole, like those who go down to the Pit.
> We shall find all kinds of costly things;
> we shall fill our houses with booty.
> Throw in your lot among us;
> we will all have one purse' (1.10-14).

In reporting the hypothetical words of a band of violent robbers the teacher dramatizes the appeal of quickly and unjustly acquired wealth. The shedding of innocent blood is an extremely serious crime (Gen. 9.6; Num. 35.33; Deut. 19.10), and the destruction of the blameless is occasionally depicted as ambush with violence (Ps. 10.8; Mic. 7.2), though only in Proverbs is there mention of joining a robber-band. Their communal life-style is thought to add to the invitation's appeal. These evil men's delight in doing their blameless victims to sudden, violent death, is compared poetically with the insatiable greed of Sheol, the nether-world, which is always hungry for new victims (see Anderson 1972; vol. 2: 860).

> my child, do not walk in their way,
> keep your foot from their paths;
> for their feet run to evil,
> and they hurry to shed blood.
> For in vain is the net baited
> while the bird is looking on;
> yet they lie in wait—to kill themselves!
> and set an ambush—for their own lives!
> Such is the end of all who are greedy for gain;
> it takes away the life of its possessors (1.15-19).

Now resuming his own discourse, the parent-teacher introduces a frequent image in Proverbs, where human life and behaviour is described as walking a certain way or path, good or evil, as, for example, in the next instruction (2.12-15). The basic way image is now extended with terms also found in Isaiah's critique of lawless Israel: 'Their feet run to evil, and they make haste to shed innocent blood' (Isa. 59.7). For the robbers, however, bloodshed is merely a means to acquire wealth quickly. The poem concludes with an elaboration of the notion that evil-doing destroys the perpetrator (1.18-19), so that taking the lives of others amounts to taking one's own life. The notion of a self-inflicted death is intended as a pedagogical warning and deterrent. In this case, death is an ethical death consequent on destroying innocent lives. Next, a nature image illustrates the great value of foreknowledge. In the animal kingdom, a bird would not be trapped by a net that is set while it watches, and if the robbers do not foresee the consequences of their headlong pursuit of wealth, this child will know them, thanks to his parents' advice, which he needs to hear and retain (1.8-9). Initially, instruction was presented as a personal adornment, but in the end, it could save a young person's life.

In this well-constructed poem, the hypothetical appeal (1.10-14) and the refutation (1.15-19) are given equal space, and word repetition reinforces the lesson. The violent lie in wait for blood, to watch without cause for the innocent one (1.11), but they lie in wait for their own blood, they watch for their own lives (1.18). The figure of a band of violent robbers is applicable to all who engage in violent oppression, to whose seductive speech an immature youth, motivated by a promise of fellowship and quick and easy wealth, might easily succumb. The parents warn that lack of caution would lead to disaster, not happiness, and they specify that it is not riches and evil companions that will make a young person happy. The following instruction will propose a positive alternative, namely wisdom (2.1-22). First, however, the topic of wisdom is introduced dramatically into the sequence of instructions by the appearance and discourse of personified Lady Wisdom.

First Discourse of Personified Wisdom (1.20-33)

In the preface, wisdom (*ḥokmâ*) is the teaching of the wise (1.2), and a personal quality inseparable from the fear of Yahweh (1.7). The reader of Proverbs now encounters a poetic personification of Wisdom (*ḥokmôt*), the Hebrew plural form being used, as in Ps. 49.3; Prov. 9.1; 24.7, which may be understood as a royal plural. Indeed, a majestic Lady Wisdom cries out in the city streets, and delivers a well-structured ultimatum to her audience.

Wisdom Appears in the Most Public Places (1.20-21)

> Wisdom cries out in the street;
> in the squares she raises her voice.
> At the busiest corner she cries out;
> at the entrance of the city gates she speaks:

While an address in the streets, bringing to mind Jeremiah proclaiming in the streets of Jerusalem (Jer. 5.1), could suggest that Wisdom is being portrayed as a prophet, yet the nature of her message will suggest that Wisdom is rather a wise teacher, like the authors of the preface (1.1-7). In the previous poem, parental teaching has a domestic setting (1.8-9), yet personified Wisdom seems to be at home in the public streets and squares of the city. Her abrupt appearance in 1.20-33 is a thought-provoking interlude in the sequence of instructions.

Wisdom Appeals to her Audience (1.22-23)

> 'How long, O simple ones, will you love being simple?
> How long will scoffers delight in their scoffing
> and fools hate knowledge?
> Give heed to my reproof;
> I will pour out my thoughts to you;
> I will make my words known to you.'

The rhetorical question 'how long' is more than a simple enquiry, and has overtones of Job's impatient longing for dawn (Job 7.4), or the psalmist's desperate prayer (Ps. 90.13). Wisdom proceeds to voice frustration over the audience's failure to attend to her words hitherto. Three groups are named, with their characteristic attitudes. The audience of Proverbs, the simple, are principally in view, and they are reproached for not yet choosing to undertake the education being offered them. The fools have already been designated as rejecting wisdom (1.7), and in the course of the book, the scoffers will appear as incorrigible, and they actively oppose wisdom teaching (9.7-8; 15.12). Wisdom pleads for a 'turning' to her reproof, that is, for a change of stance in regard to wisdom education. She appropriates the rejection of reproof experienced by wisdom teachers at the hands of their students (5.12), and expresses a desire to speak her mind.

First Indictment and the First Consequence of Heedlessness (1.24-28)

> 'Because I have called and you refused,
> have stretched out my hand and no one heeded,
> and because you have ignored all my counsel
> and would have none of my reproof,
> I also will laugh at your calamity;
> I will mock when panic strikes you,
> when panic strikes you like a storm,
> and your calamity comes like a whirlwind,
> when distress and anguish come upon you.
> Then they will call upon me, but I will not answer;
> they will seek me diligently, but will not find me.'

Wisdom adopts the rhetoric of a prophetic discourse to voice her reproach. 'Because' introduces the complaint, and the consequences of the audience's behaviour are spelled out, all in the style of a prophetic reproach (e.g. Jer. 7.13-14). While refusing to heed a call is also a theme of Jeremiah's temple address (Jer. 7.13), Wisdom's call has the educational setting of Proverbs, and represents the invitation to prospective students to learn wisdom (1.2). Giving counsel is the prerogative of the wise (15.22), and reproof is also inherent to wisdom education (10.17). The first consequence of failure to respond is depicted as Wisdom's gloating when the inevitable calamity strikes (1.26). In Proverbs, mocking may be reprehensible (see 24.17), and certainly parents do not laugh over a failed education (10.1). Rejected Wisdom's glee over the fate of the heedless and the mockers is a rhetorical threat, suggesting that the pitiful state to which their heedlessness has reduced them will, in fact, be irreversible, should the present opportunity be neglected. In a later instruction, a belated admission of remorse over the neglect of instruction has a tone of hopelessness (5.12-13). Wisdom teaching will save from misfortune (2.12, 16), but only if chosen and valued (2.1-5). The motif of the future undoing of the heedless has already been voiced (1.18-19), and the wisdom teacher will reiterate this conviction throughout the following instructions (5.7-14; 6.32; 7.24-27).

A Second Indictment and Consequence (1.29-31)

> 'Because they hated knowledge
> and did not choose the fear of the LORD,
> would have none of my counsel,
> and despised all my reproof,
> therefore they shall eat the fruit of their way
> and be sated with their own devices.'

Having at first named heedlessness as the cause of the listeners' misfortune, Wisdom proceeds to refer to their rejection of the entire process of wisdom education. They do not accept what is taught (knowledge), they lack the pre-requisite attitude (the fear of Yahweh), and they scorn their teachers' counsel and reproof. The metaphor of eating the fruit of one's behaviour, and being satisfied, suggests experiencing in oneself the consequences of one's behaviour (13.2; 18.21).

Conclusion: Misfortune or Security (1.32-33)

> 'For waywardness kills the simple,
> and the complacency of fools destroys them;
> but those who listen to me will be secure
> and will live at ease, without dread of disaster.'

To conclude the discourse, Wisdom once again refers to the simple and the fools, and succinctly links their attitude with its consequences. The simple have turned away from the final appeal to 'turn' to wisdom (1.22), and refused to make the transition from love of simpleness to the choice of wisdom. In a prophetic context, the term complacence may signify a state of prosperity, satisfaction, and heedlessness (Jer. 22.21), and here the term suggests the fool's self-righteousness confidence (12.15). In the antithetical concluding couplet, those who heed Wisdom's voice will dwell secure. This phrase expresses an ideal situation, both for the individual, and society (Ps. 16.9).

Neither Wisdom's calling out, nor even her perhaps threatening hand gesture (1.24), make her easy to visualize as a person. She can, however, be listened to, and her voice has sufficient authority to enable her warnings and promises to remain in the memory of the well-disposed. While some of the expressions and the rhetorical structure of her discourse have the ring of a prophetic discourse, on the whole the vocabulary is that of a wisdom teacher. Personified Wisdom represents wisdom teaching, the teaching of the book of Proverbs, and her voice speaks for its authority. When Wisdom declares three times, in different ways, that the hearers' misfortune will inevitably follow wrongdoing, namely heedlessness, arrogance and self-satisfaction (1.26-28, 29-31, 32), there is a call here for youths to accept responsibility for their lives and fortunes. The parental teaching resumes in the second instruction, which, following Wisdom's discourse, will be presented as wisdom teaching.

Second Parental Instruction: Wisdom, a Treasure, and its Fruits (2.1-22)

This admirably crafted wisdom poem presents the son with a summary outline of the process of becoming wise, beginning with a dedicated quest, and including the perception that wisdom is a gift of God. The beneficial personal qualities that come with wisdom are listed, and the poem concludes with a picture of the mature and wise adult. The process is presented as an understandable whole through the literary device of being included in a single Hebrew sentence of twenty-two lines, the number of consonants in the Hebrew alphabet. There are six sections, each beginning with a conjunction, or other expression, that enable the reader or hearer to recognize the beginning of a new thought-unit in the unfolding sentence. Some of the principal concerns of the following parental instructions are sketched here, and the poem begins with the parent-teacher introducing wisdom to a youth as a treasure to be eagerly sought and asked for.

The Quest for Wisdom (2.1-4)

> My child, if you accept my words
> and treasure up my commandments within you,
> making your ear attentive to wisdom
> and inclining your heart to understanding;
> if you indeed cry out for insight,
> and raise your voice for understanding;
> if you seek it like silver,
> and search for it as for hidden treasures

At the beginning, we find verbal and thematic links to the end of the first instruction, and thematic links with the entire preface (1.2-7). First, 'accepting' (*lqh*) instruction (2.1) uses, in a different sense, the term for 'takes away' (life) in 1.19, while 'treasure up' (*spn*) (the parental advice) repeats the term used in 1.11, 18 for 'lying in wait for' (a human life). Also in regard to the first instruction, while coveting unlawful gain has been shown to end in misfortune (1.8-19), now wisdom, wise advice and commands are a young person's true and lasting treasure. Secondly, the programme of wisdom instruction outlined in the preface (1.2-7) is re-presented as a process, beginning with a youth's ardent desire, and ending with a mature adult flourishing in Israelite society (2.21-22). This first section of the programmatic poem introduces wisdom as the goal of a quest, and it is structured as a series of three conditionals, creating anticipation of what follows, and allowing space for the youth's personal choice and decision. The quest begins with treasuring the parental teaching (2.1-2). The necessary dedication is elaborated with the help of terms in parallel with wisdom, namely, understanding and insight (2.2-3), and through the use of a sequence of body images: the ear is to be made attentive to wisdom, the heart inclined to understanding (2.2), and these qualities are to be called out to, as one might cry out to an absent, but much needed person (Lam. 1.19).

Wisdom as Yahweh's Gift (2.5-11)

> then you will understand the fear of the LORD
> and find the knowledge of God.
> For the LORD gives wisdom;
> from his mouth come knowledge and understanding;
> he stores up sound wisdom for the upright;
> he is a shield to those who walk blamelessly,
> guarding the paths of justice
> and preserving the way of his faithful ones.
> Then you will understand righteousness and justice
> and equity, every good path;
> for wisdom will come into your heart,
> and knowledge will be pleasant to your soul;
> prudence will watch over you;
> and understanding will guard you.

This section is structured as two extended 'then' clauses of conclusion or result (2.5, 9), carrying the poem forward by declaring the outcomes of accepting the initial conditionals. In an unexpected development, the teacher now refers to Yahweh as the wisdom teacher, for it is Yahweh who now utters words of wisdom (2.6). It is as if, at a certain point in the quest, wisdom will be experienced as a gift of God, and the decision to live in the fear of Yahweh will be confirmed. The link between wisdom and the fear of Yahweh, expressed as a statement of principle at the end of the preface (1.7), is now integrated into the process of acquiring wisdom, which entails the father's teaching, the child's efforts, and the granting of wisdom by God (Fox 1994: 242). The wise one attempts to capture in words the experience of the interplay of human effort and the divine disposition of things, and here recourse is had to a thought-provoking juxtaposition of the two aspects, of human effort (2.1-4) and the divine response (2.5-11). In the second 'then' section (2.9-11), wisdom is not merely an external adornment, as was the parental teaching in the first instruction (1.8-9), but a capacity residing in the human heart and soul, enabling a youth to actually savour righteousness, and readily put it into practice. The prudence and good judgment that are integral to wisdom will have a protective role, and this will be delineated in the remaining sections of the poem.

The Fruits of Wisdom (2.12-19)

> It will save you from the way of evil,
> from those who speak perversely,
> who forsake the paths of uprightness
> to walk in the ways of darkness,
> who rejoice in doing evil
> and delight in the perverseness of evil;
> those whose paths are crooked,
> and who are devious in their ways.
> You will be saved from the loose woman,
> from the adulteress with her smooth words,
> who forsakes the partner of her youth
> and forgets her sacred covenant;
> for her way leads down to death,
> and her paths to the shades;
> those who go to her never come back,
> nor do they regain the paths of life.

The Hebrew sentence continues with two parallel consequence clauses, each of which is introduced by 'saving you' (*lᵉhaṣṣîlᵉkā*, 2.12, 16), and they detail the protection wisdom offers a youth as life unfolds. After the previous instruction, the necessity of protection comes as no surprise, nor is it surprising that the foreseen peril is identified as seductive talk. The wise one knows that a young person trying to live in wisdom and the fear of Yahweh will encounter men and women whose behaviour is very different from his, and who will seek to entice him to join their company. It is as if the teacher is competing with these alluring voices, and only the youth who has experientially savoured wisdom (2.10), and treasured his parents' advice (2.4), will not be led astray. The description of the exultant evildoers (2.14-15) matches their depiction in 1.10-14. The second and parallel passage (2.16-19) introduces the threat posed by the alluring woman. She is not described as evil, rather as a stranger (*zārâ*) and an alien (*nokriyyâ*), subsequently to be revealed to be an adulteress (6.24-32; 7.5-20), or a prostitute (5.1-23). The recurring motifs of the path to Sheol and the house described as Sheol's threshold (5.5; 7.27) are also introduced. The terms of the woman's description closely match Malachi's admonition to unfaithful husbands (Mal. 2.14), and, like the prophet, the wise one highlights the religious dimension of the marriage contract. Both the strange woman and the evildoers are literary stereotypes, not rounded characters, and they are presented summarily in a tightly-structured, poetic outline of the scope of wisdom teaching. The parent-teacher has most at heart that the child or youth should find life, happiness, and wisdom in a stable marriage with the wife of his youth. (One may compare 2.17 with 5.18.)

Conclusion with a Development (2.20-22)

> Therefore walk in the way of the good,
> and keep to the paths of the just.
> For the upright will abide in the land,
> and the innocent will remain in it;
> but the wicked will be cut off from the land,
> and the treacherous will be rooted out of it.

The first couplet takes up in a positive summary the way imagery used in the previous two warnings, followed by two couplets of motivation. Throughout this instruction, wisdom has been described in terms of the youth's personal safety. The conclusion, however, introduces the motif of land possession, to include integration into the fabric of Israelite society as one of wisdom's benefits. In the concluding antithesis, images of sudden and premature death evoke the fate of the evildoers whose company a wise one has rejected. Following this comprehensive outline of the process of becoming wise, the next instruction will develop the motif of wisdom and the fear of Yahweh.

Third Parental Instruction: On Loyalty and Faithfulness (3.1-12)

> My child, do not forget my teaching,
> but let your heart keep my commandments;
> for length of days and years of life
> and abundant welfare they will give you
> Let not loyalty and faithfulness forsake you;
> bind them about your neck,
> write them on the tablet of your heart.
> So you will find favour and good repute
> in the sight of God and of people (3.1-4).

As the fear of Yahweh is integral to Israelite wisdom (1.7), the parent now devotes an instruction to developing the child's relationship to Yahweh, through the practice of loyalty and faithfulness. In a call for attention, the child is urged to memorize what his teacher is about to say, the heart being the organ of retention. Then the child is promised, that by putting this teaching into practice, he will live long and happily, expressed in the phrase 'years of life and length of days', terms for the reward of those who cleave to the love of Yahweh in Deuteronomy (Deut. 30.20). Loyalty and faithfulness are qualities that refer to the steadfast solidarity binding partners in a certain relationship. These qualities define God in the context of the covenant (Exod. 34.6), and in 'the proverbs of Solomon' (10.1–22.16), loyalty and faithfulness define a king's relationship to his subjects, since they lend support to his reign (20.28). Here, in a context of Yahweh-piety, a parent recommends to a child, a father to a son, their constant practice, using three metaphors. First, in the poetry of Proverbs, abstract nouns are endowed with mobility (2.10; 3.21), and so to say that these qualities are not to forsake the child is a lively image of the child always practising them. Secondly, the abstract terms are given size and shape, being worn about the neck, as an ornament would be worn. Binding suggests retention, just as when the greatest commandment of the law is to be bound upon the hand, so as to be ever kept in mind (Deut. 6.8). As neck ornaments, too, loyalty and faithfulness would be a sign of a child of God's status, and would earn the wearer honour and high regard (see Gen. 41.42). Third, the tablet of the heart image suggests that loyalty and faithfulness need to be impressed unforgettably on the mind, or held in the memory.

> Trust in the LORD with all your heart,
> and do not rely on your own insight.
> In all your ways acknowledge him,

and he will make straight your paths.
Be not wise in your own eyes;
fear the LORD, and turn away from evil.
It will be a healing for your flesh
and a refreshment for your body (3.5-8).

The teacher proceeds to detail some aspects of the practice of loyalty and faithfulness towards God. He refers to a tension between a true and religious wisdom, which rests on trust in Yahweh, and a self-opinionated, irreligious self-sufficiency. This tension appears in an extreme form in the conflict between wisdom and the fool (1.7), and the wise one and the scoffer (9.7-8). Living in the fear of Yahweh, with respect for the Creator's ordering of things, has tangible benefits, like walking safely, and avoiding pitfalls and tracks that lead nowhere. Indeed, one will thereby appear a more complete human being, as suggested in the image of wholesome flesh and bones (body, NRSV).

Honour the LORD with your substance
and with the first fruits of all your produce;
then your barns will be filled with plenty,
and your vats will be bursting with wine.
My child, do not despise the LORD's discipline
or be weary of his reproof,
for the LORD reproves the one he loves,
as a father the son in whom he delights (3.9-12).

The blessings of religious wisdom are expanded beyond personal well-being to include the enjoyment of the fruits of the land, taking up again the motif of the possession of the land that concluded the previous instruction (2.21). The wise parent-teacher is a Torah-observant Jewish landholder, and knows that offering the first fruits is an acknowledgment that the land and the harvest are Yahweh's gifts (Deut. 26.12-15), and that the ritual of the first fruits ensures that the rest of the harvest will be abundant. Well-stocked barns and overflowing wine vats are images of agricultural prosperity, as in Joel 2.24. Later teachings will highlight the need for industry in this regard (10.5, 24.30-34), however in a context where wisdom is a gift of God (3.5-8), also a bountiful harvest is considered in this light, and the son is advised to offer the first-fruits, in a rare teaching in Proverbs concerning a ritual obligation.

Finally, the parent recommends maintaining trust in time of trial, when loyalty and faithfulness will be put to the test, and when the binding and inscribing images used at the outset (3.3) are very relevant. In 'the proverbs of Solomon' the administration of discipline and reproof will be seen to be integral to wisdom education (13.1), and is a loving father's obligation (13.24). Yahweh, a wisdom teacher (2.6-7), will not fail to administer correction and reproof, which is to be accepted in loyalty and faithfulness. If adversity can be accepted as a reflection of Yahweh's training for maturity, the outcome will be wholesome.

Interlude: The Benefits of Wisdom (3.13-20)

> Happy are those who find wisdom,
> and those who get understanding,
> for her income is better than silver,
> and her revenue better than gold.
> She is more precious than jewels,
> and nothing you desire can compare with her.
> Long life is in her right hand;
> in her left hand are riches and honour.
> Her ways are ways of pleasantness,
> and all her paths are peace.
> She is a tree of life to those who lay hold of her;
> those who hold her fast are called happy.
> The LORD by wisdom founded the earth;
> by understanding he established the heavens;
> by his knowledge the deeps broke open,
> and the clouds drop down the dew.

A moment of exclamation and admiration, expressed in the poetic form of the beatitude, now breaks the sequence of the parental instructions. To pass from simpleness to wisdom (1.4) entails a dedicated search for what is of priceless value (2.1-5), and now the young are offered encouragement in this pursuit, in a poem of praise of the happy situation of the one who has succeeded in the quest, for, as is reiterated, wisdom is not only desirable, but really attainable (3.13, 18). The term 'revenue' (*tᵉbû'â*, 'produce' in 3.9) is now used metaphorically for the benefits of wisdom, which is described as the most desirable of all possessions, through the precious jewels comparison (3.15). Wisdom confers fullness of life, a benefit that has been intimated in the promise of land possession (2.21), of bodily wholeness (3.8), and a prolonged life-span (3.2). In this beatitude, Lady Wisdom makes her second appearance. As previously, her features are not described, except for her gestures, which have greatly changed since her first threatening appearance (1.24). Now Wisdom's hands, both right and left, suggesting completeness, are, like the hands of the worthy wife (31.20), giving hands (3.16). The visual symbolism need not be pressed too far, as it is difficult to imagine Wisdom actually holding her gifts, expressed in abstract terms. The first is the promise of a life full of years, and then wealth and honour. Paradoxically, Wisdom's wealth is given to those who choose wisdom above riches, as was said of Solomon (1 Kgs 3.10-13). Honour is the social respect and esteem gained by manifesting wisdom, while foolish conduct will be shown to earn disgrace (3.35; 6.33). Again it is said (as in 2.10), metaphorically, in the image of Wisdom treading peaceful paths (3.17), that the practice of wisdom is pleasurable, not difficult. She also treads paths of peace, suggesting that wise conduct establishes social concord and reconciliation. The final image of Wisdom, the tree of life, suggests that she is the source of the realistically attainable, successful life offered the Yahweh-fearing wise one in the book of Proverbs. Throughout the poem, Lady Wisdom is variously described, as a person bearing gifts, as one walking her pleasant ways, and as a tree of life. Cumulatively, she is the generous patron of the disciple who clings to her, and without such strong attachment, her gifts could never materialize. The comprehensive subject of the beatitude is not personified Wisdom, but the fortunate person who has attained wisdom. The repetition of 'happy' (3.13, 18) marks the conclusion of the beatitude.

The poem on attainable wisdom concludes on a contemplative note (3.19-20), with a couplet whose theme is the pervasive, ordering, wisdom of God. The terms 'wisdom' and its equivalents, 'understanding' and 'knowledge', are linked with four components of the created universe. The disciples are invited to sense their tread on the earth's firm surface, to lift up their gaze to the heavens' vast expanse, to imagine the seas, fountains and rivers welling up from the subterranean depths, and to feel the lightly falling rain drop from the skies. They will then be in touch with the wisdom of God, and have a taste of its pleasantness and peace.

Fourth Parental Instruction: Sound Wisdom and Prudence as Respect and Benevolence (3.21-35)

After the first two cautionary poems (1.8-19, 20-33), the immature youth has been encouraged to engage in the quest for wisdom (2.1-22). The third instruction (3.1-12) builds on the equivalence of wisdom and the fear of Yahweh (1.7), urging one who desires wisdom to enter into a trustful relationship with Yahweh (3.5-12). While the practice of justice and uprightness has been recommended (1.3; 2.7-10), the wise teacher up to this point has not discussed the implementation of wisdom in daily life and personal relationships. A parent now gives the immature child advice on living wisely with one's neighbour, that is, with other people, through the cultivation of respect for their rights and persons, under the guidance of sound wisdom and prudence (3.27-32), all being brought into the ambit of a life lived in a relationship of trust in Yahweh. The instruction may be divided as follows:

(a) exhortation to retain the parental teaching about sound wisdom and prudence, with incentives (3.21-26);
(b) four specific applications of sound wisdom (3.27-32);
(c) divine sanctions (3.33-35).

Exhortation to Retain the Parental Teaching (3.21-26)

> My child, do not let these escape from your sight:
> keep sound wisdom and prudence,
> and they will be life for your soul
> and adornment for your neck.
> Then you will walk on your way securely
> and your foot will not stumble.
> If you sit down, you will not be afraid;
> when you lie down, your sleep will be sweet.
> Do not be afraid of sudden panic,
> or of the ruin of the wicked, when it comes;
> for the LORD will be your confidence
> and will keep your foot from being caught.

This instruction concerning sound wisdom and prudence concerns the personal qualities of the wise already referred to (1.4; 2.7). The active eyes are 'an image of turning one's attention to something' (Ps. 119.6, 15; see Ryken, 'Eye, sight', *DBI*: 256). Such eager, watchful attention may suggest the ability to learn from the close observation of wisdom in practice, and the following teachings on living peacefully with others. Practising sound wisdom and prudence is life to the soul, terms used to describe the effect of the divine breath on the lifeless first human (Gen. 2.7). The neck ornament image suggests that the practice of sound wisdom and prudence will enhance one's bearing and appearance, and gain admiration and respect (3.22), while making one safe and secure (3.23-26). The exhortation develops the image of wise conduct as walking along a path, where the choices made through sound wisdom are the traveller's protection, as in 2.7-8. In using the metaphor of life as a way to travel, the teacher depicts 'the physical realities of walking down a path' (see Ryken, 'Path', *DBI*: 631), like striking one's foot (3.23, as in Ps. 91.12), and where the traveller can be assured of a pleasant and untrammelled sleep at the day's end (3.24). Sound wisdom prevents the panic and ruin that could overtake an unwise traveller (3.25), terms also used by personified Wisdom to threaten those who do not heed instruction (1.26-27). The exhortation concludes with a reference to Yahweh, Creator of the universe (3.19-20), as a reliable guide along the path of life, which is set with snares for the inexperienced.

Four Specific Applications of Sound Wisdom (3.27-32)

> Do not withhold good from those to whom it is due,
> when it is in your power to do it.
> Do not say to your neighbour, 'Go, and come again;
> tomorrow I will give it'—when you have it with you.
> Do not plan harm against your neighbour
> who lives trustingly beside you.
> Do not quarrel with anyone without cause,
> when no harm has been done to you.
> Do not envy the violent
> and do not choose any of their ways.
> For the perverse are an abomination to the LORD,
> but the upright are in his confidence.

Sound wisdom and prudence apply in situations where others' rights are concerned. The advice to pay or restore promptly what is due brings within the scope of parental wisdom teaching the Torah injunction not to defraud one's neighbour, or hold back the defenceless hireling's wages (Lev. 19.13). Then, plotting evil in one's heart is the antithesis of respect and benevolence. Another anti-social practice is beginning an unprovoked quarrel. Whereas the biblical legislation covers legal aspects of disputes that have occurred (Exod. 21.18; Deut. 19.15-21), sound wisdom is preventive. An unprovoked quarrel must not even begin. Later in Proverbs quarrels will be traced back to an irascible disposition (15.18; 30.33). Lastly, the presence of violence in society and the lure of quickly gotten wealth have been the subject of an instruction (1.8-19). All the above disruptions of social *shalom* are presented as deviations along the path of life, and the traveller who foolishly digresses will have lost Yahweh's protection. One who respects other people, however, continues the journey in Yahweh's intimate company.

Divine Sanctions (3.33-35)

> The LORD's curse is on the house of the wicked,
> but he blesses the abode of the righteous.
> Towards the scorners he is scornful,
> but to the humble he shows favour.
> The wise will inherit honour,
> but stubborn fools, disgrace.

The instruction concludes with an accumulation of three antitheses, referring to those who respect the rights of others, and those motivated by greed and self-interest. Proverbs shows great interest in the quality of life within a household (see later, on the proverbs of 'Life in the Household'), which may even be reflected in its external appearance (24.30-34). Here the point is made that the state of one's own house is an indication of one's regard for other people. In a context where social relations are viewed within the context of one's relationship to Yahweh (3.26, and 3.5-12), a household's prosperity is seen to reflect Yahweh's blessing, while misfortune is attributed to the divine curse. Scorners are the incorrigible rejecters of wisdom and wisdom teaching, and with no fear of Yahweh (1.22, 29), whereas the humble live in respect of the Creator and the intrinsic requirements of social harmony. To respect another's life and property is to gain social esteem, while greed and violence earn opprobrium. Youths would do well to build their lives in the fear of Yahweh, and with trust in Yahweh, and the practice of prudence and sound wisdom, through practising respect and benevolence towards other people.

Fifth Parental Instruction: Wisdom as a Family Heritage (4.1-9)

The family and household setting of the earliest stage of a child's education receives particular emphasis in this instruction. Apart from the address, 'children' (4.1), there is a second reference to the mother (4.3, and see 1.8), and a flashback to the father's own example and early experience, so that the parental wisdom is now transmitted to a new generation as a precious family heritage.

> Listen, children, to a father's instruction,
> and be attentive, that you may gain insight;
> for I give you good precepts:
> do not forsake my teaching (4.1-2).

This passage takes up three terms from the book's preface. First, the term 'instruction' (*mûsār*) is defined as a father's teaching, as already in 1.8-9. Secondly, this instruction will offer the 'insight' (*bînâ*) promised in the preface. Finally, the father adds a few words on the quality of his instruction. He offers excellent 'advice' (*leqah*, 4.2; see also 1.5). For its part, the child needs to be attentive, and faithful to what is taught.

> When I was a son with my father,
> tender, and my mother's favourite,
> he taught me, and said to me,
> 'Let your heart hold fast my words;
> keep my commandments, and live' (4.3-4).

The linking of wisdom teaching with the imagery of earliest childhood suggests that children need to aspire as soon as possible to the wisdom they were not born with, so that the life given at birth can be adequately nurtured, and be an adequate preparation for a long life, blessed with personal and social well-being. For this reason, the choice of wisdom is projected back to this early stage. Authority is added to the father's wisdom teaching by a reference to his own early experience, and his teaching is presented in a form meaningful to the very young, namely, as the words of his own father, the child's grandfather. The two motifs in the grandfather's remaining words are: (i) commitment to getting wisdom, and (ii) wisdom's incomparable value.

> 'Get wisdom; get insight: do not forget, nor turn away
> from the words of my mouth.
> Do not forsake her, and she will keep you;
> love her, and she will guard you.
> The beginning of wisdom is this: Get wisdom,
> and whatever else you get, get insight' (4.5-7).

As to a beginner, the father proposes the first step in the process of becoming wise, namely, to resolve to do so (4.7). The other 'beginning' of wisdom, the fear of Yahweh (1.7), is only implicit in this present instruction. Throughout Proverbs, wisdom is said to be acquired (e.g. 15.32; 23.23). The term 'acquire' ('get') may have the specific meaning of 'buy' (17.16). Here, however, Wisdom is to be acquired by choice and personal investment, and ranked in value above all other property a youth could aspire to obtain (4.7).

> 'Prize her highly, and she will exalt you;
> she will honour you if you embrace her.
> She will place on your head a fair garland;
> she will bestow on you a beautiful crown' (4.8-9).

The instruction concludes with several metaphors for the choice of wisdom, and for wisdom's rewards (4.6, 8-9). In this intimate familial setting, wisdom teaching is personified, firstly, as a generous and beneficent Lady Wisdom, as was Wisdom in the beatitude (3.13-18), and a child's commitment is elicited through the terms indicating a preferential choice of wisdom, namely, not forsaking, loving, prizing, and embracing. The later term (*ḥbq*) may simply expresses clinging to an object (Job 24.8), but also, embracing a person through affection (Laban and Jacob in Gen. 29.13, the beloved in Song 2.6). In the present context, the attractiveness of Wisdom rests on the benefits she confers, expressed as guarding, exalting and honouring. The honour attached to holding fast to Wisdom, and so to wisdom teaching is imaged in the proudly worn garland and the crown, for it is only through a life-time's practice of wisdom that a tender, untried youth (4.3) will mature in social relationships to the point of being one day esteemed in the city gates (31.23). Secondly, however, the poetic, female personification of Wisdom as the beloved suggests that the choice of wisdom, as a way of life, will be activated particularly when a youth's affections are engaged, a topic that will be developed in the three proximate instructions on marriage and sexuality (5.1-23; 6.20-35; 7.1-27). The immature one would do well to remember this image of embracing Wisdom when seized (*ḥzq*) by the adulteress (7.13). Before that, two instructions present the topic of a child's life-long growth to maturity in terms of the metaphor of a journey along a way or path (4.10-19; 20-27).

Sixth Parental Instruction: The Two Ways and their Travellers (4.10-19)

A Call for Attention (4.10-13)

> Hear, my child, and accept my words,
> that the years of your life may be many.
> I have taught you the way of wisdom;
> I have led you in the paths of uprightness.
> When you walk, your step will not be hampered;
> and if you run, you will not stumble.
> Keep hold of instruction; do not let go;
> guard her, for she is your life.

Once again the father-teacher presents himself as one whose only concern is for the life and happiness of his son-pupil (see 1.8-9; 3.1-2), and so he begins by trying to impress on his immature hearer the need to heed the instruction, which will be couched more in terms of a warning about danger than of the rewards of wisdom

(Barucq 1964: 69). Through the frequent use of the path imagery, this teaching appears to be an anxious parent's final words of advice to a young adult setting out on the journey of life. The traveller's foot could be trapped in a concealed snare, or, if he runs to escape a threat, there is the risk of a fall. Once the youth leaves his parent's presence, however, the parental teaching will be his guide. The term 'keep hold of' may be used with an abstract object, without personification (see Job 27.6), yet holding on to instruction as a life-source recalls Wisdom being a tree of life to those who lay hold of her (3.18). In short, the personified parental instruction is equivalent to Lady Wisdom as a young person's life companion and protection.

Company to Avoid (4.14-17)

> Do not enter the path of the wicked,
> and do not walk in the way of evildoers.
> Avoid it; do not go on it (*'br*);
> turn away from it and pass on (*'br*).
> For they cannot sleep unless they have done wrong;
> they are robbed of sleep unless they have made someone stumble.
> For they eat the bread of wickedness
> and drink the wine of violence.

Whereas children are not born wise, and they need Wisdom's protection to succeed in life (4.5), neither are they born evil, but become so by keeping the wrong company. Once again the path image is used in the description of evildoers (see 1.15-16; 2.12-15). The youth is at the crossroads, a place for decision, for the wrong path lies before him. The four imperatives, with the repeated 'pass on', evoke a parent's concern. The travellers on that path are caricatures of human beings. Sleep is denied, in the pursuit of evil-doing, and their food and drink is wickedness and violence.

Conclusion: The Two Paths (4.18-19)

> But the path of the righteous is like the light of dawn,
> which shines brighter and brighter until full day.
> The way of the wicked is like deep darkness;
> they do not know what they stumble over.

The imagery in the final antithesis changes from the two sorts of companions to the quality of the path itself. Walking in wisdom and righteousness (4.11) is very attractive, like walking in a light which never diminishes, but its protective brightness only increases. If one foolishly associates with violent men, as in 1.8-19, it will be like the experience of walking in complete darkness, hopelessly exposed to any and every obstacle. In summary, in this instruction, the path image is developed in terms of undesirable travel companions, and security is guaranteed by heeding the wisdom of parents, making that their companion. Otherwise, the young will fall prey to evil associations, and the promise of a young life will come to nothing.

Seventh Parental Instruction: A Portrait of the Wise Traveller (4.20-27)

> My child, be attentive to my words;
> incline your ear to my sayings.
> Do not let them escape from your sight;
> keep them within your heart.
> For they are life to those who find them,
> and healing to all their flesh (4.20-22).

This instruction develops the path image in a positive sense, focusing on the commitment and sense of purpose needed on the journey. In the poem, the blessed life of the wise is symbolized with images of the body members and the physical appearance, from the ear and eyes to the feet, with two mentions of the eyes, the heart and the foot. The instruction begins with the call for attentiveness, and for the retention of the teaching, expressed with imagery of the ear and the eyes. It is as though the eyes need to be fixed on a written text attached to the young traveller's person (see 3.21). Advice is also stored in the heart, the organ of memory, where it is constantly ruminated, and is to be 'found' when needed, that is, used in decision-making, as explained below. Travelling with such active engagement with one's companion and guide, the parental teaching, or Lady Wisdom, will enhance a young person's health and vitality.

> Keep your heart with all vigilance,
> for from it flow the springs of life.
> Put away from you crooked speech,
> and put devious talk far from you.
> Let your eyes look directly forward,
> and your gaze be straight before you.
> Keep straight the path of your feet,
> and all your ways will be sure.
> Do not swerve to the right or to the left;
> turn your foot away from evil (4.23-27).

In the body of the instruction, there is a sense of threatening danger, of the need to safeguard the heart. Besides the already mentioned function of storing what was heard, the heart has a role in wise decision-making (4.27). Without vigilance, the wrong choice may easily be made, and a life may be lost (as later, in 5.22-23; 6.32). The notion that the way of wisdom is intersected by the way of the wicked (4.14-15) is recalled, and once again, the beguiling invitation to join wrong-doers is a particular danger to avoid, and such conversations are to be shunned. The wise one walks with eyes fixed on journey's end, yet at the same time watching his step to avoid stumbling. Above all, at intersections, the moments of decision, he does not swerve. The next instruction will present one of the principal blessings of wisdom, the happiness to be found with 'the wife of one's youth' (5.18) and a threat that could jeopardize its attainment.

Eighth Parental Instruction: The Profligate and the Spouse of one's Youth (5.1-23)

In this instruction, the wise father seeks to impress on his son that sexual fulfilment is to be sought in marriage, not in encounters with other women. He seeks to impart his wisdom (5.1) with some urgency, as, more than previously, he identifies himself with his teaching, and makes three appeals to the father-son relationship. His two concerns are to show the 'simple', inexperienced youth that discretion in managing his sexual tendencies is essential for his own happiness and welfare, and that unless he is alert, he will fall victim to the engaging words of a wayward woman. He also seems concerned that an unenlightened young person could think sexual aberration to be perhaps a merely private matter, and without damaging personal consequences, so that the 'knowledge' (5.2) he wishes to share concerns those consequences. To teach a lesson on sexual restraint, he proceeds in a poetic and figurative manner to build a contrast between the wholesome privacy of sex with an ideal wife, and the unforeseen and comprehensive social alienation and personal loss that befalls a libertine. The seductive woman traps her victim through flattery and pleasure. She is not working alone, but in partnership with a ruthless, alien man, to exploit, through prostitution, the unsuspecting youth or husband. It is difficult to set the imagery describing the alien couple in a known social situation, neither does the foreign man need to be understood as the foreign woman's husband, which would make the instruction refer to adultery and its consequences, which, however, is the subject of a later instruction (6.20-35) (see Alonso Schökel and Vílchez Líndez

1984: 204). The addressee is, nonetheless, a husband, or potentially so, and compared with the 'wife of youth', this woman is a complete stranger. The poem is structured as follows:

> 5.1-2: summons to attention;
> 5.3-14: the first couplet: the exploiters—the strange woman and her partner, the strange man;
> 5.15-19: centrepiece; a man and the wife of his youth: blessing, fruitfulness, and ongoing delight;
> 5.20-23: concluding appeal, and reflection on the fate of the libertine.

Summons and First Couplet (5.1-14)
Within the overall structure outlined above, the poem begins to unfold with an appeal for the pupil's attention, and a description of the strange woman (5.1-6).

> My child, be attentive to my wisdom;
> incline your ear to my understanding,
> so that you may hold on to prudence,
> and your lips may guard knowledge.
> For the lips of a loose woman (*zārâ*) drip honey,
> and her speech is smoother than oil;
> but in the end she is bitter as wormwood,
> sharp as a two-edged sword.
> Her feet go down to death;
> her steps follow the path to Sheol;
> she does not keep straight to the path of life;
> her ways wander, and she does not know it (5.1-6).

Here is a first mention of the disciple's lips as organs of retention, perhaps suggesting the repetitive oral recitation of the instruction (5.2). The strange woman's wiles are described with reference to the sense of touch and taste, to which her flattering words appeal for their pleasant smoothness and sweetness, when they drip like honey from her mouth and lips. The aftermath of yielding to her words, however, is completely different, for she leaves a bitter, piercing taste in his mouth. The outcome is symbolized in the direction taken by her shiftless feet, along a path that leads her victim to death and Sheol, which is clearly seen by the teacher, though apparently not by the woman herself. This is the view he wants to share with his young disciple (5.1), for this encounter is an important moment for the exercise of the discretion (5.2) and heart-vigilance every wise way-farer needs (4.23), and the poem provides a specific example of the two intersecting ways evoked at the end of the previous instruction (4.26-27).

The fate of the libertine (5.7-14) completes the description of the libertine and the loose woman.

> And now, my child, listen to me,
> and do not depart from the words of my mouth.
> Keep your way far from her,
> and do not go near the door of her house;
> or you will give your honour to others,
> and your years to the merciless,
> and strangers will take their fill of your wealth,
> and your labours will go to the house of an alien;
> and at the end of your life you will groan,
> when your flesh and body are consumed,
> and you say, 'Oh, how I hated discipline,
> and my heart despised reproof!
> I did not listen to the voice of my teachers
> or incline my ear to my instructors.
> Now I am at the point of utter ruin
> in the public assembly' (5.7-14).

Once the fatal attraction of this woman's conversation is described, the rhetorical 'and now' introduces a conclusive development, which requires the pupil's greatest attention, and the advice is for every inexperienced youth (in Hebrew, 'sons', 5.7), though the warning continues in the singular in 5.8. We are not informed if the woman's house (5.8) is the same as that of the alien man, but the two have complementary roles in a process of entrapment, entailing seduction on her part and cruel extortion on his (Alonso Schökel and Vílchez Líndez 1984: 204). In another facet of the house image, a youth's life task is to build wisely his own house, namely his household, and this achievement requires that he associate with a completely different woman, namely, the wife of his youth (see below, and 14.1). The imperatives, to keep away from her (5.8) are followed by the motivations, introduced by the repeated 'lest' (*pen*, 5.9-10), rendered by 'or' and 'and' in the NRSV. These motivations are several times longer than the warning expressed in imperatives, and they have the form of an extended description of the penalties following sexual indulgence. The fate is made personal by the repeated second-person pronouns, and a citation of the foolish man's rueful words. Image after image depicts the damage incurred, namely loss of honour, financial ruin, and a situation of life-destroying, pitiless exploitation. Once again, as in 1.10-19, the technique of word repetition illustrates the inherent consequences. Having entered the house of an alien woman (*zārâ*, 5.3, 20a; *nokriyyâ*, 5.20b), his strength and labours will go to the house of an alien man (*nokrî*, 5.10b) and they will satisfy the hunger of aliens (*zārîm*, 5.10a). He groans, or rages in disappointment and frustration, and in his misery he testifies, in a first-person avowal, to the accuracy of Wisdom's description of the scoffer and the fool (1.25, 30; compare 1.7). He refers in his lament to the rupture of the fatherly relationship of care and concern offered by his teachers (5.13, and see 4.2; 5.1), and his social death will occur when he earns the reprobation of the local community (5.14), gathered to pronounce judgment in such a case.

Centrepiece: A Man and the Wife of his Youth: Blessing, Fruitfulness, and Ongoing Delight (5.15-19)

> Drink water from your own cistern,
> flowing water from your own well.
> Should your springs be scattered abroad,
> streams of water in the streets?
> Let them be for yourself alone,
> and not for sharing with strangers.
> Let your fountain be blessed,
> and rejoice in the wife of your youth,
> a lovely deer, a graceful doe.
> May her breasts satisfy you at all times;
> may you be intoxicated always by her love.

The wise father proceeds to describe the sexual fulfilment he wishes for his son. The exchange of intimate, mutual sexual love is symbolized in the water images. The spouse is a well, a cistern, a fountain, set within the household, as in an enclosed garden, where a man may drink to satiety the life-giving, pleasurable waters. The flowing streams are his generative powers, to be shared exclusively with his wife, for his own advantage, and not squandered on outsiders (strangers). The father invokes a divine blessing on his son's 'spouse of youth', that she may be endowed with vitality and fruitfulness (Gen. 17.16, and see Ruth 4.11). Animal images complement the water images. The hind and doe suggest female grace and beauty, in the context of a 'celebration of marriage's sexual pleasures' (see Ryken, 'Pleasure', *DBI*: 652). In the light of this blissful prospect, a man has no need to seek, or be cajoled into sex outside the relationship with the wife of his youth, and this partnership is ongoing, for life (at all times, always), the contrast with other relationships being emphasized by the repetition of 'intoxicated' in the following final, personal appeal.

Concluding Appeal, and Reflection on the Fate of the Libertine (5.20-23)

> Why should you be intoxicated, my son, by another woman (*zārâ*)
> and embrace the bosom of an adulteress?
> (*nokriyyâ*; 'adventuress', RSV)
> For human ways are under the eyes of the LORD,
> and he examines all their paths.
> The iniquities of the wicked ensnare them,
> and they are caught in the toils of their sin.
> They die for lack of discipline,
> and because of their great folly they are lost.

The teacher recalls the father-son relationship that shapes all his concern, and which the libertine has so sadly rejected, and the scene changes from the intimate pleasures of the wife of youth (5.19) to the poor substitute of the embrace of a strange woman. The final words addressed to the son are a reflection on sexual transgression in the light of the religious aspect of wisdom (5.21), a reference to misfortune as the inherent consequence of evil-doing (5.22), and the use of the specific language of wisdom education (5.23). Unlike the strange woman who heeds (*tᵉpallēs*) not the path she takes, God, creator of the universe (3.19-20) examines (*mᵉpallēs*) every human's path, so that debauchery is also impiety, a sinful absence of the knowledge and fear of Yahweh. Besides, there is a flow-on effect of transgression, so that people are caught like a hunted animal, but in a trap they set for themselves. Finally, it is folly and lack of discipline to ignore the consequences of one's choices, once they have been made known through instruction.

Concluding Comments

The urgency of the message is matched by the care of the composition. There is a telling use both of word repetition, and rhetorical variation. Two descriptions of the libertine's fate enclose the depiction of the joys of marriage. To admonitions in the form of commands are added sections introduced by the deterrent 'lest' (5.9, 10 RSV), and a series of third-person verbs of exhortation (5.16-18). This instruction is also enlivened by a rhetorical question (5.20), three appeals to the audience (5.1, 7, 20), and a first-person citation of the offender's bitter, final words (5.12-14). In the next instruction a concerned parent presents another grave threat to the success of a child's life-project, namely financial imprudence.

Ninth Parental Instruction: On Going Surety (6.1-5)

In the previous teaching, an imprudent man has come to ruin by
undertaking a crushing financial obligation to a third party in
return for the favour of an unknown woman. He has placed himself in the power of strangers (*zarîm*, 5.10) trapped by incontinence
(5.22). The present instruction is an earnest warning of a very concerned father (6.1, 3) to avoid another peril, namely offering one's
property as surety for another's debts.

> My child, if you have given your pledge to your neighbour,
> if you have bound yourself to (lit. struck hands, i.e. shaken
> hands with) another (*zār;* compare 5.10),
> you are snared by the utterance of your lips,
> caught by the words of your mouth (6.1-2).

The situation referred to in the hypothesis (see 1.10-14 for this
style) is going surety with a creditor for another's debt. There was
every chance, the wise one apparently believes, that the debtor
would default on the loan, which would then be the responsibility of the guarantor. De Vaux envisages the situation as follows. 'In Biblical law the surety is the person who, when the debt
matures, intervenes (the root *'rb*), in favour of the insolvent debtor
and assumes responsibility for the payment of the debt, either by
obtaining it from the debtor or by substituting himself for him' (de
Vaux, 1961: 172).

> So do this, my child, and save yourself,
> for you have come into your neighbour's power:
> go, hurry, and plead with your neighbour.
> Give your eyes no sleep
> and your eyelids no slumber;
> save yourself like a gazelle from the hunter,
> like a bird from the hand of the fowler (6.3-5).

The verbs now suggest haste and insistent appeal for release from
the given undertaking. The son is to imagine himself, as an imprudent backer, to be like a hunted animal caught in a trap, the example used being the prized and rare gazelle (1 Kgs 4.23), and then
to have the immense relief of escaping through immediate, decisive action. He would need to prevail upon the debtor to repay the
loan immediately, with accruing interest, thus freeing the surety.
This is one situation in Proverbs from which a foolish person is
urged to be saved after the event. In another poetic text, though
from a later era, Ben Sira depicts the dire consequences of assuming responsibility for the debt. 'Being surety has ruined many who

were prosperous, and has tossed them about like waves of the sea; it has driven the influential into exile, and they have wandered among foreign nations' (Sir. 29.18). As in the previous instruction, the financial arrangements are quite quickly and imprecisely sketched in the poetry, but the trapped animal imagery conveys a sense of the unexpected, serious outcome of imprudently agreeing to guarantee another person's loan.

Tenth Parental Instruction: The Paralysis of the Quest for Wisdom (6.6-11)

> Go to the ant, you lazybones;
> consider its ways, and be wise.
> Without having any chief or officer or ruler,
> it prepares its food in summer,
> and gathers its sustenance in harvest (6.6-8).

A second instruction on avoiding financial peril concerns sloth. The previously growing intensity of the paternal address to the 'child' is now temporarily eased, as the teacher directly addresses a slothful youth, thereby asking the immature audience to imagine themselves to be such. Even people represented by this character type can rise to wisdom and success, however, if they take instruction from harvest ants, it having previously been demonstrated that contemplation of animals can lead to wisdom (5.19; 6.5). 'One of the most vivid portraits in the entire book is that of the self-starting and industrious ant' (Ryken, 'Proverbs, book of', *DBI*: 681), as, during the summer harvest, they ply ceaselessly to and from field to the ant-nest, carrying individual grains for storage until winter. They require no leader (the term for leaders in society in Isa. 3.6), nor overseer (taskmasters in Exod. 5.6) to ensure that the work is done, nor ruler (those having authority over others, Jer. 33.26). The lesson is then drawn.

> How long will you lie there, O lazybones?
> When will you rise from your sleep?
> A little sleep, a little slumber,
> a little folding of the hands to rest,
> and poverty will come upon you like a robber,
> and want, like an armed warrior (6.9-11).

Resuming the direct address, and adopting the style of Personified Wisdom (1.22), the teacher taunts the slothful person while he slumbers in serene content. His time, however, has run out, and any additional sleep will spell calamity. On his journey through life, the sluggard will be overtaken by two unwelcome fellow-travellers, want and poverty, who will threaten his life, and seize his property. While in the 'proverbs' the lazy person may be portrayed with humorous disparagement (19.24; 22.13; 26.15), in the end, sloth is incompatible with wisdom (26.16), and is completely absent in the portrait of the model of wisdom that concludes the book (31.10-31). The sloth that has a conspicuous place in the programme of wisdom instruction is evidently a serious character flaw, and not a relatively harmless temperamental characteristic, as could be implied by 'lazybones' (NRSV). For the gravity of sloth in Proverbs, see Strola 2005: 7, 28-29.

A Portrait of a Scoundrel (6.12-15)

The wise one now uses a cautionary third-person description of a state of physical and moral degeneration, making the scoundrel the antithesis of the one who walks in the way of wisdom (4.20-27).

> A scoundrel and a villain
> goes around with crooked speech,
> winking the eyes, shuffling the feet,
> pointing the fingers,
> with perverted mind devising evil,
> continually sowing discord;
> on such a one calamity will descend suddenly;
> in a moment, damage beyond repair.

The term translated as 'scoundrel' refers to baseness of one type or another, being used in the description of the ill-natured Nabal (1 Sam. 25.17), those who instigate idolatry (Deut. 13.13), and in 'the proverbs of Solomon' this unprincipled villain is a lying witness (19.28). Like the wise traveller (4.20-27), his human form is sketched incompletely, the whole person being sufficiently represented by the eyes, mouth, heart, fingers and feet. Even these members are not depicted in their shape and form, but are seen only as engaged in anti-social activity, and they are brought together into a single, symbolic body. The villain's contorted mouth utters misleading words (6.12, compare 4.24). He cannot look straight ahead (compare 4.25), for he winks his eyes through duplicity and evil intent. He turns his feet towards every evil, shuffling this way and that (compare 4.26). His hands are not evident, but his fingers make sinister signals (6.13). His perverted heart (mind) is abandoned to unrestrained evil devising (6.14). Whereas one who walks the way of wisdom retains his teacher's words, and finds in them life and healing (4.22), the villain's appearance indicates that he has rejected this source of vitality, and when calamity strikes, his body will be beyond healing, and incapable of further evildoing (6.15).

Yahweh's Abominations (6.16-19)

> There are six things that the LORD hates,
> seven that are an abomination to him:
> haughty eyes, a lying tongue,
> and hands that shed innocent blood,
> a heart that devises wicked plans,
> feet that hurry to run to evil,
> a lying witness who testifies falsely,
> and one who sows discord in a family.

Following a list of vices incompatible with wisdom, that are unified as activities of a single scoundrel's body members, the God-fearing wise one now provides another pedagogical aid, a numerical list, in the form of an arithmetic progression from six to the complete, or perfect seven (see also Job 5.19-27). These seven ways of behaving without regard to the fear of Yahweh are also unified with the use of the expression, Yahweh's abomination. This is the second use of a phrase (see 3.32) which is very frequent in 'the proverbs of Solomon' (10.1–22.16), where it refers to who, or what is hated or rejected, like a prohibited sacrifice (15.8), but also to social and ethical transgressions, like thinking evil (15.26), arrogance (16.5), or corruption in judges (17.15). In the present list, the abomination refers to such socially destructive activity, which is considered an affront to the Creator's wise disposition of the world and all that is in it (3.19-20). This behaviour closely matches that of the scoundrel in the previous poem (6.12-15). The first six abominations (6.16-19a) concern the perverse use of the eyes, the tongue, the hands, the heart, the feet, and possibly the function of exhalation. Yahweh, too, is described in bodily terms in that the feeling of loathing is attributed to Yahweh's *nepeš*, 6.16 ('to him', NRSV, i.e. the living body).

Haughtiness, the first abomination, is a malfunction of the human eyes (6.17). One may be wise in one's own eyes (3.7), and haughty eyes signify an unreal estimation of one's place in the world, without reference to Yahweh the Creator (3.7, 19-20). Secondly, Yahweh abhors the lying, destructive tongue (6.17). Proceeding from the organs of the head to the upper limbs, the third abomination is hands shedding innocent blood (6.17). Fourth, a heart that plots evil (6.18) breaches the relationship between neighbours (3.29). The fifth abomination describes the pursuit of evil as an abuse of the feet (6.18, as in 1.16). The first five abominations form a list beginning with the functions of the head organs, and finishing with the feet. The sixth abomination, giving false witness, is an abuse of the function of breath-exhalation in a more literal translation of the verb *yāpîaḥ* (6.19), as in the RSV, 'a false witness who breathes out lies'. Yahweh's final abomination is the one sowing discord between brothers (6.19, a trait of the scoundrel in 6.14). Implicitly, harmony between friends and associates is Yahweh's delight (3.27-33).

While the use of bodily organs to symbolize human behaviour may be understood as an aspect of the concreteness of biblical poetry, in the view of the wise ones, living in the fear of Yahweh entails a socially constructive use of the created bodily functions. Not included in this list are sins of sexual folly, a topic which is resumed in the following instruction on adultery.

Eleventh Parental Instruction: The Adulteress and her Injured Husband (6.20-35)

> My child, keep your father's commandment,
> and do not forsake your mother's teaching.
> Bind them upon your heart always;
> tie them around your neck (6.20-21).

Yahweh's abominations have been described in a symbolic listing of the eyes, tongue, hands, heart and feet (6.16-19). Body imagery is found again in the parental instruction on adultery. Here the household teaching of father and mother is to be bound to the heart, for retention, and, in the parallel expression, attached to the neck, for continual reference. Wisdom is not a personal adornment for the head and neck (as in 1.8-9), but, as in 3.3, the ever-ready subject of a young person's thought and meditation, as are the divine words in the Torah, which are attached to his person, like the divine words in the Torah (Deut. 6.6-8). In this wisdom instruction, there is no reference to a divine prohibition (Deut. 5.18), but rather, adultery is senseless (6.32), and every youth needs to know that this act of folly will provoke the husband's revenge (6.33-35).

> When you walk, they will lead you;
> when you lie down, they will watch over you;
> and when you awake, they will talk with you.
> For the commandment is a lamp and the teaching a light,
> and the reproofs of discipline are the way of life (6.22-23).

So intimately present to one on the way of wisdom, the parental teaching once again becomes a personified guide and instructor, as in 4.10-13. Moreover the parental teaching has a role that
the Torah assigns to Israelite parents themselves, to speak of the
commandments throughout the day (Deut. 6.7). Teaching is also
like a lamp that helps one see the next step ahead. The claim that
discipline and reproof are life-giving, gains credence in the light
of the description of the 'death' of the youth who rejected them
(5.23).

> to preserve you from the wife of another,
> from the smooth tongue of the adulteress.
> Do not desire her beauty in your heart,
> and do not let her capture you with her eyelashes;
> for a prostitute's fee is only a loaf of bread,
> but the wife of another stalks a man's very life (6.24-26).

In this instruction, the strange woman (*nokriyyâ*) is an unchaste
married woman, an adulteress, who is described as the protagonist
in a seductive encounter. As regards her physical appearance, only
her beguiling words are mentioned, with the image of entrapment
being applied to her appealing glances. For the man's part, the folly
of adultery is shown to begin in his unrestrained sexual desires. At
this point the wise one makes an appeal to reason by comparing the
cost of adultery with that of frequenting prostitutes. The financial
cost of the latter is minimized to a symbolic loaf of bread, so as to
emphasize the life-threatening consequences of adultery.

Further Illustrations of the Consequences of Committing Adultery (6.27-35)

> Can fire be carried in the bosom
> without burning one's clothes?
> Or can one walk on hot coals
> without scorching the feet?
> So is he who sleeps with his neighbour's wife;
> no one who touches her will go unpunished.
> Thieves are not despised who steal only
> to satisfy their appetite when they are hungry.
> Yet if they are caught, they will pay sevenfold;
> they will forfeit all the goods of their house.
> But he who commits adultery has no sense;
> he who does it destroys himself.
> He will get wounds and dishonour,
> and his disgrace will not be wiped away.
> For jealousy arouses a husband's fury,

and he shows no restraint when he takes revenge.
He will accept no compensation,
and refuses a bribe no matter how great.

The outcomes of adultery are in the nature of things, flowing from the act itself, and the teacher illustrates this by comparing the act of adultery with touching fire, which inevitably scorches the skin. Touching may also imply a violation of a third person's rights (Zech. 2.8), an aspect which is also present in this instruction, which highlights the husband's rage and insatiable prosecution (6.34-35). By an extended comparison of adultery with theft, the teacher demonstrates how Wisdom's promise of a full life with riches and honour (3.16) is no empty claim. The basis of the comparison is that adultery, like theft, was considered a violation of a man's property rights. The Torah legislation fixes the monetary compensation for theft (Exod. 22.1-4; Lev. 6.1-7), which can amount to fivefold restitution in the case of theft of a beast (Exod. 22.1). In the present context, even though the compensation for theft may entail financial ruin, it will be complete. Once the offence of adultery is discovered, however, retaliation is at the husband's discretion, and is fired by his implacable wrath. No amount of monetary compensation will appease him. The adulterer will also be subject to physical abuse, possibly at the hands of the husband, or his household, or associates, and public scorn. The city gates are where reputations are on display (24.7-9), and where the adulterer would be despised. A man may recover from a beating, but the adulterer's shame will not be erased from public memory, and he suffers a social death. The gravity of the penalty illustrates the import of having 'no sense' in Proverbs (6.32). This adulterer lacks the practical wisdom to resist the encouraging words of a married woman, through not foreseeing the inevitable consequences of indulging his personal desire. Senselessness is a defect in the mind and judgment, resulting in a grave violation of the social order, for which both the husband and society will exact compensation. The following, final instruction on adultery aims to dispel any illusion that the husband's absence could save the offender from the grave ensuing consequences.

Twelfth Parental Instruction: Wisdom, the Beloved, and the Seductress (7.1-27)

In ch. 7, the last of three instructions on sexuality, a hapless youth fails to find Wisdom, his true life-companion (7.4) when he foolishly agrees to enter the house of another woman. The 'strange woman' re-appears, this time as the wife of an absent, travelling husband, and she is the protagonist in an encounter with a youth as yet un-committed to wisdom. The teacher begins by recommending two ways to avoid misfortune, first by memorizing his advice, and then by cultivating a special relationship with Wisdom. First, the follow-ing advice is to be treasured like the pupil of one's eye, a precious, vulnerable, body member.

> My child, keep my words
> and store up my commandments with you;
> keep my commandments and live,
> keep my teachings as the apple of your eye;
> bind them on your fingers,
> write them on the tablet of your heart (7.1-3).

In a second metaphor, symbolically binding wisdom teaching on the finger would have a practical purpose, to ensure that it would be faithfully copied onto the tablet of the heart (7.3), just as loyalty and faithfulness were written on the tablet of the heart (3.1-3). This image suggests a deep, perhaps indelible penetration into a youth's consciousness.

> Say to wisdom, 'You are my sister,'
> and call insight your intimate friend,
> that they may keep you from the loose woman ['iššâ zārâ],
> from the adulteress [nokriyyâ] with her smooth words (7.4-5).

In a more personal and affective image of his relationship to Wis-dom, the young person is urged to consider Wisdom to have the sta-tus of a dear friend, the beloved, by naming her 'sister' (Song 4.9). The need for such a close relationship is demonstrated in the fol-lowing narration.

> For at the window of my house
> I have looked out through my lattice,
> and I saw among the simple ones,
> I observed among the youths,
> a young man without sense,
> passing along the street near her corner,
> taking the road to her house
> in the twilight, in the evening,
> at the time of night and darkness (7.6-9).

The wise one shapes the instruction as a didactic narrative, by assuming a narrator's role. Previously, the strange woman has been briefly described (5.3-6), or hardly described at all (6.24-25), but in the present poem she is brought to life, given centre-stage in the eye-witness description of a street-scene. The teacher has positioned himself so that every word the temptress says can be heard and reported. First, however, her victim is introduced. The designation, 'without sense' (7.7; see 6.32) indicates to the reader that this youth, selected from a group of equals (7.7), will succumb.

> Then a woman comes toward him,
> decked out like a prostitute, wily of heart.
> She is loud and wayward;
> her feet do not stay at home;
> now in the street, now in the squares,
> and at every corner she lies in wait.
> She seizes him and kisses him,
> and with impudent face she says to him... (7.10-13).

At first view, the approaching woman seems to be a harlot. While her distinctive clothing is not described, she could not have been wearing a veil (Gen. 38.15) as her face is exposed (7.13). Her restless inability to stay in her house, through her need to find victims, is criticized. She is not a kinswoman, and her kiss of greeting is followed by an invitation to erotic love.

> 'I had to offer sacrifices,
> and today I have paid my vows;
> so now I have come out to meet you,
> to seek you eagerly, and I have found you!
> I have decked my couch with coverings,
> coloured spreads of Egyptian linen;
> I have perfumed my bed with myrrh,
> aloes, and cinnamon.
> Come, let us take our fill of love until morning;
> let us delight ourselves with love.
> For my husband is not at home;
> he has gone on a long journey.
> He took a bag of money with him;
> he will not come home until full moon.'
> With much seductive speech she persuades him;
> with her smooth talk she compels him (7.14-21).

This is not a casual encounter. The woman has sought out the youth, saying that she has discharged, through a vowed communion sacrifice, or peace offering, her obligation to God on the granting of a favour (Lev. 22.18-23). Her real intent, however, is not to share her festal table prepared on this occasion, but rather, her carefully arranged bed, and the description of its exotic, embroidered covering and perfume has sensuous appeal. Sound repetitions bind half-verses together: *šelāmîm*, 'peace offerings', and *šillamtî*, 'I have fulfilled' (7.14); *rābadtî*, 'I have covered' my bed with 'coverings' (*mar*ᵉ*baddîm*, 7.16). The invited guest will have his fill, but it will be of illicit love. She dismisses the deterrent of a betrayed husband's revenge elaborated in the previous instruction (6.33-35), by saying that he will be away for some time to come, since he has provided for a long absence, so that secrecy is assured. In pictorial language the teacher shows the effect of her words.

> Right away he follows her,
> and goes like an ox to the slaughter,
> or bounds like a stag toward the trap
> until an arrow pierces its entrails.
> He is like a bird rushing into a snare,
> not knowing that it will cost him his life (7.22-23).

A heedless youth may indeed be misled by the smooth words of a 'strange woman', as the teacher has always said (2.16; 5.3; 6.24). The narration now focuses on the youth, not the woman he is following, and his naivety contrasts with the wise one's awareness of the danger. He illustrates the young man's foolish ignorance by comparing him with three animals in peril. Neither the ox, nor the stag, nor the bird can be expected to know where it is heading, but tragically, the youth has ignored advice, and is on the level of the ignorant animal victims.

> And now, my children, listen to me,
> and be attentive to the words of my mouth.
> Do not let your hearts turn aside to her ways;
> do not stray into her paths.
> for many are those she has laid low,
> and numerous are her victims.
> Her house is the way to Sheol,
> going down to the chambers of death (7.24-27).

After the narration of this fatal encounter, the teacher draws the lesson. It was not an exaggeration to ask that his teaching be written on the tablet of the youth's heart (7.3, compare 7.25), or that he be in love with Wisdom (7.4). In the wise one's experience, a large number of uncommitted youths have been led astray through senseless, sexual indulgence, and their lives seriously affected (compare 1.32). The teacher refers to the 'death' that follows in symbolic terms, that is, Sheol and the chambers of death, without referring to the husband's rage (6.32-35), nor to physical, financial and social ruin (5.9-14), which constitute the premature death signified by previous references to death (2.18; 5.5). He bluntly states that death is linked directly to this act of adultery, emphasizing the ethical death that is an aspect of the previous descriptions, without excluding that the other aspects will be incurred, even when this transgression seems undetected in the short term. Without knowing it, one who has rejected the love of Wisdom has been an easy prey to seduction, and is on a downward path to the abode of the dead (7.27).

Concluding Comments on the Parental Instructions

In the above instructions, wise parents have sought to train their son, or sons, in the wisdom, righteousness, and piety declared to be the aim of the book (1.1-7, 8-9). If a youth were to take to heart this advice, he would have established his own household. His marriage would be secure (5.1-23), threats to his financial security are warded off (6.1-5), and his future assured by personal diligence (6.6-11). Liaisons with other women are avoided (6.20-35), and he dwells trustfully with his neighbour (3.27-31). His household enjoys the blessing of Yahweh (3.32-33), and he dwells securely in the land (2.21). Folly, or failure in life, and impiety, are described in terms of yielding to the alluring words of the violent and perverse (1.10-19; 2.12-15), or of another woman (2.16-19; 5.3-14; 6.20-35), with consequent financial ruin and the loss of a household (5.9-10). Through disregard for the parental advice and teaching (5.12-13), a foolish, now adult son would not have foreseen the consequences of his senseless acts and choices (5.1-2, 7.22-23). One could agree with the comment that in the book as a whole, the household imagery constitutes a basic, pervasive metaphor.

> Founding a house (and the related theme of finding a spouse) was the great task of the young in Proverbs' society. Founding (or governing) a house becomes a basic metaphor for any reader of Proverbs, young or old, male or female. Everyone is charged with the task of building 'a house' in the sense of a personal and communal life. Each person can draw an analogy for his or her own life (Clifford 1999: 108-109).

In the following two poems of Personified Wisdom, Wisdom calls the untutored to her house of instruction (8.1-36), where a banquet of learning is prepared (9.1-6).

Second Discourse of Personified Wisdom: From the City Gates to Wisdom's Gates (8.1-36)

As the first section of Proverbs draws to a close, the wise authors set aside the style of parental wisdom teaching, in order to present their unlearned audience with a different form of instruction, taking their promise of the use of figurative language (1.6) to a new level of development. The extended poetic personification of the abstract, Wisdom, in chs. 8–9, has been anticipated, however, in Wisdom's first discourse in 1.20-33, and in the personification of Wisdom in 3.13-18; 4.8-9. In the context of the previous parental instructions, the structure of Wisdom's discourse in 8.1-36 is broadly recognizable as a teacher's discourse, falling into three sections. In the first section (8.1-21), Wisdom summons her audience (8.1-3), claims a hearing (8.4-11), and extols the benefits of acquiring wisdom (8.12-21). In the second section (8.22-31), the centre of the discourse, Wisdom establishes the basis of the claims she has made, speaking now of her privileged, unique relationship to the Creator and to humans. The discourse closes when Wisdom, the teacher, issues an invitation to her audience to come to her house of instruction (8.32-36). Her audience is, rhetorically, all of humanity, but more concretely and specifically, the audience of the book of Proverbs, notably the simple, and includes all those who have followed the course of wisdom instruction thus far. The wisdom extolled in this discourse is intimately associated with the fear of Yahweh, and personified Wisdom speaks, both rhetorically and in the terms of self-attribution, as no wisdom teacher has yet spoken. Wisdom's second discourse is, however, a sustained invitation to heed wisdom instruction. By the end, Wisdom has faded from public view, and the reader is left with the image of eager students waiting to be admitted to her house of instruction.

A Discourse in a Public Space (8.1-3)

> Does not wisdom call,
> and does not understanding raise her voice?
> On the heights, beside the way,
> at the crossroads she takes her stand;
> beside the gates in front of the town,
> at the entrance of the portals she cries out:

Whereas the wise and righteous Job took his seat at the gate of the city, and all stood in awe at his majestic, liberating words (Job 29.7-25), personified Wisdom takes her stand near the gates, not, like Job, to administer justice, but with the aim of gaining the widest possible audience. This most public space is sketched in a quick succession of five phrases of location. The heights is a generalized expression for the prominent position occupied by a town on a hill-top. The focus narrows to the open space just outside the walls and gate, where the approaching roads merge, and where a motley crowd could be found, comprising people engaged in commerce in the market (20.14), or taking their leisure, or seeking justice in the court situated within the structure of the gates (22.22) (see Lang 1986: 22-23). In 'the proverbs of Solomon', Wisdom teaching will refer to many human activities and situations, and later in the discourse she will make a point of her bonds with all of humankind (8.31).

The Speaker Summons the Audience and Claims a Hearing (8.4-11)

'To you, O people, I call,
and my cry is to all that live.
O simple ones, learn prudence;
acquire intelligence, you who lack it (lit. fools).
Hear, for I will speak noble things,
and from my lips will come what is right;
for my mouth will utter truth;
wickedness is an abomination to my lips.
All the words of my mouth are righteous;
there is nothing twisted or crooked in them.
They are all straight to one who understands
and right to those who find knowledge.
Take my instruction instead of silver,
and knowledge rather than choice gold;
for wisdom is better than jewels,
and all that you may desire cannot compare with her.'

For the present, personified Wisdom has a particular message for the recipients of wisdom teaching, the simple and fools, and that in view of their humanity. To the simple (1.4), Wisdom repeats the aim of the wise ones who penned the book, to impart prudence to them. Fools are included in the human audience, even though the wise ones consider fools to hold instruction in disdain (1.7). The speaker then declares her credentials (8.6-8), not claiming to be the mouthpiece of a king, as an ambassador would (2 Kgs 18.19), but proclaiming that her character is irreproachable, and her words reliable. As the audience is targeted by people making deceitful claims for attention (2.12), Wisdom's admirable personal probity as a messenger enhances the authority of the wisdom teaching being offered in Proverbs, to the extent that the teachers, the wise ones, reflect the model of Wisdom in this respect. The concluding two verses of this preamble (8.10-11) come finally to some of the specific topics of wisdom teaching, namely instruction, knowledge, and wisdom (1.2, 7). Compared with the activity of the vendors trading around the gates (Lang 1986: 22-23), Wisdom's offering is of price-less value, and here Wisdom reiterates the precious metals compar-ison already used by the wise teacher (3.15).

Wisdom's Self-portrait and the Benefits of Choosing Wisdom (8.12-21)

'I, wisdom, live with prudence,
and I attain knowledge and discretion.
The fear of the LORD is hatred of evil.
Pride and arrogance and the way of evil
and perverted speech I hate.
I have good advice and sound wisdom;
I have insight, I have strength.
By me kings reign,
and rulers decree what is just;
by me rulers rule,
and nobles, all who govern rightly.
I love those who love me,
and those who seek me diligently find me.
Riches and honour are with me,
enduring wealth and prosperity.
My fruit is better than gold, even fine gold,
and my yield than choice silver.
I walk in the way of righteousness,
along the paths of justice,
endowing with wealth those who love me,
and filling their treasuries.'

In 8.12-16, Wisdom claims that the educational aims of the book are her personal qualities. These aims include prudence, knowledge and discretion (1.4), insight (1.2), sound wisdom (3.21), and the fear of the Lord, so closely linked to wisdom (1.7). Then, like a wise, God-fearing teacher, Wisdom detests Yahweh's abominations (6.16-19). Further, she is a wise, morally upright, and trustworthy coun-sellor, present in the wise and effective exercise of royal justice, a role which a queen-mother will share towards the end of Prov-erbs (31.1-9). In the final verses of this section, Wisdom's gifts are detailed in between the term 'love', placed at the beginning and the end (8.17, 21), to make the point that those who love Wisdom enter into a reciprocal relationship with her, which includes receiving her gifts. The advantages of a young man's regarding Wisdom as the beloved have been demonstrated in the previous instruction (7.4), and the idea of reciprocal love (8.17) has a context in Proverbs' edu-cational vocabulary, in that a wise one will love his teacher (9.8), but a wise father will also love his child (3.11-12). The gifts that follow from loving Wisdom have already either been said to flow from living according to the parental teaching, for example, righteousness and justice (as in 2.9), or attributed to Wisdom, as wealth and honour (3.16). The theme of seeking and finding wisdom has also been introduced in the instructions (2.4-5). Understanding Wisdom as a female personification of the teaching and values proposed throughout Proverbs does not fully account for the accumulation of attributes in this self-presentation. Personified Wisdom is more than a convenient method of offering in summary the qualities and benefits of wisdom teaching. Her rhetoric lingers, and in the hearers' imagination she is a figure to be chosen and loved, one whose memory will help determine life-choices, by reinforcing the message of the wise parents who have preceded her, and of the following wisdom teachings. In the wider biblical context, the rhetoric of her lofty personal claims compares in form, if not content, with the prophetic style of divine self-exaltation (Isa. 45.5). It is difficult also to overlook the attribution of the qualities in 8.16 with those attributed to the Spirit of God in Isa. 11.2, and to God in Job 12.13, 16 (see Gilbert 1981: 13). It is this relationship of Wisdom to Yahweh that is clarified in the next section of the discourse.

Yahweh's Wisdom in the World's Creation (8.22-31)

At this point, the wise ones enhance the identity of personified Wisdom with images of the process of the creation of the world. Wisdom, as a poetic figure, is now pictured in a delightful, close relationship with Yahweh, as he created the awesome universe (3.19-20), and she can extend a loving and attractive invitation to humans, especially the 'simple', to take delight in assiduously acquiring wisdom (8.32-36).

> 'The LORD created me at the beginning of his work,
> the first of his acts of long ago.
> Ages ago I was set up,
> at the first, before the beginning of the earth.
> When there were no depths I was brought forth,
> when there were no springs abounding with water.
> Before the mountains had been shaped,
> before the hills, I was brought forth—
> when he had not yet made earth and fields,
> or the world's first bits of soil.
> When he established the heavens, I was there,
> when he drew a circle on the face of the deep,
> when he made firm the skies above,
> when he established the fountains of the deep,

when he assigned to the sea its limit,
so that the waters might not transgress his command,
when he marked out the foundations of the earth,
then I was beside him, like a master worker;
and I was daily his delight,
rejoicing before him always,
rejoicing in his inhabited world
and delighting in the human race.'

The imagery in the first part of this section (8.22-26) suggests that Wisdom was created in remotest time, before anything else at all existed, and so could be present beside the Creator as the ordered world emerged from nothing. In the second part (8.27-31), Wisdom's presence during creation is emphasized. All the while, not only was Wisdom a witness, but she was the Creator's intimate, being at his side, not as a mere spectator, but actively delighting in God's handiwork, the world and its human inhabitants. Wisdom is a privileged witness to the order with which Yahweh endowed the universe.

In this account of her origins, Wisdom leads the pupil on a journey of the imagination to the edges of the cosmos, as it was then understood. First, a quick succession of temporal phrases (8.22-23) highlights Wisdom's priority, also capturing the freshness of Wisdom's creation: 'the first', 'long ago' and 'ages ago' make the ultimate leap backwards in time. Then, a *tabula rasa* is established by eliminating from view the world's watery parts (8.24), that is, the cosmic surrounding waters, as well as the springs by which these waters are released on to the earth, and then the land parts of the world (8.25-26). The submerged mountain tops were originally the first of the land to emerge from the subsiding waters, then the hills, and finally the fields, and they now are all removed from a view which focuses on pre-existent Wisdom. Now Wisdom can depict the divine builder constructing the universe in her presence. The primeval abyss is assumed to exist, and Yahweh empties it by tracing, like a master-builder, a line where the firmament will be placed on the waters. Then the builder makes the skies firm, as they will need to keep the waters out. He then strengthened the springs previously removed from view (v. 24) so that they will safely bring up the lower cosmic waters to the surface of the earth (see Clifford 1999: 96). Wisdom then saw Yahweh attend to the land by a command restricting the ocean to certain areas, and so the dry land appears. This is consolidated when Yahweh laid, or according to the Greek reading, made firm, the earth's foundations, that is, the pillars holding up the earth out of the underlying water. The personal presence of Wisdom throughout this creation process is the highlight of the entire passage. She is the first of creation, it is she, the speaker, who removes the visible world from the pupil's gaze, and the ensuing description of Yahweh's work is introduced with 'I was there' (8.27), and concludes with 'I was there beside him' (8.30). Thus Wisdom is a privileged witness when Yahweh imposed order on the universe.

The Hebrew terms used to describe Wisdom's birth and her role in creation may be either textually construed or interpreted in different ways. Wisdom clearly comes to birth (8.24-25), and she is the beloved daughter of Yahweh, his happiness and joy. In the previous verse, instead of being 'set up' (8.23 NRSV), Wisdom may have been arguably 'poured forth', in molten form, like an artefact, or again, to continue the birth metaphor, she may have been 'woven' in the womb. The ambiguity continues in the concluding 8.30-31, the climax to which all the preceding leads. Wisdom is in Yahweh's presence, rejoicing at every stage of Yahweh's work, like those other witnesses to creation in the creation account in Job, 'when the morning stars sang together and all the heavenly beings shouted for joy' (Job 38.7). None of the proposed interpretations of the difficult Hebrew term *'āmôn* is completely consistent with the imagery as a whole, whether, for example, the NRSV 'master worker', which would be a more appropriate description of Yahweh than of Wisdom, or 'sage', that is, 'a divine or semi-divine bringer of culture and skill to the human race' (Clifford 1999: 101), or 'nurseling' which accords with the previous birth imagery. The point of the conclusion of the discourse, and of the whole passage, may be summarized: 'Wisdom invites her disciples to have a relationship with her analogous to the one she has with Yahweh' (Clifford 1999: 98). She knows how Yahweh intended the universe to function, and just as those who bring order to society are indebted to Wisdom (8.15) (Gilbert 1981: 14), so will Wisdom, if embraced, bring order into the lives of the young.

Concluding Appeal (8.32-36)

> 'And now, my children, listen to me:
> happy are those who keep my ways.
> Hear instruction and be wise,
> and do not neglect it.
> Happy is the one who listens to me,
> watching daily at my gates,
> waiting beside my doors.
> For whoever finds me finds life
> and obtains favour from the LORD;
> but those who miss me injure themselves;
> all who hate me love death.'

Wisdom's final 'and now' introduces a persuasive appeal, and she resumes speaking like a wisdom teacher (compare 8.32a with 7.24a). The simple have no good reason to remain in their uncommitted state, nor the fools to remain obstinate. In view of their humanity to which Wisdom has appealed (8.31), they can no longer linger in the city gates. Let them become model students, waiting for her at those other gates, the gates of Wisdom's house of instruction. The next figurative lesson (9.1-6) introduces Wisdom as a hostess issuing an invitation to enter her house. Inside, a feast of life awaits her guests.

Two Hostesses and Two Meal Invitations (9.1-18)

The first section of Proverbs comes to a close with a poetic diptych (Alonso Schökel and Vílchez Líndez 1984: 245), each panel of which displays a female character, the one of Wisdom, the other of a Foolish Woman, the contrasting panels being neatly balanced by the women speaking to the same audience. Between the panels is a group of educational adages, offering an experienced instructor's advice to other wise teachers, about dealing with wise and foolish students. This instructional theme relates to the women's messages in the panels, where each woman makes a summary, final appeal to those who have not yet committed themselves to the pursuit of wisdom, notwithstanding all the previous parental instructions, and despite personified Wisdom's two carefully composed, and well-motivated appeals.

The First Panel: Wisdom's Banquet (9.1-6)

> Wisdom has built her house,
> she has hewn her seven pillars (9.1).

Personified Wisdom's previous discourse at the city gates closed with a summons to her house of instruction (8.34). The house image is now developed differently, in a scene of the festal inauguration of Wisdom's newly constructed house. Architecturally, the perfect number of seven pillars refers to the one or more rows of internal pillars supporting the rafters, and creating aisles that enhanced the living area. The exceptionally large, gracious, and hospitable inner space suggests a palace of the ruling elite as the model for the image (see Holladay, 'House, Israelite', *ABD*, III: 316). In Jewish tradition, Wisdom's house becomes a royal palace, when, in the Tosefta, Prov. 9.1 is cited alongside the parable of 'a king who built a palace and dedicated it; and prepared a meal and [only] afterward invited the guests' (*Sanh.* 8.9 in Neusner 2002: 1174; see Gilbert 1981: 24).

> She has slaughtered her animals,
> she has mixed her wine,
> she has also set her table.
> She has sent out her servant-girls, she calls
> from the highest places in the town (9.2-3).

The reader is not meant to delay admiring the architecture, for another five verbs in rapid succession (9.2-3) lead to the moment when Wisdom, the hostess, is sending out her delegated handmaidens to invite the guests, from the highest, most public point in the city. The preparations are quite specific. The expression, 'she has slaughtered her animals' (*ṭābᵉḥâ ṭibḥāh*, 9.2) is regular for killing an animal and preparing the meat for a meal (Gen. 43.16; 1 Sam. 25.11), which is indicated in 'dressed her meat' (NAB). Wisdom has also enriched the wine with spices for a special occasion, and finally, the table has been prepared, needing only the guests to arrive. The occasion for this banquet is not simply to celebrate, as a king might, the completion of an important building project (2 Chron. 7.8), but the meal is designed to nourish a particular group of guests, the immature and senseless. Wisdom is the second woman in chs. 1–9 to issue a meal invitation, whose real intent is then specified (see 7.14, 18). The servant girls speak in the first person, as if Wisdom were personally speaking (9.4a-5). They call out the invitation so as to reach all the invitees, wherever they may be dispersed in the crowd.

> 'You that are simple, turn in here!'
> To those without sense she says,
> 'Come, eat of my bread
> and drink of the wine I have mixed.
> Lay aside immaturity, and live,
> and walk in the way of insight' (9.4-6).

The immature and the senseless, the addressees of the book of Proverbs (1.4), are the ones amongst the crowd most in need of instruction. The festal meal is now generalized as bread, which symbolizes Wisdom's teaching, and the guests are being asked to leave aside childhood immaturity, and commit to a life nourished by that teaching. The meal invitation scene is a poetic, narrative exposition. At the end of chs. 1–9, personified Wisdom, who has been seen issuing from the Creator's hands in first-born freshness, to be the privileged witness of the rest of creation, as Yahweh's delight, and who in turn delights in humans (8.22-31), now re-presents to the immature amongst them the fundamental challenge proposed both in her previous two discourses, and in the parental instructions, to leave immaturity, accept wisdom instruction, and live successfully and happily. The quality of the life Wisdom promises has been detailed in the previous poems, and it includes a right relationship with Yahweh (3.5-6), longevity (3.16), physical vitality (3.8), wealth and social well-being (3.2-4), and peaceful possession of the land (2.21).

The Second Panel: The Foolish Woman's Invitation (9.13-18)

> The foolish woman is loud;
> she is ignorant and knows nothing.
> She sits at the door of her house,
> on a seat at the high places of the town,
> calling to those who pass by,
> who are going straight on their way (9.13-15).

In Hebrew, two disparaging abstract nouns are used in Folly's description, 'foolishness' (*kᵉsîlût*) and 'ignorance' (*pᵉtayyût*), words which are found only in this place in the Bible, and they suggest that she represents the essence of folly. The satirical expression, she 'knows nothing', has been said of the wayward women (5.5-6; 7.22-23), as is Folly's trait of noisiness (7.11). Her slothful inactivity, as she sits on a chair to issue the invitation, contrasts with Wisdom's effective preparations (9.1-3), but both her location and audience are the same as Wisdom's. The immature walking past would need to turn aside to accept, as they would to enter the house of the promiscuous woman (5.8).

> 'You who are simple, turn in here!'
> And to those without sense she says,
> 'Stolen water is sweet,
> and bread eaten in secret is pleasant' (9.16-17).

The meagre, symbolic meal cannot compare with Wisdom's generous fare, and the theft and secrecy implied in the adulteress's invitation in ch. 7 now become incitements to illicit pleasure. Folly knows, however, that this fare can appeal to the senseless, and that she needs only to sit on her chair and offer it.

> But they do not know that the dead are there,
> that her guests are in the depths of Sheol (9.18).

This hostess cannot, like Wisdom (9.6), advise the guests of the outcome of accepting her nourishment, and this gap is filled by the wisdom teacher's comment. Sheol, the abode of the dead, identifies this woman's house with the wayward women's house (2.18;

5.5; 7.27), and those who accept will be like the senseless one 'not knowing' his fate (7.23). At this point, the audience needs to choose which of the invitations to accept. Personified Wisdom's counterpart is an adulteress or a prostitute, like the loose woman of the instructions. While the latter is not the only threat to the attainment of wisdom (see, for example 2.12-15), a woman character type is a suitable antithesis to Woman Wisdom. As well as being sexually deviant, she personifies all the unrighteous and irreligious traits of folly referred to in the previous poems, for example, sloth (6.10), the deceitful promise of rapid satisfaction (1.13), and smooth and deceitful speech (1.11-14).

Intermediate Passage: A Sage's Counsel to Teachers and Students (9.7-12)

In the passage separating the two panels, the counselling voice of the wise one who composed the preface (1.1-7) re-emerges into the foreground. The first three sayings are addressed to fellow teachers, a contribution to the promise made to the wise in the preface (1.5a), and the second three to students. An experienced teacher has wanted to include these comments on the educational process, here at the end of chs. 1–9.

> Whoever corrects a scoffer wins abuse;
> whoever rebukes the wicked gets hurt.
> A scoffer who is rebuked will only hate you;
> the wise, when rebuked, will love you.
> Give instruction to the wise, and they will become wiser still;
> teach the righteous and they will gain in learning.
> The fear of the LORD is the beginning of wisdom,
> and the knowledge of the Holy One is insight.
> For by me your days will be multiplied,
> and years will be added to your life.
> If you are wise, you are wise for yourself;
> if you scoff, you alone will bear it.

The advice to teachers makes a rhetorical unit, in that 9.8a looks back to 9.7, and 9.8b looks forward to 9.9. The first adage (9.7) converts the advice in 1.7b into a warning for the teacher: attempting to educate the unwilling will only damage oneself. The second saying (9.8) also concerns educating the recalcitrant, but from the perspective of the harm done to the relationship between a teacher and the disciple. In one instruction, the libertine, too late, laments the rupture of this relationship (5.13). On the other hand, teaching a willing student establishes a good relationship (9.8b). In the third saying (9.9) a teacher is seen as an agent of growth (as in

1.5), provided, of course, that the pupil is upright, a reminder that wisdom teaching has an intrinsic ethical aspect, and a pupil without that will make little progress. The advice to students (9.10-12) is rhetorically a slightly confusing group of three sayings, in that they comprise a third-person reflection, followed by two counsels addressed directly to students in the second-person, in the first of which the speaker refers to himself in the first-person (9.11). First, there is a recall of the basic religious dimension of the process of becoming wise (1.7; 2.6). Knowing God amounts to knowing the behaviour that pleases God, and respecting the order of the created world. The appeal to a healthy self-interest in 9.11 would sit perfectly as the conclusion to Wisdom's invitation above. Once Wisdom has again secured the audience's attention, the teacher adds a final, fatherly reminder that throughout the process of instruction and rebuke, a wise teacher has the pupil's welfare at heart (9.12).

While a rich fare of wisdom teaching has already been provided in the first nine chapters, the invitation to Wisdom's house of learning in the final chapter of the book's first section also looks ahead to the following 'proverbs of Solomon' (10.1–22.16). The simple ones who have renounced their immaturity are qualified to share the banquet of wisdom offered in the following section.

Proverbs 10.1–22.16: The Proverbs of Solomon

Introductory Comments

'The proverbs of Solomon' will be discussed according to a number of topical groups, rather than by commenting sequentially on the unfolding text. The following topics are identified: Formation in Wisdom, Life in the Household, The Benefits of Righteousness, Yahweh and the King, The Power of Language, Poverty and Prosperity, and Joy and Sadness. The location and distribution of the sayings on any particular topic will, however, be noted, and by way of preview, it may be mentioned that many sayings on the subject of righteousness are found in chs. 1–15, and rarely after that. In the second half of the section (16.1–22.16), where relatively few righteousness proverbs are found, topics that were only introduced in the first half, for example, the plight of the poor, are much more numerous. Topics that are evenly distributed throughout the section, for example, on the need to accept discipline and instruction, are developed with some urgency towards the end, on the threshold of 'the words of the wise' (22.17–24.34).

The reader may at first be more aware of the rhetorical difference between this section and the longer instructional poems in chs. 1–9, rather than of the broadening of the themes in the first section. The prevailing form of expression is the two-line proverb in the third person: 'A wise child makes a glad father, but a foolish child is a mother's grief' (10.1). In chs. 10–15, the two half-verses are usually in a relation of antithetical parallelism, as above. In the second half of the section (16.1–22.16), however, the second half-verse usually develops the thought of the first, often providing a more particular focus, or developing the thought of the first affirmation: 'The LORD has made everything for its purpose, even the wicked for the day of trouble' (16.4). Rhetorical touches enliven the parallelism, for example, a proverb may include an exclamation: 'To make an apt answer is a joy to anyone, and a word in season, how good it is!' (15.23). Alliteration also adds to the appeal of many of the Hebrew proverbs, and more significantly, makes them memorable, able to be recalled as guides to decision-making in later life: *bā'-zādôn wayyābō' qālôn* ('"When pride comes, then comes disgrace", but wisdom is with the humble', 11.2). Amongst the proverbs one very occasionally finds the second-person imperative, so frequent in the first nine chapters: 'Leave the presence of a fool, for there you do not find words of knowledge' (14.7). From ch. 16 on, the number of imperatives increases: 'Commit your work to the LORD, and your plans will be established' (16.3; see also 19.18, 27; 20.16; 22.6). The citation of a character's spoken words, found in the first and the last parental instruction in chs.1–9 (1.11-14; 7.14-20), also occurs in the 'Proverbs'. '"Bad, bad," says the buyer, then goes away and boasts' (20.14). In summary, Solomon's proverbs are mostly sayings in the third person, without reference to an audience. Many of them, however, are enlivened through the music of the language, by exclamation, and dramatic speech forms. While in the following topical commentary the rhetorical aspects are frequently noted, attention will also be given to elucidating the metaphorical language, understanding which has an important role in the education of the young to wisdom (1.6).

Formation in Wisdom

In chs. 1–9, a father and mother are teachers, and these chapters comprise, for the most part, a series of wisdom instructions addressed by a father to their son. In 'the proverbs of Solomon', cited words of instruction are rare, becoming more frequent in the second half of the section. Many of the two-line, pithy sayings, on the other hand, are concerned with the process of acquiring wisdom, and they refer, in their third-person style, to instruction and discipline, to the value of wisdom, to a teaching father, a mother, and a son, and to other characters appearing in the first nine chapters, including the simple one and the wise one, the scoffer and the fool. Approximately forty of the three hundred and fifty proverbs comprising this section are dedicated to this topic, and they are distributed throughout the section. In a progressive reading of the proverbs concerned with wisdom education, a number of clusters may be identified, as below, preceded by a note on the setting of these sayings.

The Household Setting

As in chs. 1–9, the theme of the household is important in 'the proverbs of Solomon', beginning with the first proverb: 'A wise child makes a glad father, but a foolish child is a mother's grief' (10.1).

The motif of the emotional effect on the parents of the behaviour of grown children is absent in the instructions, which were concerned with a son's future life and welfare (e.g. in 1.15-19), and the relationship between the generations is alluded to only in the context of wisdom teaching as family heritage (4.3-4). Nonetheless, in the light of the previous descriptions of wisdom and folly, and of a child's success and failure, the parents' emotional involvement in their son's behaviour in 'the proverbs of Solomon' is understandable. This topic is developed with a subsequent reference to the joy and satisfaction awaiting a father (15.20), with three references to a father's grief (17.21, 25; 19.13), and another allusion to a sorrowing mother (17.25), who bears the brunt of a fool's contempt for wisdom and instruction (15.20; see also 1.7). The cost to mothers and fathers of a failed education receives greater emphasis than the joy of success. Sayings in the second section reiterate the previous descriptions of a child's failure, when we read depictions of the fool's financial failure (21.20), his domestic failure (14.1), and his inability to foresee and avoid misfortune (14.16) (Barucq 1964: 117).

A Wise Young Person Enters Willingly into the Process of Education which Includes Discipline and Reproof (chs. 1–15, noting 10.8, 17; 12.1; 13.1, 14, 18, 24; 15.5, 10, 12, 32, 33)

The vocabulary of the Torah and the prophets in the context of instruction, noted already in regard to the use of the term *tôrâ* as parental teaching (1.8), occurs also in regard to the terms instruction and discipline, which occur as translations of the Hebrew *mûsār*. In the Bible generally, discipline may come in the shape of God's liberating acts for the people (Deut. 11.2), or as a prophetic interpretation of national disaster, which is not understood by Israel, and rejected (Jer. 7.28; 17.23; 32.33). Job's affliction is said to be a discipline sent to him, as an individual, by God, which he would be advised to accept (Job 5.17). In the book of Proverbs, on the other hand, discipline is addressed to the young and immature, and it has an indispensable role in their formation. Discipline or instruction is administered by parents or teachers, and it is embraced, or rejected by their children, young and old. The term 'reproof', or 'correction' (*tôkahat*), occurs in parallel with 'instruction' or 'discipline', and while the two terms are difficult to distinguish, reproofs have been defined as integrating perspectives often contrary to one's own instincts (Clifford 1999: 155).

As at the beginning of the instructions (1.8-9), it is also now noted very early that the wisdom that gladdens a parent (10.1) can only be acquired by accepting teaching and direction: 'The wise of heart will heed commandments, but a babbling fool will come to ruin' (10.8). The wise one takes to heart the advice of his elders, but the fool ('the fool of lips'), endlessly expressing the folly in his heart, has little inclination to listen to instruction, where he would learn a salutary lesson about the outcomes of his behaviour. An antithetical proverb, applying the word-pair 'forsaking' and 'keeping' (4.6) to the process of acquiring wisdom, captures the life-and-death importance of accepting instruction and reproof: 'Whoever heeds instruction is on the path to life, but one who rejects a rebuke goes astray' (10.17). In another early proverb (12.1) the 'love'–'hate' word-pair illustrates that wisdom requires a decisive choice to accept the attendant discipline and reproof: 'Whoever loves discipline loves knowledge, but those who hate to be rebuked are stupid' (12.1). In the psalms the stupid is paralleled with the fool (Pss. 49.10; 92.6), as ignorant of God's presence in human affairs. Those who do not understand the necessity of rebuke are just as stupid. The proverb moves briskly, with the first half-verse comprising four two-syllable words and the second half-verse concluding with the emphatic two-syllable *bāʿar* ('stupid').

Two concentrations of proverbs, in chs. 13 and 15, are concerned with the role of discipline and rebuke. The mocker, heedless of rebuke, is the antithesis of the wise: 'A wise child loves discipline, but a scoffer does not listen to rebuke' (13.1). This first reference to the scoffer sets the term 'scoffer' in a wisdom education context. In the psalms, the scoffers ridicule the followers of God's law (Ps. 1.1), and in Isaiah the adult opponents of God and the prophet (Isa. 28.22) pay no heed to God's designs. In Proverbs, while the scoffers are scorned by God (3.34), this is because of their rejection of training in wisdom (1.22; 9.7). Acceptance of correction is made more purposeful when sayings concerning discipline and reproof are found in proximity to other proverbs stating the gravity of the issues entailed, namely, life or death (13.14), social esteem, or poverty and dishonour (13.18). The image of the fountain suggests that the teaching of the wise is a never-failing source of life for those who implement it: 'The teaching of the wise is a fountain of life, so that one may avoid the snares of death' (13.14). In the antithesis, death is like a hunter laying traps and snares for the unwary. Notwithstanding the teacher's frequent praise of the benefits of wisdom (e.g. 3.13-18; 4.8-9), and the appeals of personified Wisdom (8.1-36; 9.1-6), it is now acknowledged that discipline and correction are uncongenial to the young. Several sayings, building on the antithesis, 'heeding instruction' and 'ignoring reproof' (10.17; 13.18; 15.5), reiterate the serious issues here at stake, which include one's acceptance into the wider community (see 5.9; 6.33): 'Poverty and disgrace are for the one who ignores instruction, but one who heeds reproof is honoured' (13.18). Another proverb looks to a father's responsibility: 'Those who spare the rod hate their children, but those who love them are diligent to discipline them' (13.24). This sonorous proverb, with each word in the first half-verse containing an 'o' sound (*ḥôśēk šibṭô śônē' bᵉnô*), arrives at a stark conclusion. Because a loving father imparts the necessary discipline (3.12), the father who neglects this duty is said, in the poetry of antithesis, to hate his son.

The first proverb on discipline and reproof in ch. 15 concerns a youth's responsibility in this matter: 'A fool despises a parent's instruction, but the one who heeds admonition is prudent' (15.5). Then a salutary reminder is given to the simple that death is the ultimate consequence of rejecting instruction, with another allusion (see 14.15) to the fool being led inevitably along the wrong path: 'There is severe discipline for one who forsakes the way, but one who hates a rebuke will die' (15.10). As Charles Bridges commented, there is no surer step to ruin than to hate correction (Bridges 2001: 120). In contrast, 'The ear that heeds wholesome admonition will lodge among the wise' (15.31). The listening ear represents, by synecdoche, a young person who accepts correction willingly. A very different community life is sketched in the picture of the gang of violent men (1.11-14). The lesson of the benefits of correction is repeated in another proverb built on the parallel of ignoring or heeding instruction and reproof: 'Those who ignore instruction despise themselves, but those who heed admonition gain understanding' (15.32). The point made here is that while the immature may find correction very difficult to receive, correction imparts the illuminating self-knowledge that enables the young to construct their lives in a positive and fruitful manner. In the context of the proverbs about wisdom as instruction and discipline, the equivalence of wisdom and fear of Yahweh (1.7) is expressed by the idea that one who fears Yahweh will experience continuous teaching and training in wisdom: 'The fear of the LORD is instruction in wisdom, and humility goes before honour' (15.33). The fear of God goes beyond a reverential attitude to God, to include the effort to live in harmony with other people, within the whole created order. Such realistic humility is recognized and is the foundation of community respect.

Wisdom's Advantages (16.16, 21, 22, 23)

After the many proverbs concerning the place of discipline and reproof, a number of sayings in ch. 16 extol wisdom, discipline's reward. Here the wise ones educate by sharing their own experience of wisdom's value, once it is acquired. One who exclaims, 'How much better to get wisdom than gold! To get understanding is to be chosen rather than silver' (16.16), is speaking from experience. Next come a pair of proverbs built on the metaphor of the organic link between heart, mouth and lips. The wisdom residing within the heart gains people's attention through the spoken word, imaged in the mouth and lips: 'The wise of heart is called perceptive, and pleasant speech (lit. sweetness of lips) increases persuasiveness' (16.21, see also 16.23). Finally a proverb speaks in highest terms of practical good sense (*śēkel*). 'Wisdom (*śēkel*) is a fountain of life to one who has it, but folly is the punishment (*mûsār*) of fools' (16.22). Instruction in wise conduct (*haśkēl*, 1.3), a term related to *śēkel*, is promised in the preface (1.3), and numerous proverbs praise the person possessing this practical good sense in its adjectival form (*maśkîl*), translated as 'prudent', 'wise', 'one who deals wisely' (10.5, 19; 14.35). In the antithesis (16.22b) there is a parody of the vocabulary of instruction, when the only discipline or instruction (these terms being a more appropriate translation of *mûsar*, than the NRSV choice of 'punishment') that fools receive is their own folly, teaching them very well to become more and more foolish. Indeed fools are at ease with their hatred of knowledge (1.22, 32), and they will not accept a wholesome discipline (15.32), the necessary condition for acquiring good sense.

The Incorrigible (17.10, 16, 21, 25)

Much experience seems to have taught the wise ones that some youths are incorrigible, so that any objective comment on their condition is difficult: 'A rebuke strikes deeper into a discerning person than a hundred blows into a fool' (17.10). Another colourful expression of frustration is found in a saying on a fool's condition. Here a wise one cannot comprehend the incongruity between what a certain person has, namely, money at his disposition in view of purchasing wisdom, and what he has not, namely practical good sense, and any desire to better himself (15.21). These deficiencies place wisdom beyond his reach, allowing him to think that wisdom can be purchased like merchandise: 'Why should fools have a price in hand to buy wisdom, when they have no mind to learn?' (17.16). In a serious word of advice to one who aims to establish a household, the theme of the long-term effects on the parents of a failed upbringing recurs: 'The one who begets a fool gets trouble; the parent of a fool has no joy' (17.21, see also 17.25).

Fourth and Final Group (chs. 19–22): Exhortations to a Father and a Son (19.18, 20, 25, 27, 29; 21.24; 22.6, 10, 15)

A greater concentration of the sayings concerning wisdom education comes as 'the proverbs of Solomon' draw to a close, so that the three principal protagonists in the process of formation in wisdom, the father, the son, and the scoffer, are in strong relief. The last mentioned well-known character-type (see ch. 15, for example) reappears in five sayings. This term seems to name a wisdom teacher's opponent (13.1; 15.12). Sadly, his punishment may benefit others (21.11), but not himself. He is seen as a threat to the teacher's authority, because he has his own plan for education (14.6), without any recourse to the wise (15.12). Though he is intractable, reiterating his fate at the end of the section of the proverbs was apparently considered a useful warning to the well-disposed (19.25; 21.11; 22.10). This final group also includes five exhortations in the second-person style of chs. 1–9, two addressed to the learner (19.20, 27) and three to the parent-teacher (19.18, 25; 22.6). Rhetorically, these exhortations are an echo of the longer instructions in chs. 1–9, and they anticipate the second-person style of the following 'words of the wise'.

'Discipline your children while there is hope; do not set your heart on their destruction' (19.18). This a word of encouragement to parents. If they have hope for their children, this will sustain them in the arduous task of training them. (Other expressions of hope as a source of confidence are read in Ruth 1.12 and Job 11.18). The wise one has a message of hope for children also, to encourage them to accept discipline and instruction: 'Listen to advice and accept instruction, that you may gain wisdom for the future' (19.20). Holding up for consideration the outcomes of choices, for good or for ill, is a frequent educational technique in Proverbs (e.g. 5.11; 14.12). On the other hand, even a deserved beating would not improve a scoffer's attitude (13.1; 15.12), and the teacher would receive little thanks for attempting it. The uncommitted simple, however, may be impressed by witnessing the scorner's fate: 'Strike a scoffer, and the simple will learn prudence; reprove the intelligent, and they will gain knowledge' (19.25). The second half-verse asserts that the intelligent will profit simply by being reproved (as in 12.1; 15.5, 31, 32). The final words to the child are a warning. 'Cease straying, my child, from the words of knowledge, in order that you may hear instruction' (19.27). The teaching of elders needed to be retained, as a guide to living long after an initial education (22.6), and the best outcome was when parents' wisdom was transmitted to the next generation (4.3).

Following a saying about a scoffer in a legal context (19.28), the legal imagery continues in the fate that society inflicts on the intractable: 'Condemnation is ready for scoffers, and flogging for the backs of fools' (19.29). In another saying, criticism turns to vituperation: 'The proud, haughty person, named "Scoffer", acts with arrogant pride' (21.24). A scoffer is the embodiment of arrogance, emphasized by the sound repetition in the first and last words (*zēd...zādôn*). The training which parents impart is envisaged as initiation into a permanent way of living, one which mature parents would pass on to their own children (4.3): 'Train children in the right way, and when old, they will not stray' (22.6). In the final scoffer saying in the section, his behaviour is as disruptive as that of the hothead (15.18): 'Drive out a scoffer, and strife goes out; quarrelling and abuse will cease' (22.10). If the saying were to be addressed to a person of authority in a group, a king could be envisaged (Ps. 101.5). The saying, however, may amount to an observation: there is no point in trying to come to terms with arrogance, and it is wise to stem discord by acting quickly (17.14). The final saying in 'the proverbs' concerning the training of the young reverts to the theme of discipline and reproof, the subject of so many proverbs in the first half of the section: 'Folly is bound in the heart of a boy, but the rod of discipline drives it far away' (22.15). For a youth to decide wisely in situations which could ultimately be destructive, the space of his heart would need to be unencumbered with folly, so that the heart could have treasured the advice that alone could save him (3.3; 6.21; 7.3). The metaphor of the rod is used for discipline, which, like a shepherd's rod (Ps. 23.4), drives away the threat posed by such besetting folly.

Concluding Comments

The theme of formation in wisdom, so prominent in chs. 1–9, receives sustained expression in 'the proverbs of Solomon', which are dedicated to training in wisdom through the literary form of the two-line proverb in the third person. A reader could easily infer from the proverbs on wisdom that parents are always considered to be wise and just, and that the development of children hinges on their willingness to learn from and imitate their parents. While unworthy parents would be included in the various unfavourable character types in this section, the latter are never referred to as parents. In the presentation of parents and children in the proverbs in this section, the urgent second-person appeals to the audience found in the earlier instructions give way to apparently neutral observations in the third person, proposed apparently for the audience's calm consideration, and verification. An inspection of the disposition of the sayings on this theme, however, dispels any impression of objective neutrality on the part of the authors. Over the course of the first five chapters of 'the proverbs of Solomon' many of the observations teach the importance of a willingness of the young to accept training and reproof. It was considered useful to advise those attracted by Wisdom's words at the end of the first section (chs. 8–9) that there was no easy path to wisdom and maturity. A third group of sayings targets the unteachable, named scoffers and fools, who appear now as outsiders in respect to the wise ones and youths who are well-disposed. In the final group of proverbs dealing with wisdom education, the wise ones address words of encouragement to parents and children, those engaged in the task, taking them into their confidence through a change to the second-person style. The need for discipline is reiterated at the very end of the section, so that the attentive reader of the sayings on formation in wisdom will be disposed to be attentive to the theme of wisdom education when it re-appears in the following section, 'the words of the wise' (22.17–24.34).

Life in the Household

The proverbs on training in wisdom have concerned the upbringing of children. It pertains to the fullness of life held out in Proverbs that a father and mother should see their grown children mature in wisdom and righteousness. Another group of proverbs, which will now be discussed in the order in which they occur, concerns the relationship of parents, grown children and grandchildren, and of husband and wife, rather than the specific aspect of wisdom education. It is difficult to discern a topical development in the sequence of family relationship proverbs, and the three paragraphs in the following commentary represent a quantitative division. The conclusion takes the form of a thematic summary. 'A child who gathers in summer (*baqqayiṣ*) is prudent, but a child who sleeps in harvest (*baqqāṣîr*) brings shame' (10.5). In the word-pair 'prudent' and 'shameful' (see also 17.2), the term 'wise', *maśkîl* ('prudent'), relates closely to wise dealing (*haśkēl*, 1.3), that is, wisdom in decision and practice. A wise young person knows the importance of working in harmony with the seasons, and can act accordingly. The penalty of household sloth, bringing shame on the family, goes beyond the financial ruin attaching to sloth in the previous proverb (10.4), and may include the son's disgrace (13.18), and the mother's sense of failure (10.1). A proverb on a disruptive householder closes a group of four proverbs beginning the participial 'one who' + verb, and these proverbs illustrate the outcome of the behaviour of typical persons (11.26-29). 'Those who trouble their households will inherit wind, and the fool will be servant to the wise' (11.29). Here a youth's future, for good or for ill, is tied to success in household management. Greed is one cause of such disruptive behaviour (15.27), and is the antithesis of the wise housewife's thoughtful and generous provision (31.20-22). Paradoxically, the hoarder will have the empty air as an inheritance (NAB), that is, will be left without household, or possessions, which is affirmed in a proverb on generosity (11.24). The parallel half-verse pictures such a one being subject, as a servant or slave, to a successful householder, one who has what counts most in household affairs, practical wisdom. Next, 'A good wife is the crown of her husband, but she who brings shame is like rottenness in his bones' (12.4). As a wife's practical wisdom brings honour on her husband (31.23), so can her foolish behaviour inflict humiliation, which, through the image of the state of his bones, sours a man's whole experience of life. 'The good leave an inheritance to their children's children, but the sinner's wealth is laid up for the righteous' (13.22). A good, or righteous head of family, who has not brought the household down though foolish behaviour, will leave the inherited family property to his own children and grandchildren. Here the family's future, even to the second generation, is secured by acting righteously, not by seizing ill-gotten gain, for example (10.2). In the antithesis, the sinner is said to leave nothing to his children, but the householder's ill-gotten wealth will fall to a righteous, or honest householder. This somewhat surprising description of the outcomes of antithetical behaviour, expressed in terms of the replacement of the unworthy by one more worthy, is a notion found also in Job 27.17. This proverb is linked to the previous proverb, 'Misfortune pursues sinners, but the just shall be recompensed with good' (13.21 NAB), by chiastic repetition of the terms 'good' and 'sinner'.

The wise woman builds her house, but the foolish tears it down with her own hands (14.1). The proverb uses contrasting women-types, and the imagery of house-building and house-demolition, to illustrate effectively the decisive role of a wife and mother. A woman's wisdom is defined in terms of her ability to create household harmony and prosperity. Other proverbs concern the aspects of a husband's responsibilities (13.22; 15.27), and of Yahweh's involvement (19.14). 'Those who are greedy for unjust gain make trouble for their households, but those who hate bribes will live' (15.27). Bribery and greed have specific contexts in the psalms (Ps. 10.3), and in prophecy (Isa. 33.15), but the present saying refers to the trouble that greed brings on a family, whereas a household maintained on honest earnings will flourish. 'A wise servant will rule over a disgraceful son, and will share the inheritance as one of the brothers' (17.2). This proverb, whose sonorous first half-verse has three 's' sounds (*'ebed-maśkîl yimśōl b⁰bēn mēbîš*), again extols practical household wisdom. The shameful conduct is not defined, but, when the family property is distributed, the son's share will go to the servant, perhaps one born in the household, who knows how to manage affairs, and who has earned his master's confidence, like Abraham's unnamed servant (Gen. 24.2). 'Grandchildren are the crown of the aged, and the glory of children is their parents' (17.6). The half-verses begin with the similarly sounding 'crown' (*'⁰ṭeret*) and 'glory' (*tip'eret*), and two pairs of 'm' sounds resound throughout. The long life flowing from righteousness (16.31) includes the honour and happiness of seeing one's children's children. For their part, such children take pride in their parents (20.7), as A. Cohen noted: 'No words could present a more powerful incentive for a man to live honourably, that his children should have reason to be proud of him' (Cohen 1985: 112). 'A stupid child is ruin to a father, and a wife's quarrelling is a continual dripping of rain' (19.13). A mother and father are both said to be grieved by their foolish son (17.25), but this proverb, through another image of the house-structure (14.1), dwells on the worst that can happen to a man, when his wife's constant aggravation adds to his sorrow. 'A house and wealth are the inheritance of ancestors, but a sensible wife is from Yahweh' (19.14). On the other hand, a good wife coming to a man is like an unpredictable gift of Yahweh, just as Rebekah's family perceived a divine dimension in the events surrounding her betrothal (Gen. 24.50). A woman's prudence, or household ability, is the quality most esteemed.

'Those who do violence to their father and chase away their mother are children who cause shame and bring reproach' (19.26). The Torah legislation stipulates grave penalties for disrespect and stubborn disobedience to parents (Exod. 21.15; Lev. 20.9; Deut. 21.18-21), but this proverb has an instructional aim, as it provides an extreme example of how a youth's disgraceful conduct can tear a family asunder. It seems that an adult son disowns and drives out his parents, and seizes the family property before it is bequeathed. 'If you curse father or mother, your lamp will go out in utter darkness' (20.20). This household proverb contains the image of the brightly burning household lamp as a symbol of the household's prosperity, as in the final poem in the book (31.18). The snuffed out lamp, on the other hand, plunges the house into complete darkness, which symbolizes a disrespectful child's premature death. 'An inheritance quickly gained at the beginning will not be blessed at the end' (20.21 NIV). Here the word-pair 'beginning'–'end' is used to express the outcome of greed, or haste to get rich, for Proverbs is critical of unworthy haste (6.18; 19.2), and haste occasioned by covetousness is singled out (1.16). In this saying, prosperity, in terms of God's visible blessing, is denied the householder who seizes his inheritance, so that his unrighteous greed for gain is thwarted. 'It is better to live in a corner of the housetop than in a house shared with a contentious wife' (21.9). A youth can expect to encounter undesirable men in the wider society (2.12-15), and the promise of domestic happiness (5.15-19) may be unfilled if children turn out badly (17.21, 25), or if one's spouse is not seen to be Yahweh's gift (19.13-14). Poetically speaking, it is better to live outside in the dripping rain, or in a desert (21.19), than to dwell with a contentious wife. 'Precious treasure remains in the house of the wise, but the fool devours it' (21.20). The well-stocked house of the wise, demonstrating Yahweh's blessing on one who seeks righteousness (10.22), is the antithesis of the empty house of the pleasure seeker. 'The mouth of a loose woman is a deep pit; he with whom the LORD is angry falls into it' (22.14). The couplet is bound together by the occurrence of three 'u' sounds, and numerous 's' and 'z' sounds (*šûḥâ ᵃmuqqâ pî zārôt zᵉ'ûm yhwh yippol-šām*). Falling into the trap of a loose woman's mouth is an image of the unexpected damage incurred by a man's sexual folly. If a good wife is Yahweh's gift to a man (19.14), at the other extreme, the ills entailed in consorting with another woman are seen to be an indication of Yahweh's displeasure.

The simple had much to learn, and the wise were offered food for thought in the proverbs on life in the household. It seems that the honour, or public standing of the house and family is a major concern. A son's neglect of the household property would soon become evident, and this brings shame on all the family, as much as grave disrespect to his parents. Good children, however, are their parents' crowning glory. At the core of every flourishing household is a prudent wife and mother, the most tangible sign of Yahweh's blessing. In these proverbs, the husband's role appears to be just as important. He needed to be aware that greed and haste, far from securing the family's future, would surely compromise it, as much as would his consorting with another woman. Finally, if the young could only build the house of their own lives on a foundation of righteousness, nowhere is the outcome more apparent than in having a secure and productive household, where righteousness overflows into new generations.

The Benefits of Righteousness

While it was affirmed in chs. 1–9 that Yahweh made the world in wisdom (8.22-36; 3.19-20), and that wisdom brings success to those who chose it, it becomes apparent in the first chapters of 'the proverbs of Solomon' (chs. 10–14), that, in the world of human desire and interaction, it is righteousness that succeeds. In that respect, righteousness has the status of wisdom in chs. 1–9, while wisdom's role continues also in 'the proverbs of Solomon'. In some proverbs, Yahweh rewards those who practise righteousness, while in other proverbs the creator's involvement is not expressed, but the imagery passes directly from an action to its outcome. These two ways of presenting outcomes are illustrated in the two proverbs in ch. 10 on righteous desire (10.3, 28). In some proverbs, the abstract, righteousness, is defined, for example, both wisdom and righteousness are linked to the way people speak more than to any other topic (see 10.11, 20, 21 and the speech proverbs discussed as a separate topic below). Righteousness is also involved in the choice of company people keep (12.26), their treatment of animals (12.10), and the acquisition of and use of money (11.4). The life flowing from righteousness is illustrated in terms of reputation (10.7), stable possession of property (10.30), or survival of the family line (11.21, see Clifford on 11.21), whilst the outcomes of wickedness are represented as unattractive and destructive. The proverbs are crafted to remain in the memory as aids to decision-making.

> The statements of wisdom are memorable, not merely by virtue of their brevity, but by virtue of their poetic structure. They are designed to be memorised, designed to bring out their moral truth powerfully. They sink from the conscious mind of the student to the subconscious mind of the adult in later years, only to be recalled to the conscious mind later in life at each moment of moral decision (Craigie 1979: 9).

These sayings are discussed below in two groups, in the order in which they appear in the text.

Only Righteousness Provides Security (10.2, 3, 6, 7, 16, 25, 30; 11.4)
A first group of eight proverbs is marked out by the near-repetition of 10.2 in 11.4, both being proverbs of honesty and injustice. A

caution about the appeal of ill-gotten gain also begins the parental instructions (1.8-19). 'Treasures gained by wickedness do not
profit, but righteousness delivers from death' (10.2). In delivering from death, righteousness has the role of wisdom and instruction in chs. 1–9 (5.23). The terse saying evaluates lives of greed
or of honesty in a single moment, on the grounds of the eventual
outcomes. The following proverb, 'The LORD does not let the righteous go hungry, but he thwarts the craving of the wicked' (10.3),
is similar to the previous one in the opening sounds, for *lō'-yar'îb*,
'[Yahweh] does not allow to be hungry' (10.3) echoes *lō'-yô'îlû*,
'[riches] are of no profit' (10.2). It is hardly surprising that the
wholesome satisfaction of desire should be cited in order to add to
the appeal of ethical justice, for in the imagery of chs. 1–9 every
attempt was made to make wisdom desirable (see 2.4; 3.14-15),
and bad choices are said to begin with disordered desire (6.25).
'Blessings are on the head of the righteous, but the mouth of the
wicked conceals violence' (10.6). Here the benefits of righteousness are expressed in terms of the blessing, or good will, whether
of God or of one's fellows, which is said to adorn the head as a
crown, the head being the most visible, and representative part of
the human body (Schroer and Staubli 2001: 83). The scoundrel's
lying mouth, misrepresenting his destructive, evil intent (6.1),
makes the antithesis of the blessing-crowned head of the righteous. 'The memory of the righteous is a blessing, but the name of
the wicked will rot' (10.7). The term 'blessing' is again linked with
having a good reputation. Righteous people are said to live on in
the memory of their children and of the community, and people will
ask that God bless them as God blessed the righteous Abraham
(Gen. 12.2). The wicked, however, leave an odious reputation, their
name rotting with their decaying bones. 'The wage of the righteous
leads to life, the gain of the wicked to sin' (10.16). This is another
proverb on righteous and unjust gain, and its consequences of life
and death (as 10.2), the terms 'wages' and 'income' being used for
the consequences of certain behaviour. Not only is unjust profit
of no ultimate gain (10.2), but the outcome is sin, a term previously linked to death (5.22), whereas honest labour is life-giving
for all concerned. Another of righteousness's attractions is a sense
of confidence in one's future, expressed in the metaphor of survival
in a tempest (1.27): 'When the tempest passes, the wicked are no
more, but the righteous are established forever' (10.25). It seems
that in the course of their lives, both righteous and wicked can
expect to find themselves in life-threatening situations, but only
the ethically just person will withstand the raging wind, like a

building set on firm foundations. Next, 'The righteous will never be removed, but the wicked will not remain in the land' (10.30). Here the image of the security promised the righteous is the stable possession of their land and property, as Toy noted: 'The prosperity of a man was inseparably connected with his share in the soil' (Toy 1904: 218). It is not denied that the unjust can prosper for a time, but they will suffer dispossession, and their descendants will be without inheritance. 'Riches do not profit in the day of wrath, but righteousness delivers from death' (11.4). Previously, perishing on the day of calamity has been attributed to rejecting wisdom teaching (1.27). The first half-verse of the proverb eliminates wealth as a life-support in such dire circumstances, leaving only righteousness, the assumption being again, that also the righteousness will experience severe adversity. A comparison may be drawn in prophecy of the uselessness of acquired riches to save the corrupt on the day of Yahweh's wrath (Zeph. 1.18).

Only Righteousness Confers Life and Security— Reiterated (11.5, 6, 8, 10, 18, 21, 31; 12.3, 7; 13.9; 14.34)

'The righteousness of the blameless keeps their ways straight, but the wicked fall by their own wickedness' (11.5). Righteousness and blamelessness are two qualities of the ethically ideal human being (Gen. 6.9; Job 12.4), while walking straight is an image of both living righteously and securely, for evil lies to the right and left (4.27), and going astray leads to death (10.17). Previously it was said that the choice of wisdom, and trusting in Yahweh keeps one's way straight (3.6), and now righteousness has this role. The antithesis refers to the life-journey of the wicked, where it is their own behaviour that is the traveller's undoing. In the next proverb, where wickedness is defined as scheming evil, it is inferred that the righteous behaviour that keeps the upright out of trouble is a disposition of benevolence towards other people: 'The righteousness of the upright saves them, but the treacherous are taken captive by their schemes' (11.6). The idea that only righteousness ensures one's well-being is repeated in the next proverb, with an unexpected development in the antithesis: 'The righteous are delivered from trouble, and the wicked get into it instead' (11.8). The use of the metaphor of substitution to express antithetical outcomes was noted above in a proverb of the household (13.22), where, in the case of reward, the unworthy person is replaced by the worthy. In the present proverb, the wicked suffer the misfortune they had intended to inflict on their innocent victims, which is another way of expressing the fundamental notion enunciated at the outset, that plotting evil is self-destructive (1.18-19). 'When it goes well with the righteous, the city rejoices, and when the wicked perish, there is jubilation' (11.10). The Hebrew preposition *bᵉ* introduces each half-verse, and the 'a' vowel concludes the last word in each verse, (*qiryâ*, 'city', and *rinnâ*, 'jubilation'). The success of the righteous and the equally certain downfall of the wicked have a social dimension, triggering waves of jubilation throughout the whole community, signified by the city, where its life is most intense. 'The wicked earn no real gain, but those who sow righteousness get a true reward' (11.18). This proverb takes up again the language of wages (10.16), and builds an antithesis on the words *šeqer*, 'falsehood', that is, false wages, in 11.18a, and *śeker*, 'wages', or 'reward' in 11.18b, to contrast what is real with what is only apparent. The wicked, for example, the fraudsters in 11.1, may think they profit for a time, but honest work alone brings a genuine return. In 11.21 the outcomes of righteousness and wickedness are expressed in a word-pair with legal connotations, 'not be unpunished' and 'escape' (see also 19.5): 'Be assured, the wicked will not go unpunished, but those who are righteous will escape'. The need to assure the reader suggests that this point is difficult to make. In another proverb, too, the wise ones use a rhetorical argument to reiterate this conviction, despite appearances to the contrary: 'If the righteous are repaid on earth, how much more the wicked and the sinner!' (11.31). These events will happen within the life-times of those concerned. 'No one finds security by wickedness, but the root of the righteous will never be moved' (12.3). In the emphatic second half-verse the security of the righteous person is depicted in the image of the firmly rooted plant, withstanding nature's destructive forces. The alliteration, *reša'*, 'wickedness', and *šōreš*, 'root', ties the half-verses together and is an aid to memorizing this saying. 'The wicked are overthrown and are no more, but the house of the righteous will stand' (12.7). The two antithetical verb forms enclose this proverb, which begins with the overturning of the wicked, and ends with the image of the standing house of the righteous. The household imagery is more intimate in the next righteousness proverb: 'The light of the righteous rejoices, but the lamp of the wicked goes out' (13.9). The joyfully shining household lamp evokes the life and happiness enjoyed by upright people, while in the antithesis the extinguished lamp symbolizes the end of a household and family line. 'Righteousness exalts a nation, but sin is a reproach to any people' (14.34). A good reputation is one of the advantages held out to the young if they choose to act uprightly in moments of decision.

Whereas the individual was said to achieve honour through wise action (4.8), the proverb envisages the collective dimension, in that the whole community is honoured, not only their city, as in 11.10-11, but their nation, a term identifying the community that would be created by sharing in Abraham's righteousness (Gen. 18.17-19).

Concluding Comments

In a casual reading of 'the proverbs of Solomon', the sayings about righteousness may appear repetitious. These proverbs, situated within the first half of the section (chs. 10–14), reiterate for the benefit of the undecided that there is no wisdom without wisdom's ethical dimension, named righteousness (1.3; 8.20), and the choice of righteousness amounts to a choice of a full and happy life, the only alternative being a premature death, which need not be understood in chronological terms, but rather, as in chs. 1–9, as ethical, religious, and social death and grave personal misfortune. The fullness of life that flows from righteousness is depicted in images of a flourishing household (10.25; 12.7), of the permanent possession of the land (10.30; 12.3), and of being part of a vibrant community (11.10-11). The righteous person earns honest wages (11.4, 18), enjoys the satisfaction of desire (10.3), receives abundant blessings (10.6), and most frequently, walks a straight way with guaranteed security, despite threats (11.3, 5). The wealth of the wicked is worthless (11.18), their craving is not satisfied (10.3), their bones rot (10.7), and their household is devastated (10.25, 30). When they stumble and fall (11.5; 13.6), the whole city rejoices in their overthrow (11.10). The confident promises of eventual prosperity or misfortune attached to antithetical types of behaviour can be understood to have an educational purpose. The wise authors and collectors of these sayings have chosen their language to help form the consciences of the young. The sayings guarantee to them that injustice and oppression are not the foundations of a full and happy life, and that the appeal of rapid wealth, at the expense of justice, is an illusion. In the light of the sayings in the second section of 'the proverbs of Solomon' (chs. 25–29), however, it could also be argued that in the present first section of the 'proverbs', the wise authors aim to present to the young, in a simplified form, a more profound conviction, resting on life-times of experience. This is, that humans are created to live in an ethical universe, and that in the end, despite all appearances to the contrary, good will triumph, and must be believed in.

Yahweh and the King

> 'My child, fear the LORD and the king, and do not disobey either of them' (24.21).

The Yahweh Proverbs

Approximately one in seven of the three hundred and seventy-five couplets in 'the proverbs of Solomon' (10.1–22.16) refer to Yahweh. About half of these are found in the first half of the section (thirty sayings from 10.3–16.11), with a concentration towards the end of the first half and the beginning of the second half (with thirteen proverbs from 15.25–16.11). There, in the centre of the section, an almost sequential group of ten Yahweh sayings (16.1-7, 9, 11) is meshed into the following group of five royal proverbs (16.10, 12-15). These two groups are linked thematically, in that in the royal proverbs, the ideal king is depicted as having divine qualities, enabling him to govern as Yahweh's agent, sharing in Yahweh's intimate knowledge of his subjects, loving righteousness, kindness and fidelity, and requiring worthy behaviour of his servants. The sayings on Yahweh and the king will be discussed together, beginning with the Yahweh proverbs.

In the Yahweh proverbs as a whole, Yahweh is depicted under two aspects. Most often Yahweh is the one who sanctions various forms of righteous behaviour, e.g. righteous desire (10.3), commercial honesty (11.1), and compassion (14.31). In a significant minority of sayings, however, Yahweh's activity transcends human capacity, and his knowledge surpasses the limits of human knowledge. For example, Yahweh knows the depths of the human heart (15.11), and only Yahweh can bring plans to fruition (16.3). Proverbs of this type extend from 15.11 to 21.31, and they will be the subject of this discussion. They offer the simple and the wise an incentive to live in the fear of Yahweh. They also associate the fear of the Lord with the quality of humility (15.33; 22.4), the antithesis of arrogance, which in the view of the wise is incompatible with wisdom (16.5; 21.24, compare 1.7).

a. *An Initial Pair of Proverbs on Yahweh's Knowledge of Creation (15.3, 11).* In the first saying, all-seeing eyes are attributed to Yahweh, to suggest his intimate knowledge of every person's moral worth: 'The eyes of the LORD are in every place, keeping watch on the evil and the good' (15.3). The two 'o' vowels at the beginning (*bᵉkol-māqôm*), and the two 'im' plural endings of the last two words (*rāʿîm wᵉṭôbîm*) make this saying memorable. The second saying is built on the 'how much more' expression, passing from what can be readily conceded to a new conclusion. Though Sheol, and its synonym, Abaddon, the abode of the dead, are imagined to lie deep in the impenetrable earth, yet Yahweh's vision extends even there, and Yahweh sees their inhabitants as clearly as though he were present, yet Yahweh's knowledge of the human heart, exclaims the wise one, is even more intimate. 'How much more human hearts!' (15.11b).

b. *The Central Block of Yahweh Sayings (16.1, 2, 3, 4, 5, 7, 11).* By way of thematic introduction, the first saying (15.33) affirms that the attitude of the fear of Yahweh is, in itself, equivalent to a course of wisdom instruction, and, paradoxically, humility is the gateway to social esteem. In a neatly balanced antithesis, 'The plans of the mind belong to mortals, but the answer of the tongue is from the LORD' (16.1), the final phrase in Hebrew stands out. A wise one has sensed the presence of Yahweh when people speak in socially constructive ways. 'All one's ways may be pure in one's own eyes, but the LORD weighs the spirit' (16.2). People may judge the quality of their actions and way of life to be as pure as the oil in the lamp of the tabernacle sanctuary (Exod. 27.20), but only God's evaluation penetrates to the spirit, to the core of their motivation. This saying about fallible human judgment qualifies the affirmations that the wise can determine the end of the way by their conduct (1.31), and they can see their way with clarity, through instruction (6.23). A rare saying in the imperative echoes the parental advice, to trust in God for success in life (3.5-6): 'Commit your work to the LORD, and your plans will be established' (16.3). Here the advice is that in times of distress, having an attitude of trust addresses effectively any concern people may have about succeeding. Somewhat similar is the sentiment in the psalms, 'Commit your way to the LORD; trust in him, and he will act' (Ps. 37.5). God's activity is seen to be a necessary complement to human effort. The next two proverbs attempt to respond to the challenge posed to the God-fearer by the apparent good fortune of people who seem to live without fear of God. 'The LORD has made everything for its purpose, even the wicked for the day of trouble' (16.4). The advice given in this pithy saying is similar to the conclusion reached by the victim of oppression in Ps. 73.19, 'How they are destroyed in a moment, swept away utterly by terrors!', so that the lives of the godless do not provide a reason to abandon trust, even when it does not appear that the world was created in wisdom (8.22). Likewise, the downfall of the arrogant, literally 'those haughty of heart', is certain, as expressed in the concluding legal metaphor: 'All those who are arrogant are an abomination to the LORD; be assured, they will not go unpunished' (16.5). The expression 'be assured', or, more literally, 'my hand upon it' (Cohen), again reinforces a point that was apparently very difficult for the young to accept.

'By loyalty and faithfulness iniquity is atoned for, and by the fear of the LORD one avoids evil' (16.6). This proverb echoes the advice, that it is not the ritual cleansing of the burning coal on the lips that expiates sin and removes guilt (Isa. 6.7), but rather the practice of the loyalty and faithfulness supporting a relationship with Yahweh (3.3-7). 'When the ways of people please the LORD, he causes even their enemies to be at peace with them' (16.7). Later in Proverbs, there is advice about specific ways to relate to one's enemies (24.17; 25.21-22). This saying evokes the wonder of reconciliation, a situation of Yahweh's making, which befalls those who live in the fear of Yahweh. 'The human mind plans the way, but the LORD directs the steps' (16.9). Normally speaking, the planning of a journey determines one's path (4.11-12). The proverb, however, creates an antithesis between human foresight and reaching journey's end, to make the point that planning should not exclude an attitude of the fear of Yahweh. 'Honest balances and scales are the LORD's, all the weights in the bag are his work' (16.11). Crafted weights and scales are said to be the works of Yahweh, like the created elements (Ps. 103.22), and every human being (Job 34.19). This creation image, at the least, suggests Yahweh's personal interest in the administration of commercial justice (see also 11.1), at a time when weight-standards varied, and fraudulent practice was widespread. Traders acting in the fear of Yahweh will use their weights and scales justly, as instruments of the Creator's ordering of society.

c. *Proverbs of Yahweh's Transcendence in the Second Half of 'the Proverbs of Solomon' (16.33; 17.3; 19.21; 20.12, 24, 27; 21.30, 31).* The above type of proverb becomes more numerous in the second half of the section. 'The lot is cast into the lap, but the decision is the LORD's alone' (16.33). This saying reflects the belief in the Bible that the casting of lots was one of the few legitimate means of divine revelation, and that though throwing the lots was a human action, the revelation was a direct message from God (see Bidmead, 'Lots', *EDB*: 824). The apparent dichotomy illustrates the Creator's pervasive presence in human affairs. 'The crucible is for silver, and the furnace is for gold, but the LORD tests the heart' (17.3). Images of furnace and melting pot conjure up the process of smelting and refining in obtaining the genuine precious metal. This comparison illustrates Yahweh's sure and penetrating gaze into the human heart. Next, in the first of two proverbs of Yahweh's effective purpose (19.21; 21.30), the antithesis is between the many plans of the human heart and the one, effective purpose of Yahweh. 'The human mind may devise many plans, but it is the purpose of the LORD that will be established' (19.21). This saying does not refer, like Isaiah, to the difficulty of ever knowing the mind of God (Isa. 55.8), but affirms that Yahweh's plan alone will be put into effect, which reinforces the previous advice to entrust one's projects to Yahweh (16.3).

The next proverb of Yahweh's pervasive presence refers to the sight and hearing, to which great importance is attributed in Proverbs. 'The hearing ear and the seeing eye—the LORD has made them both' (20.12). Like the mind, the ear is the organ of cognition (18.15), and knowledge is also acquired through the eyes (3.4; 4.21), which can express a range of attitudes and emotions, both uplifting (15.30; 22.9), and destructive (16.30; 17.24; 21.4). One who fears Yahweh will come to a wondering recognition of the Creator's presence in these vital activities. The next Yahweh proverb, 'All our steps are ordered by the LORD [lit. 'are from the LORD']; how then can we understand our own ways?' (20.24), uses the expression 'from Yahweh' to distinguish outcomes from an exclusive human mastery of them. Here the overall unfolding of a God-fearer's life seems to be a matter for wondering contemplation, which is quite different from a sense of satisfaction in human achievement. Next, 'The human spirit [lit. 'breath'] is the lamp of the LORD, searching every inmost part' (20.27). Yahweh's gift of the breath of life (Gen. 2.7) empowers the Creator, as it were with the light of a penetrating lamp, to scrutinize the darkest recesses of the personality. The lamp as an image of Yahweh's scrutiny is also a prophetic image (Zeph. 1.12). The second proverb of Yahweh's effective purpose, 'No wisdom, no understanding, no counsel, can avail against the LORD' (21.30), resounds with three negations, ranging over three aspects of human decision-making, as if the latter were at odds with the mind of God. Yet wisdom and understanding stem from the fear of Yahweh (9.10), and these gifts should be implored of Yahweh (2.6). The negations and the tensions simply make the point that a God-fearer will plan undertakings with respect to Yahweh's purpose. The final proverb in this series illustrates with military imagery the failure of human effort not made with respect for Yahweh's intentions. 'The horse is made ready for the day of battle, but the victory belongs to the LORD' (21.31). The expression, 'prevail against Yahweh' cannot be understood as belittling the role of wise counsel (20.18).

Concluding Comments on the Yahweh Proverbs

The introductory saying on humility and the fear of Yahweh (15.33) is the key to approaching the proverbs of Yahweh's transcendence in the centre, and in the second half of the first section of 'the proverbs of Solomon'. A sage imbued with these attitudes, has sensed the mystery of Yahweh's presence in ordinary human affairs, giving occasion to those proverbs where human effort and achievement seem insufficient or inadequate. In the sight of other teachings, however, it is unlikely that the intention was to lessen the appreciation of effort and persevering commitment in the attainment of wisdom (2.3-4). The disciple who memorized these proverbs, would, however, have an incentive to implore wisdom from Yahweh (2.5-6), a wisdom that is inseparable from the fear of Yahweh, and humility (1.7).

The Royal Proverbs

'By me kings reign, and rulers decree what is just' (8.15).

It is particularly incumbent on the king to fear Yahweh, and subjects need to respect the king's authority. In the royal proverbs, Yahweh's activity for his people is reflected in the king's judgments and choices, so that it would be wise to live with respect for both Yahweh and the king (24.21). The distribution of the royal proverbs throughout the section (10.1–22.16) corresponds with the arrangement of the above proverbs of Yahweh's transcendence, in that the central block of five sayings (16.10, 12-15) is preceded by a pair of royal proverbs (14.28, 35), and after the central group, there follow numerous sayings (seven) in the second half of the book. The well-instructed reader of 'the proverbs of Solomon' (10.1–22.16) will approach 'the words of the wise' (22.17–24.34) with a sense of wonder before Yahweh's surprising presence in human life and affairs, and a healthy respect for the one who represents Yahweh in the administration of justice.

The royal proverbs will be discussed as a single group (14.28, 35; 16.10, 12, 13, 14, 15; 19.12; 20.2, 8, 26, 28; 21.1; 22.11). 'The glory of a king is a multitude of people; without people a prince is ruined' (14.28). Kings and princes are usually synonymous (8.15; 31.4; Ps. 2.2), and the word-pair in this antithesis is used to enhance the ideal of a stable society, led by a successful ruler, a notion expressed with animal imagery towards the end of Proverbs (30.31). 'A servant who deals wisely has the king's favour, but his wrath falls on one who acts shamefully' (14.35). The first of four proverbs of the king's wrath (see also 16.14; 19.12; 20.2) declares that the royal authority is sustained by prudent and wise-dealing royal officials and administrators, and a king has little tolerance of the unworthy. The phrase, 'king's servants' designates the officials (NRSV) of Solomon's household (1 Kgs 10.5), and this proverb applies to any official given responsibilities in the royal administration. 'Inspired decisions are on the lips of a king; his mouth does not sin in judgment' (16.10). Since the king's role is to enact Yahweh's just governance, a king's decision, at the best, was compared with an oracle, as though the judgment were not his own. The king's cooperation with his God needed to be expressed in the justice and fairness of his edicts (1 Kgs 3.28).

Next, the word-pair 'abomination'–'delight', used elsewhere in a single saying, and attributed only to Yahweh (11.1, 20; 12.22; 15.8), is distributed over two adjacent proverbs, the first beginning with 'abomination', the second with 'delight'. 'It is an abomination to kings to do evil, for the throne is established by righteousness' (16.12), and 'righteous lips are the delight of a king, and he loves those who speak what is right' (16.13). Just as many proverbs of righteousness are coined to educate the young to act honestly and justly to secure the household, the first of these sayings could envisage a future king. Wise and righteous courtiers had an important role in the royal administration, and their behaviour illustrates, in a subordinate way, the truth of Wisdom's words, 'by me kings reign' (8.15). In requiring counsellors to tell him the truth, the king asks no less than Yahweh whom he represents (12.22). A pair of proverbs continues the theme of the king's anger. 'A king's wrath is a messenger of death, and whoever is wise will appease it' (16.14). 'In the light of a king's face there is life, and his favour is like the clouds that bring the spring rain' (16.15). The messenger of death metaphor describes an outburst of divine anger on the occasion of the plagues of Egypt (Ps. 78.49-50 NAB), while in the ancient Near East, the anger of the absolute monarch could be just as fatal (Est. 7.10). Though a wise woman could change the king's mind (2 Sam. 14), wise indeed would be the courtier who could calm the king's anger (20.2). Yet that seems to be the case in the second of the above proverbs, where threat is changed to an uplifting promise of life, reflected in a profound change in the king's countenance. Seeing the king's face was the privilege of intimates admitted to his presence (2 Sam. 14.24, 28, 32).

Yet other images illustrate the king's aroused anger, and the uplifting effect of his favourable regard: 'A king's anger is like the growling of a lion, but his favour is like dew on the grass' (19.12). In another pair of proverbs, agricultural images make the point of the king's inspired judgment. The king's gaze, which recognizes the evil locked in the hearts of suppliants, is compared with the wind, or the winnowing-fork, that separated the chaff from the grain: 'A king who sits on the throne of judgment winnows all evil with his eyes' (20.8). This is the only proverb of the king's sight, and it gives him Yahweh's vision to recognize evil (15.3). Another agricultural image also illustrates the king's penetrating judgment: 'A wise king winnows the wicked, and drives the wheel over them' (20.26). A farmer appropriately driving the wheel-thresher over the sheaves to separate the grain is in harmony with the divine wisdom (Isa. 28.28-29). The king discerns the wicked in his entourage, and they are swept away like the chaff. 'Loyalty and faithfulness preserve the king, and his throne is upheld by righteousness' (20.28). In the psalms, righteousness and justice are the foundations of Yahweh's rule (Ps. 89.14), whereas in Proverbs, these are royal qualities to be demonstrated by the king in regard to his subjects.

Other agricultural imagery evokes the king's relationship with Yahweh. 'The king's heart is a stream of water in the hand of the LORD; he turns it wherever he will' (21.1). Two images are combined. In one image, the heart, or mind of the king is being held in God's hand, so completely is he at God's behest. In another image, God, like a wise farmer, manually directs the flow of water in a chan-nel. The NIV separates the images. 'The king's heart is in the hand of the LORD; he directs it like a watercourse wherever he pleases.' 'Those who love a pure heart and are gracious in speech will have the king as a friend' (22.11). In the Solomon narrative, the 'king's friend' is one of Solomon's principal officials (1 Kgs 4.5, and see 2 Sam. 15.37). Yahweh's king would be advised by a wise courtier, the goodness of whose heart is transparent (17.3, and see the proverbs of the king's judgment), and whose speech is pleasing (15.26).

The royal proverbs occur mostly in the second half of the book. They would stem from the royal court, and they are the creation of scribes enamoured of the ideal of peace and stability attainable through the administration of a just and Yahweh-fearing king. These sayings, depicting a king who rules by wisdom (8.15), high-light his rapport with Yahweh, his keen judgment, and his awesome presence, and they are illustrated in the narrative of Solomon's judgment: 'All Israel heard of the judgment that the king had ren-dered; and they stood in awe of the king, because they perceived that the wisdom of God was in him, to execute justice' (1 Kgs 3.28). Later in Proverbs, a queen-mother will be more specific about the role of the king as a judge, when she refers to the future king's duty to defend the cause of the poor (31.1-9). In the proverbs considered above, however, care for the poor is not mentioned as a royal quality, although care for the poor is a trait of every wise person, as will be discussed below in the proverbs on 'Poverty and Prosperity'.

The Power of Language

Some fifty of the three hundred and seventy-five proverbs in 'the proverbs of Solomon' (10.1–22.16), including more than one third of the proverbs in ch. 10, concern the way people speak, and the power of the spoken word, for good or for ill. Socially beneficial speech is attributed to the wise and righteous, and destructive speech to the fool and the wicked, so that wisdom and righteousness are linked to the exercise of speech more than to any other topic. The relatively high number of speech proverbs corresponds to the role of speech in human life, described by Clifford as 'the quintessential human activity' (Clifford 1999: 193). The benefits of the wisely spoken word extend from the individual, to the many in the community, and to the entire city. The victims of malicious speech may be neighbours, close associates, members of the same household, or of wider society. Moreover, the wise are said to draw life for themselves from the way they speak, with judicious expression of the wisdom in their heart, using words with moderation and restraint, and at the opportune moment. Fools are their own worst enemy, and their character is shown in their ceaseless, inane chatter, an expression of irrationality and emptiness.

The number and wide distribution of the proverbs of speaking suggests that learning to speak with wisdom was considered an important component of wisdom education. The majority of these sayings occur in the first half of 10.1–22.16 (thirty-six proverbs), with twenty-two in the second half. The many speech proverbs in chs. 10–15, with strongly antithetical parallelism, contrast the social and personal consequences of the speech of righteous and wicked, the wise and the fool. The antithetical speech proverbs continue in ch. 12. They introduce a concern for telling the truth, and they describe speech as the expression of a person's inner disposition. Images of the body organs, the tongue, lips, and mouth, or the heart symbolizing the underlying thoughts, help to build the poetic parallelism in the speech proverbs. The next concentration of speech proverbs is found in ch. 15, and these sayings, while still composed in the antithetical style, refer to ways of speaking that are timely, gracious, considered, and life-giving. The benefits which wise speech brings to others are again described in ch. 16, where the contrasting ways of speaking are located in different proverbs, and not within the same proverb, as in chs. 10–15. The beauty and appeal of correct speech, then, appears more clearly in the middle of the section. A number of the proverbs of speaking in ch. 16 describe also the destructive speech of the wicked and perverse. The ten speech proverbs in ch. 18 continue to employ reinforcing, or synonymous parallelism, not contrasting or antithetical parallelism, and they describe in picturesque language the benefits of wise speech, and the effects of foolish speech. In ch. 20, the reader is cautioned about gossiping, and in the final proverb on this topic, the quality of one's language is said to be the key to self-preservation. Nine groupings of speech proverbs may be recognized.

How one's Speech Affects Other People (10.8, 11, 13, 14)

A first group is framed by two proverbs about the speech of the wise and the foolish (10.8, 14). In the first, 'the wise of heart', one who ponders the teacher's words, is antithetically paralleled with the 'fool of lips', whose ceaseless chatter renders him incapable of receiving instruction, and who 'will come to ruin', as though the created world cannot tolerate such empty speech. In another proverb (10.11), right and just speech enlivens the hearers, like spring water about which communities cluster. The mouth, or words, of the wicked seem to cover up the thoughts of the heart, full of violence and destruction. In the next proverb, 'On the lips of one who has understanding wisdom is found, but a rod is for the back of the one who lacks sense [heart]' (10.13), two bodily surfaces are contrasted, perhaps humorously. The lips are one surface, seen as supporting wisely uttered words (see Ryken, 'Lips', *DBI*: 515), while the fool's back receives a beating. The term 'heartlessness' in Proverbs suggests thoughtlessness, irrationality, or stupidity (Schroer and Staubli 2001: 44). Finally in this group, the wise silently store up knowledge in the heart, or memory, until it can be usefully expressed, whereas in the last words, fools are imagined as carrying about a time bomb concealed in their mouth, which, as soon as they speak, explodes on themselves and everybody round about (Waltke 2004: 462). 'The wise lay up knowledge, but the babbling of a fool brings ruin near', or, 'is impending terror' (10.14).

What People Say Spells Life or Death (10.18-21, 31)

The speech proverbs in a second group illustrate the relation of a person's thoughts to their verbal expression. The first saying parallels concealing and uttering, both used negatively, to depict the fool. The hidden malevolence in this character's heart, or thoughts, is expressed in lies and spreading slander, rather than just speaking it, for a bad report quickly spreads, like the spies' message to Moses about the land (Num. 14.36). 'Lying lips conceal hatred, and whoever utters slander is a fool' (10.18). In view of the numerous proverbs of destructive speech, it is not surprising that restraint is praised. 'When words are many, transgression is not lacking, but the prudent are restrained in speech' (10.19). The three last words of this musical saying contain three 's' sounds (*wᵉḥōśēk śᵉpātāyw maśkîl*). As body members, the heart and tongue can be imagined to be weighed, like precious metals. 'The tongue of the righteous is choice silver, but the heart of the wicked is of little value' (10.20 NIV). Once again the wise ones move from heart to tongue, from inner disposition to its expression in words, and both together symbolize a communicating person (Clifford 1999: 115). In the next saying, a person's lips are visualized as producing food, or fruit for others to live on. Fools, however, have nothing to offer others, and they die themselves from lack of nourishment. 'The lips of the righteous feed many, but fools die from lack of sense' (lit. 'heartlessness', making a 'lips–heart' parallel) (10.21). The last saying in this group is built with images of plant cultivation and pruning, with the mouth and the tongue in parallel: 'The mouth of the righteous brings forth wisdom, but the perverse tongue will be cut off' (10.31).

Destructive Speech and the Restraints of Loyalty (11.9, 11-13)

Four types of destructive speakers appear again in ch. 11, the antithesis of four other character types, whose speech is personally or socially beneficial. 'With their mouths the godless would destroy their neighbours, but by knowledge the righteous are delivered' (11.9). Here the wise author first observes that humans, in their spoken word, possess an instrument of social destruction or of liberation. Slander is not contrasted with helpful speech, however, but with knowledge, or wisdom, which has the power to save oneself, or others, from perverse speakers, as in the parental instruction (2.12), though the proverb does not suggest how this deliverance is achieved. The next speech proverb, built on the biblical image of the city, illustrates how, ideally, a shared language can create human solidarity and communion with the divine. On the other hand, communities are torn apart by malicious speech. Both upright and wicked are plural in Hebrew. 'By the blessing of the upright a city is exalted, but it is overthrown by the mouth of the wicked' (11.11). Next, people are destroyed not only by violence, slander, and perversity, but also by derision. Both the wicked (18.3), and the poor (14.21), can be recipients of social contempt, and the advice is to

refrain from such arrogant language in all cases. 'Whoever belit-
tles another lacks sense, but an intelligent person remains silent'
(11.12). Finally in this sequence, silence can be an expression of loyalty: 'A gossip goes about telling secrets, but one who is trustworthy in spirit keeps a confidence' (11.13). A breach of confidence may
involve relaying scandal, an expression used in Jeremiah's bleak
description of complete social discord (Jer. 9.4).

Speech as True and False, and Speech as Expressive of an Interior Disposition (12.6, 13, 14, 17, 18, 19, 22, 23)

The antithetical speech proverbs continue in ch. 12. These sayings express a concern for telling the truth, they describe speech as
the expression of a person's inner disposition, and they look at the
effect of the spoken word on others. In the first proverb, violence is
attributed, by synecdoche, to destructive speech, likening that to
concealed highway robbers (11.9). 'The words of the wicked are a
deadly ambush, but the speech of the upright delivers them' (12.6).
Slander could be included in acts of destructive violence (11.9).
Together with the antithesis, the proverb evokes the invitation to
participate in violence (11.9), and a person having the wisdom to
reject this fatal trap (2.12). The final pronoun is ambiguous, however, and could refer to the courageous intervention of a third
person on behalf of the innocent (14.25; 24.11). The rash speaker
appears for the first time in a proverb introduced by the expression,
yēš + participle, 'there is one who'. Everything this character type
says damages people. 'There is one whose rash words are like sword
thrusts, but the tongue of the wise brings healing' (12.18 RSV). In the
Torah legislation, the rash oath renders one unfit to worship God
(Lev. 5.4), whereas the wise ones are more concerned for the effect
on human relationships. Two proverbs focus on the effect of people's words on themselves, for good or for ill (12.13-14). In the first,
the contrast between the speech of the evil one (*ra'*) and righteous
one (*ṣaddîq*) is emphasized by the final position of these terms in
the Hebrew half-verses, which are sonorous through sound repetition, *bᵉpeša' šᵉpātayim môqēš rā' wayyēṣē' miṣṣārâ ṣaddîq*: 'The evil
are ensnared by the transgression of their lips, but the righteous
escape from trouble' (12.13). The image of the concealed trap on the
path of life, a trap ironically set for others by the malicious speaker,
illustrates the self-destructive power of evil speech. Second, a
saying with reinforcing parallelism enhances the personal value of
speaking wisely through an imaginative comparison with manual
labour, the work of one's hands. Lips uttering good words are like
a tree bearing nourishing fruit, with repetition of the 'p' and the 'i'

sounds (*mipp*ᵉ*rî pî-'îš*), just as people are sustained by their manual labour: 'From the fruit of his lips a man is filled with good things, as surely as the work of his hands rewards him' (12.14 NIV). In two of the proverbs in this sequence, a person's speech is an expression of character and inner disposition (12.17, 23). The first takes up the pervasive motif of telling the truth in legal proceedings (as in 6.19; 25.18): 'Whoever speaks the truth gives honest evidence, but a false witness speaks deceitfully' (12.17). The saying makes the point that people's habitual truthfulness will be their best resource when they need to give witness, even at personal cost. Second, a sage wryly notes that those who have least to contribute often say the most: 'One who is clever conceals knowledge, but the mind of a fool broadcasts folly' (12.23). One saying creates the antithesis by comparing the truth and falsehood in the temporal aspect. Truth once uttered seems to share in the stability of creation, so that even if the truth is challenged, it will endure, compared with falsehood which will be quickly overtaken by reality, and exposed. 'Truthful lips endure forever, but a lying tongue lasts only a moment' (12.19). Finally the gravity of lying is given a religious dimension: 'Lying lips are an abomination to the LORD, but those who act faithfully [lit. 'doing the truth'] are his delight' (12.22). The expression 'doing the truth', rather than 'telling the truth' suggests that people who tell the truth are showing just one facet of their fidelity in other obligations and relationships.

The Calm Response, and Beautiful Expression (15.1, 2, 4, 7)

The speech proverbs in the first of the two chapters in the middle of 'the proverbs of Solomon' (chs. 15–16) picture the contribution that words can make to human well-being and psychological wholeness. Such proverbs are in the nature of immediately observable empirical findings. There are observations on the gentle answer (15.1, 4), on eloquent expression (15.2), on the sharing of wisdom (15.7), on words that are timely (15.23), gracious (15.26), and considered (15.28). A person's facial expression can say as much as the spoken word (15.30). For the first time in the book, a proverb observes the effect of speech in relation to human emotion, namely anger, and it is wise to take note of the power of words in this regard: 'A soft answer turns away wrath, but a harsh word stirs up anger' (15.1). The critique of anger is not unexpected, for anger disrupts the social harmony esteemed by the wise ones (15.18, and in the evil-doer description in 6.14), and loss of self-control is incompatible with wisdom (14.29). A harsh or abrasive word is equally powerful, sparking the fire of anger, which may be difficult to contain. A graphic, antithetical proverb shows a wise one making beautiful utterances, and a fool spouting out rubbish: 'The tongue of the wise dispenses knowledge, but the mouths of fools pour out folly' (15.2). Sharing one's knowledge is part and parcel of being wise: 'The lips of the wise spread knowledge, not so the minds of fools' (15.7). In the parallel antithesis, the heart (mind) of the fool has nothing worthwhile to communicate.

Examples of Life-giving Speech (15.23, 26, 28, 30; 16.24)

An appropriate, timely word is within the power of everybody, not just the king's many advisers (15.22), and the wise one can speak from experience: 'To make an apt answer is a joy to anyone, and a word in season, how good it is!' (15.23). Next, such an utterance is a well-considered response, a point emphasized in the antithesis, showing evil gushing out of the wicked one's mouth: 'The mind of the righteous ponders how to answer, but the mouth of the wicked pours out evil' (15.28). Again the unity of mind (heart) and expression is assumed (see 15.7). In the next saying, 'pleasant words', that is, 'intended to be friendly and helpful' (Cohen 1985: 101), are opposed to 'schemes of evil', designed to injure: 'Evil plans are an abomination to the LORD, but gracious words are pure' (15.26). The term 'abomination' has here an ethical meaning, while the cultic context is elsewhere retained (15.8), which could suggest that helpful words in the situations of life beyond the temple precincts are just as pleasing to God as offering an acceptable sacrifice. Good news is first communicated through the messenger's gleaming eyes. 'The light of the eyes rejoices the heart, and good news refreshes the body' (lit. 'bones') (15.30). The image of the invigorated bones depicts the experience of general well-being, the opposite of how Job felt when he preferred dying to living with the state of his bones (Job 7.15). A second proverb illustrates, in the Hebrew body images, how pleasing words have the capacity, like delicious honeycomb, to uplift the whole person, symbolized in the restored bones (body, in most translations), as though we see the bones of an emaciated person, become once again embedded in sound flesh (Schroer and Staubli 2001: 206, on the imagery of the bones): 'Pleasant words are like a honeycomb, sweetness to the soul and health to the body' (16.24).

Destructive Character Types and Destructive Speech (16.27, 28, 29; 17.4, 7, 15)

The proverbs of life-giving speech are followed by a block of sayings illustrating the damage that words can cause. Premeditated villainous speech is depicted in a proverb combining rather awkwardly the image of digging ('concoct' in translation) in preparation for building, with that of a fire leaping out from a furnace door, and scorching anyone within range: 'Scoundrels concoct evil, and their speech is like a scorching fire' (16.27). There could hardly be a greater contrast to the refreshment good news brings (15.30). In the following proverb, slander destroys the bonds of friendship. The term *'allûp*, a 'close friend', can include intimate family relationships (2.17; Mic. 7.5). 'A perverse person spreads strife, and a whisperer separates close friends' (16.28). A proverb continues the theme of the recruitment of the gullible to lives of violence (1.10-14): 'The violent entice their neighbours, and lead them in a way that is not good' (16.29). The one who lends a willing ear to malicious talk may, however, already be corrupt: 'An evildoer listens to wicked lips; and a liar gives heed to a mischievous tongue' (17.4). If this person is a witness or a judge, the innocent will be destroyed (17.15). Finally a proverb develops the capacity of the lips to represent, by synecdoche, the whole person, to the point that the speaking lips can seem to belong to a very different person: 'Fine speech [lip] is not becoming to a fool; still less is false speech [lip] to a ruler' (17.7). A courtier with a fine sense of the integrity expected of a king and his servants has composed this proverb.

Wise Speech as Life-giving and the Speech of Fools (17.27, 28; 18.2, 6, 7, 8, 13, 20, 21)
The section 17.27–18.21 includes twelve picturesque speech proverbs that employ reinforcing parallelism, not contrasting parallelism. One saying speaks in highest praise of those who used measured words: 'One who spares words is knowledgeable; one who is cool in spirit has understanding' (17.27). The emphatic tautology, *yôdēa' dā'at*, 'knows what knowledge is' (NJB), greatly extols the value of self-control, for knowledge, a component of wisdom, is the practical knowledge of how to live wisely, and it includes the fear of Yahweh (1.7), prudence, and discretion (8.12). The image of the coolness of fresh water (25.25) evokes a refreshingly even disposition. In another saying, even the fool who manages to stay silent, to block the flow of words through his lips (15.2, 28), may for a time appear intelligent: 'Even fools who keep silent are considered wise; when they close their lips, they are deemed intelligent' (17.28). The next speech proverb quickly corrects any suggestion that a fool could actually qualify for such scant praise: 'The fool takes no pleasure in understanding, but only in expressing personal opinion' (lit. 'his heart') (18.2). Three successive water images

capture both the interiority and the social benefits of the speech of the wise. Their words come from a deep well, they flow up as a living, refreshing fountain, and they overflow their banks in generous sharing. 'The words of the mouth are deep waters; the fountain of wisdom is a gushing stream' (18.4). There could be no greater contrast to such life-giving language than the image of a mouth calling out for a beating. A fool's provocative words occasion retaliation from offended persons. 'A fool's lips bring strife, and a fool's mouth invites a flogging' (18.6).

Another proverb, as previously (12.13), illustrates the self-imposed consequences of destructive speech by picturing the lips of the malicious speaker as a trap snapping closed on that same person: 'The mouths of fools are their ruin, and their lips a snare to themselves' (18.7). Listening to gossip is criticized as much as spreading it. Body imagery illustrates the capacity that malicious gossip has to engross the eager listener: 'The words of a whisperer are like delicious morsels; they go down into the inner parts of the body' (18.8). A saying extols the art of listening by depicting the plight of one who has failed to understand, through not listening: 'If one gives answer before hearing, it is folly and shame' (18.13). This sonorous proverb has nine syllables in each half verse, with emphasis on the concluding words, *yišmāʿ* ('hearing') and *kᵉlimmâ* ('shame'). One saying is constructed around the image of the satisfied stomach, with the word 'satisfied' in each half-verse: 'From the fruit of the mouth (*mippᵉrî pî-ʾîš*) one's stomach is satisfied; the yield of the lips brings satisfaction' (18.20). The sages suggest that satisfaction in life is not gained by filling one's mouth and stomach with food, but by speaking in socially constructive ways. The four 'i' sounds (*mippᵉrî pî-ʾîš*) reinforce the message. Lastly in this sequence, the tongue is likened to one of the two trees a householder might choose to cultivate. One tree produces nourishment, the other bears noxious fruit: 'Death and life are in the power of the tongue, and those who love it will eat its fruits' (18.21).

There is Nothing More Precious (20.15, 19; 21.23)

Since wisdom is more precious than gold (16.16), or precious stones (8.11), then, in an appealing image, words of wisdom are the most valuable and beautiful adornment the lips can wear: 'There is gold, and abundance of costly stones, but the lips informed by knowledge are a precious jewel' (20.15). Lips uttering gossip or slander are the complete opposite: 'A gossip reveals secrets; therefore do not associate with a babbler' (lit. the loose lipped character, one without self-restraint) (20.19). The gossip, or scandal-monger, defined again as one who purveys damaging information (11.13), is the subject of one of the few second-person exhortations in the whole 'proverbs of Solomon' section, the advice being simply to keep away from such people, and not indulge in the pleasure of listening to detraction (18.8). The final proverb is built on the relation of mouth, tongue, and the whole person, symbolized by the throat (*nepeš*), as though the organs of speech were the doorway to a person's very life: 'He who guards his mouth and his tongue keeps himself (*napšô*) from trouble' (21.23 NAB).

Concluding Comments

The proverbs about speaking illustrate more than any others the social aspect of the anthropology of the wise authors of 'the proverbs of Solomon'. The human ideal is expressed in the image of the two cities, one in which the inhabitants are in communication with God and their fellows, the other torn to pieces by malicious speech. This serious topic, however, is developed piecemeal, within the limits of the parallel couplet. The wise ones appeal to the imagination through the use of poetic language, evocative figures of speech. With the exception of the sayings referring to truthful and false witnesses, the sayings are couched in general, widely-applicable terms. Human society is undermined by lies, slander, malicious plotting, and derision, but also by listening to such derogatory comments. Some images, like sword thrusts, or pictures of physical disintegration, express sensitivity to the pain inflicted on the victims of malicious speech. The frequent use of the term 'fool' for a variety of destructive talkers illustrates the threefold character of wisdom and folly in Proverbs as religious, ethical, and practically intellectual. Less clearly ethically based are the sayings which are critical of loquacity and unreflective speaking. In them, the sages seem to be offended as much by the demonstration of an inner emptiness as by the specific type of damaging speech. The descriptions of socially beneficial speech are referred to at the beginning of this discussion, as is the placement of such proverbs at the centre of this first section of 'the proverbs of Solomon'.

Poverty and Prosperity

In terms of the number of sayings dedicated to the theme of the pursuit of wealth, and the deprivation of the poor, that is, about one-eighth of the present section, the topic of poverty and prosperity compares with the previously discussed topics of Yahweh and the king, and the power of language. In these sayings, society includes people who have come to ruin through negligence (10.4), some who are victims of greed (13.23), and others who pretend to be what they are not (13.7). In the first half of the 'proverbs' (chs. 10–15), with a concentration of sayings about righteousness, only prosperity attained with justice gains Yahweh's blessing, and has enduring value (10.2, 22). A number of 'better than' sayings throughout the section extol righteousness, the fear of God, and truthfulness above wealth which has been acquired through injustice (15.16; 16.8; 19.22). The topic of generosity and compassion is introduced in 14.31, and continues in the second half of the 'proverbs' (19.17; 21.13; 22.9). Many of the sayings on rich and poor are memorable for their Hebrew rhythm and euphony. In their sequential order in 'the proverbs of Solomon', these proverbs may be divided into the following nine thematic groups.

Righteousness is Preferable to Wealth (10.2, 4, 15, 22; 11.4)

In the first saying, gain is subject to the criterion of honesty, and an endorsement of righteousness as the source of life is impressed on the memory. 'Treasures gained by wickedness do not profit [*lō'-yô'îlû*], but righteousness delivers from death [*taṣṣîl mimmāwet*]' (10.2). The two half-verses are linked by a repetition of 'il' sounds. Early in 'the proverbs of Solomon' (10.1–22.16), righteousness is given the role of wisdom in chs. 1–9, as the source of life and prosperity, and the point is made that Wisdom's treasures (8.21) are gained honestly. The intended audience of this saying are not the poor and oppressed, but people for whom becoming wealthy through injustice is an attractive option, like the youth in the first parental instruction (1.8-19). 'A slack hand causes poverty, but the hand of the diligent makes rich' (10.4). The terms *rā'š* ('poor') and *ta'ăšîr* ('makes rich') link the half-verses aurally, as does the repetition of 'hand', a symbol of energy. It is assumed that prosperity is attainable by honest work, and the wise one has little sympathy for preventable poverty. 'The wealth of the rich is their fortress; the poverty of the poor is their ruin' (*mĕḥitat dallîm rêšām*, 10.15). This succinct saying comprises just seven Hebrew words, flowing with rhythm and repetition of the 'm' sound. The image of the rich person living securely in a well-defended city, and of the poor (*dallîm*) dwelling in ruins (see the image of dwelling in ruins in Ps. 89.40) is a pitiful evocation of society's great inequalities. 'The blessing of the LORD makes rich, and he adds no sorrow with it' (10.22). The term *'eṣeb*, 'sorrow', can mean toil (5.10), and if, contrary to the NRSV, human effort, rather than Yahweh, is taken as the subject of 'adds to it', then labour adds nothing to the divine blessing (Barucq), a sense which is close to: 'It is the Lord's blessing that brings wealth, and no effort can substitute for it' (NAB). This saying encourages giving priority to the fear of Yahweh in all money dealings, while granted that, in the wider context, toil and effort are necessary and praiseworthy (10.4; 14.23). 'Riches do not profit in the day of wrath, but righteousness delivers from death' (11.4). It is as though those who would use money wisely need to imagine themselves in a grave, life-threatening situation, when the transient value of one's acquired wealth would become apparent. Prophecy is more explicit than this cryptic saying on the theological and physical aspects of the 'day of wrath' (Zeph. 1.18).

Imitate the Creator's Generosity (11.24, 25)

'Some give freely, yet grow all the richer; others withhold what is due, and only suffer want' (11.24). The verb for giving freely (*mᵉpazzēr*) is also used for the Creator's liberality in scattering frost over the earth's surface (Ps. 147.16), and in the canonical context, the Yahweh-fearer would do well to practise the creator's generosity. 'O' sounds complete each half-verse: *nôsāp 'ôd* ('gets more') and *maḥsôr* ('want'). Such random giving seems a part of the created order, and so the generous prosper. 'A generous person will be enriched, and one who gives water will get water' (11.25). This person is, literally, one who confers a blessing, through generous giving. Being enriched, literally being 'made fat', and being refreshed with water, are also images of Yahweh's generosity and blessing (Deut. 31.20; Hos. 6.3).

The Unprofitable Pursuit of Wealth (11.26, 28; 13.7, 11)

The next character type is the unscrupulous profiteer who hoards grain in time of need. Here the term blessing occurs again: 'The people curse those who hold back grain, but a blessing is on the head of those who sell it' (11.26). The victimized populace sense a flagrant violation of the order of nature and society, and they react, as they do when produce is allowed to move freely, by invoking Yahweh's sanctions, or a blessing, on such merchants. The saying is clinched with a concluding double 'sh' sound: *lᵉrō'š mašbîr*. 'Those who trust in their riches will wither ('will fall', in the unamended text), but the righteous will flourish like green leaves' (11.28). Again, true prosperity is the fruit of righteousness, not of grasping for wealth, or relying solely on it. The happy situation of a person of integrity is illustrated with the botanical image of the flourishing green plant, as in Ps. 1.3 and Jer. 17.8. 'Some pretend to be rich, yet have nothing; others pretend to be poor, yet have great wealth' (13.7). Other sayings critical of pretence—of one who plays the great man (12.9), of the boasting benefactor (25.14)—make a sharp contradiction between appearance and reality, and no less here, where the Hebrew is cryptic, with sound repetition. In the first half-verse *yēš mit'aššēr* ('there is one who pretends to be rich') is followed by two abrupt monosyllables of the reality behind that appearance, and in the second half-verse *mitrôšēš* ('one who pretends to be poor') is also followed by two monosyllables. In this wry observation about the grip of monetary concerns on some peoples' lives, the wise one challenges the hearer to look beyond appearances for a person's real qualities. 'Wealth hastily gotten will dwindle, but those who gather little by little will increase it' (13.11). This lilting Hebrew proverb, where the antithesis in each half-verse is in the emphatic final position, provokes thought by the absence of specific circumstances. The industrious ant (6.6-8), a model for the sluggard's instruction, could illustrate this saying about haste and greed. The ant succeeds because it works in harmony with the times and seasons, with its fellows, and with respect for the order of the world about it.

More on the Plight of the Poor (13.23; 14.20)
'The field of the poor may yield much food, but it is swept away through injustice' (13.23). The second half-verse, comprising two four-syllable phrases, is rhythmic and sonorous: *wᵉyēš nispeh bᵉlō' mišpāṭ*. The point made is that the poor may suffer not only injustice and oppression, but also bitter disappointment. The envisaged situation may be that of a poor tenant-farmer who, having worked hard on his assigned fallow ground until his tillage produces a bountiful crop, ready for consumption, sees the rich proprietor snatching it away from him (see Meinhold 1991; vol. 1: 228), and compare, 'The poor are feeding grounds for the rich' (Sir. 13.19). 'The poor are disliked even by their neighbours, but the rich have many friends' (14.20). Here is a picture of a rich man surrounded by admirers, while the antithesis reflects the sad reality of the isolation of the poor. Once again wealth, or absence of it, tends to shape people's judgment of others, and for unworthy motives.

Introducing Generosity and Compassion (14.21, 31)
'Those who despise their neighbours are sinners, but happy are those who are kind to the poor' (14.21). The topic of showing compassion, giving alms to the poor or needy, is here introduced in the

book of Proverbs. Despising people could find expression in mockery (11.12), and the term 'sin' may here, as in the parental instruction (5.22), be visualized as the crippling bonds that render impossible a generous gesture. The vitality and blessed state of the generous person likens that person to the one who has found wisdom (3.13-18). 'Those who oppress the poor (*dāl*) insult their Maker, but those who are kind to the needy honour him' (14.31). The first of the poor and needy proverbs presents them as fragile works of God, at the mercy of their fellow humans, whose own relationship to their Maker is shaped by their generosity, or inversely, by their callous mistreatment of the needy.

Challenging the Pursuit of Riches (15.16)
Of the numerous (15) 'better than' proverbs in 'the proverbs of Solomon' expressing value in terms of the priority of 'a' over 'b', some seven extol one or other of wisdom's fruits over riches gained through lies and oppression. Personified Wisdom uses this proverbial speech form to extol wisdom over wealth (8.11, 19), and the wise ones speak similarly in regard to the fear of Yahweh (15.16), righteousness (16.8), telling the truth (19.22), and good reputation (22.1). In the first such proverb, 'Better is a little with the fear of the LORD than great treasure and trouble with it' (15.16), the undefined 'trouble' (*mᵉhûmâ*) of riches can refer in prophecy to moral disorder and oppression (Amos 3.9), a sense which would evoke the picture of the band of thieves in the first parental instruction (1.8-19), so that the saying would be a caution addressed to youth about joining the company of the unscrupulous rich.

Three Rich–Poor Sayings (18.23; 22.2, 7)
This group comprises the final three 'rich'–'poor' (*ʿāšîr / rāš*) proverbs in 'the proverbs of Solomon'. In the first, a street-scene could be envisaged, or a pleading debtor on the farm: 'The poor use entreaties, but the rich answer roughly' (18.23). 'Entreaties' (*taḥᵃnûnîm*), which is etymologically related to the term for being compassionate (*ḥānan*), receives emphasis as the first word in the Hebrew saying. The poor one, in need of compassion, is obliged to entreat, becomes vulnerable, and is unfeelingly rebuffed. 'The rich and the poor have this in common: the LORD is the maker of them all' (22.2). The first half-verse of this musical six-word saying in Hebrew, with its three 'sh' sounds, quickly sketches a rich and poor person side by side, or face to face, as an image of their commonality, despite the huge difference in social class. Almost before the reader has the time to appreciate the incongruity, the second half-verse makes a cryptic,

unexpected three-word comment about their basic human equality. The saying succeeds through its brevity and an element of surprise. 'The rich rule over the poor, and the borrower is the slave of the lender' (22.7). The final rich–poor saying is amongst the most melodious of the proverbs, where the first half-verse is united with three 'sh' sounds, and the second half-verse by a repetition of the 'l+o' combination, with one final 'sh' sound recalling the first half-verse: *'āšîr bᵉrāšîm yimšôl wᵉᶜebed lōweh lᵉᵓîš malweh*. This saying evokes the plight of people reduced to slavery through personal or family insolvency, such as the insolvent Jews threatened with servitude at the time of the rebuilding of the city walls (Neh. 5.1-6).

Other Sayings on the Plight of the Poor (19.4, 6, 7)
'Wealth brings many friends, but the poor [*dāl*] are left friendless' (19.4). In the first half-verse, the first two words are linked by two 'o' sounds: *hôn yōsîp* + two plurals in 'im': *rēᶜîm rabbîm*, while the second half-verse begins and ends with a 'd': *wᵉdāl...yippārēd*. First, a group of self-serving friends is shown flocking around the wealthy, and then they flee a fellow human being in need, who is left alone in poverty. 'Many seek the favour of the generous, and everyone is a friend to a giver of gifts' (19.6). In a society where benefits hinge on the patronage of the rich and powerful, people literally 'placate the face of the generous', that is, they make them well disposed, which is reflected in their face (see 15.13). The term 'generous', *nādîb*, is used in parallel with 'rulers' in Wisdom's speech (8.16), and there could indicate an administrator and head of a powerful family. 'If the poor are hated even by their kin, how much more are they shunned by their friends! When they call after them, they are not there' (19.7). The third of three proverbs on the abandonment of the poor person (see also 14.20; 19.4) completes the picture of their isolation by adding separation from kinsfolk to separation from friends and neighbours. Helpless and dependent, they are rejected simply because they are poor, and they have no protectors at all.

There is No Righteousness without Compassion (19.17; 21.13; 22.9, 16)
As previously intimated (14.21, 31), compassion needs to be included amongst the qualities of whoever would be wise and righteous, and whoever would prosper: 'Whoever is kind to the poor [*dāl*] lends to the LORD, and will be repaid in full' (19.17). The metaphor of Yahweh's loan repayment makes a strong appeal to self-interest as a motive for generosity, and kindness could take

the form of lending without interest, as recommended in the Covenant Code on behalf of a needy Israelite (Exod. 22.25). Repetition of 'l', 'm', and 'o' sounds creates a musical second half-verse (*ûgeᵉ- mulô yᵉšallem-lô*). The hard-hearted person, on the other hand, will also be repaid in full: 'If you close your ear to the cry of the poor [*dāl*], you will cry out and not be heard' (21.13). The first half-verse depicts a poor person crying out loudly to gain the attention of one who could help, who then literally 'stops his ears', and in the next scene, that same person is in the situation of the neglected petitioner. In the next proverb, the imagery changes from hearing, and then closing one's ears, to seeing with a bountiful eye (RSV): 'A kindly eye will earn a blessing, such a person shares out food with the poor [*dāl*]' (22.9, NJB). The final saying in 'the proverbs of Solomon' (22.16) presents the young with two wrong alternatives in the use of money. They may, through greed and injustice, deprive the poor of what is their due. They may also seek advancement by giving to the rich, which is pure loss of precious resources, with no explanation offered, but is in keeping with the character of the impregnably secure (10.15), or heartless rich (18.23). Either way, practising justice and generosity are the only reliable guides to gaining wealth and security.

Concluding Comments

The topic of poverty receives fuller treatment in 'the proverbs of Solomon' than in chs. 1–9, where the poor do not appear, even though threat of poverty is extended to the elite audience of the instructions, should they become idle or imprudent (6.1-11). In 'the proverbs of Solomon', the abject isolation of the poor is emphasized, while the overall social situation is not described in any specific detail. In this regard it would be difficult to make a clear social distinction between the two terms for the poor, *rāš* and *dāl*, though it can be noted that when the topic is kindness and compassion, the preference is for *dāl*. This group of sayings is a significant component of Wisdom's promised feast of learning (9.5-6). The simple one who ponders and memorizes them will learn that a life of wisdom and integrity needs to include acts of generosity and compassion.

Joy and Sadness

In the proverbs of poverty and prosperity, the pursuit of riches is clearly not the key to wisdom and happiness. The proverbs of joy and grief add another dimension to the notion of the life and

happiness attaching to wisdom, namely emotional health and physical well-being. In some sayings, the experience of joy, or grief and
dejection, is linked with an ethical judgment on human behaviour.
The failure of a child's upbringing grieves the parents (10.1; 17.25),
just as a child's wisdom and success occasions joy. Malicious speech
can hurt deeply (12.18), and a timely word raises the speaker's spirits, and may be just as beneficial to another person (15.23). Some of
these proverbs have been discussed in the context of other themes,
for example, righteousness or the power of language. Other sayings are more concerned with the ebb and flow of the emotions in
the human psyche, and there may be no ethical judgment attached,
but the impact of emotion in personal well-being is illustrated symbolically by body imagery, like the exposure of the skeleton, or
the breaking of the spirit. Some of these sayings are linked with
wisdom indirectly, through their location in the 'proverbs' section.
In ch. 16, wisdom is a fountain of life (16.22), as promised in 3.8,
and a number of proverbs in chs. 14–17 create an awareness of the
role of emotional harmony in health and well-being. The proverbs
of joy and sadness are discussed below, as a single group, in the
order in which they occur.

'Anxiety weighs down the human heart, but a good word cheers
it up' (12.25). Being weighed down, an image of the quenching of
vitality, is attributed to the heart, here representing the whole
human personality. The heart is the only internal organ that can
be felt (Schroer and Staubli 2001: 41), so that the feeling of joy on
hearing good news is easily attributed to the heart. 'Hope deferred
makes the heart sick, but a desire fulfilled is a tree of life' (13.12).
This sympathetic observation first shows a person suffering from
dejection, which is represented metaphorically as heart sickness,
the pulsating heart being here imaged as the inner source of desire.
When desire is attained, however, there is a surge of vitality, represented in the image of the tree of life. Following three 'l' sounds
in the first half-verse, the proverb ends conclusively with two final
'a' sounds (*ta'ʷwâ bā'â*). 'The heart knows its own bitterness, and
no stranger shares its joy' (14.10). Here the personified heart is
the symbol of the inner person, bearing secrets known to Yahweh
alone (15.11), including the most profound emotions of bitterness,
affliction, and joy. What is known to Yahweh and the heart is not
shared by any outsider (*zār*), the latter emphatic final monosylla-
ble highlighting the exclusiveness of the heart's experiences. 'Even
in laughter the heart is sad, and the end of joy is grief' (14.13).
Making the point of the fragility of emotional experience, the sage,
a close observer of the human spirit, expresses that fragility with

a pair of contrasts, first, between a deep inner life and its outward expression, and second, in a temporal sequence, between the beginning and the end. The saying sounds a note of realistic caution in regard to attaining human fulfilment, which is unusual in Proverbs. 'A tranquil mind gives life to the flesh, but passion makes the bones rot' (14.30). This saying notes the overall health benefits of a tranquil personality, literally 'heart', implicitly comparing that with healing balm of Gilead (Jer. 8.22). Taken together, flesh and bones are the fundamentals of a recognizable human being, and life is attributed to the flesh, because the more the bones are embedded in sound flesh, the healthier the person appears. The antithesis describes the damaging effects of passion, such as jealousy or envy, in the rotting bones image. People subject to these emotions anticipate their complete disintegration, for normally the bones of the dead endure for a time, while soon after death there is nothing of the flesh left to see (Schroer and Staubli 2001: 209-12). The young are advised, for their health's sake, to cultivate a calm disposition, and not be consumed by jealousy (6.34), impatience, or indignation (see Job 5.2). 'A glad heart makes a cheerful countenance, but by sorrow of heart the spirit is broken' (15.13). A second proverb of the impact of the emotional life on health and well-being concerns joy and sorrow. The cheerful disposition, seated in the heart, deep within a person, registers on the face, the focus of the person in the eyes of others, whereas the broken spirit (see also 17.22; 18.14) represents a depletion of the life forces that animate the human being and symbolizes everything that is lethargic and dead, the absence of vitality and *joie de vivre*. A person subject to grief, depression and dejection has perished prematurely. 'A cheerful heart is a good medicine, but a downcast spirit dries up the bones' (17.22). Another proverb on the health benefits of cheerfulness uses the image of the dried-up bones in the antithesis to symbolize the effect of depression on one's health, as if the person were reduced to a skeleton, whereas healthy bones are moist and nourished (15.30). 'The human spirit will endure sickness, but a broken spirit—who can bear?' (18.14). A person may be able to cope with physical illness, whereas in the antithesis, dejection is represented as an unendurable affliction. Such an unfortunate person is alive, but devoid of vitality.

The sages harness their imaginative resources to convey to the simple an experience of the emotional dimension of the life promised through wisdom. Image after image suggests an integrated conception of health and well-being, at the same time dispelling any illusion of an easily acquired emotional harmony.

Concluding Comments: The Arrangement of the Sayings in 'the Proverbs of Solomon'

At the conclusion of this thematic commentary, some observations may be made on the overall thematic and rhetorical arrangement. The collection falls into two recognizable halves (10.1–15.33 and 16.1–22.16, approximately). The first part is notable for numerous proverbs of righteousness, where this quality is the key to life or death, as was the case with wisdom in chs. 1–9. The proverbs of Yahweh's transcendence and the royal proverbs are introduced in the first half, and become numerous in the second half of the 'proverbs'. These sayings inculcate humility and the fear of Yahweh and the king. The acceptance of discipline and reproof as essential to acquiring wisdom is a pervasive theme, while urgent invitations to accept instruction and discipline are made towards the end of the section. Sayings on the poor are present throughout, while the duty of generosity receives emphasis in the second half of the collection. The proverbs on the power of language are widely distributed, yet towards the end of the 'proverbs' the use of speech is associated with the priceless value of wisdom. Proverbs of household relationships occur throughout.

All told, 'the proverbs of Solomon' have added rich additional veins of wisdom to the household teaching proposed in the first nine chapters. 'The words of the wise' (22.17–24.34) will add to the treasury of wisdom found in the first two sections.

Proverbs 22.17–24.34: The Words of the Wise

Introductory Comments

'The words of the wise' (22.17–24.34), comprising also the additional 'words of the wise' (24.23-34), is a set of paternal wisdom instructions that have many similarities to the instructions in chs. 1–9. Overall, they are a series of exhortations to wise and just conduct, more numerous and briefer than the first set of instructions. As in chs. 1–9, a wise father, in urging his son to become wise, also refers to 'your mother'. Wisdom is a conspicuous topic in this section, as in the former, and in both sections wisdom is located both in the household and in the city gates. In the structure of the book, then, the sayings in the third person of 'the proverbs of Solomon' (10.1–22.16), many of which concern acquiring wisdom, are preceded and followed by a section of parental wisdom instructions. A broader range of topics of instruction is found in 'the words of the wise' than in the first set of instructions. Like them, 'the words of the wise' refer to the need of instruction, to a husband's fidelity, and to the imprudence of offering pledges, yet other teachings develop topics raised in 'the proverbs of Solomon', for example, the threat which drunkenness presents to any young person hoping to establish a household, the administration of justice, and the parental commitment to a child's education. Again, as in the 'proverbs', the young need not envy the lot of people who prosper through injustice. In the commentary, reference will be made primarily to the earlier instructions (chs. 1–9), to 'the proverbs of Solomon' (10.1–22.16), and to the Bible generally, with attention to the Torah.

Advice to a Young Israelite on Honesty and Restraint in the Acquiring of Wealth and in the Exercise of Public Office: An Adaptation of the Instruction of Amenemope (22.17–23.11)

This first part of 'the words of the wise' contains an introduction, followed by a series of approximately ten short exhortations, which have many points of similarity with the Egyptian *Instruction of*

Amenemope, written by an Egyptian official 'for his son', in view of the latter's becoming, like his father, an upright, god-fearing, and successful scribe in the Egyptian administration. While the parallels suggest that this first part of 'the words of the wise' is an Israelite adaptation of an Egyptian writing, the verbal and topical similarities to *Amenemope* will be identified in view of illustrating imagery that is not found elsewhere in Proverbs. The frequent references to acquiring wisdom in 'the words of the wise' (23.15, 19, 22-25; 24.3-7) occur after the first section. Neither is the wisdom motif a feature of *Amenemope*, where, moreover, imagery similar to that in Proverbs may have a different context than in Proverbs.

Title and Introduction (22.17-21)
In the style of the instructions in chs. 1–9, the Israelite wise one begins by claiming his son's attention, and encouraging him to retain the teaching.

> The words of the wise:
> Incline your ear and hear my words,
> and apply your mind to my teaching;
> for it will be pleasant if you keep them within you,
> if all of them are ready on your lips.
> So that your trust may be in the LORD,
> I have made them known to you today—yes, to you.
> Have I not written for you thirty sayings
> of admonition and knowledge,
> to show you what is right and true,
> so that you may give a true answer to those who sent you?
> (22.17-21).

Here the similarity to *Amenemope* is striking, as appears in the following citations:

> Give your ears, hear the sayings,
> Give your heart to understand them;
> It profits to put them in your heart,
> Woe to him that neglects them! [ch. 1]
> Knowing how to answer one who speaks,
> To one who sends a message (Prologue) (Lichtheim 2006: 148-49).

In the Proverbs text, there is no explicit reference to scribal duties, and the wise one repeats a motif of a previous instruction (2.10), that his advice can be savoured, which anticipates the honey metaphor for wisdom later in the section (24.13). The motif of trust in Yahweh, also recalling an earlier instruction (3.5), replaces references to Egyptian deities in a work that, like the other Egyptian instructions, is set in the theological framework of Egyptian religion (McKane 1970: 106). The mention of thirty sayings is the most notable echo of *Amenemope*, which comprises thirty chapters. In the following commentary, 'the words of the wise' are divided on thematic and rhetorical grounds, and an identification of thirty sections in these 'words' is not attempted.

Five Short Admonitions (22.22-29)

a. *No Abuse of Power*. The first admonition is enlivened with three 'al' sounds: 'Do not rob the poor because they are poor [*'al-tigzāl-dāl kî dal-hû'*], or crush the afflicted at the gate; for the LORD pleads their cause [*yārîb rîbām*] and despoils of life those who despoil them' (22.22-23). God's partiality to the defenders of the poor is a theme of *Amenemope* (ch. 28) (Lichtheim 2006: 161), yet this advice also recalls Yahweh's identification with the poor in 'the proverbs of Solomon' (14.31; 17.5). In the legal image, Yahweh is the powerful advocate of the defenceless, a judge sentencing the oppressor according to the principle of evil-doing redounding to the perpetrator, and this advice applies to a youth destined to be a person of wealth and power in Israelite society.

b. *Avoid Angry People*

> Make no friends with those given to anger,
> and do not associate with hotheads,
> or you may learn their ways
> and entangle yourself in a snare (22.24-25).

In *Amenemope*, self-control and kindness are the traits of the ideal man (Lichtheim 2006: 146), and the administrator is advised 'not to befriend the heated man' (ch. 9) (Lichtheim 2006: 153), nor to 'force yourself to greet the heated man' (ch. 10) (Lichtheim 2006: 154). Yet the caution harmonizes well with the proverbs on self-control (16.32), and on the capacity of anger to create yet more strife (15.18).

c. *Avoid Going Surety*

> Do not be one of those who give pledges,
> who become surety for debts.
> If you have nothing with which to pay,
> why should your bed be taken from under you? (22.26-27).

While generosity and compassion are advocated in 'the proverbs of Solomon' (19.17), this exhortation discourages offering a guarantee beyond one's means to honour, evoking the previous warnings about the imprudence of pledge-giving (6.1-5; 17.18; 20.16).

d. *Respect the Landmarks*

> Do not remove the ancient landmark
> that your ancestors set up. (22.28)

As will appear in a repetition of this advice towards the end of this first part of 'the words of the wise', the most defenceless in Israel, orphans and widows, for example, were victims of this abuse. In the Israelite context, landmarks were symbols of the original allocation of property to Israel's ancestors (Deut. 19.14; 27.17), and the inherited land of the defenceless was subject to unscrupulous appropriation at the hands of the rich and powerful. *Amenemope* also cautions a future administrator against practising this injustice (ch. 6) (Lichtheim 2006: 151).

e. *In Praise of the Skilled Worker.* The wise one engages his audience with a rhetorical question, and links the question and the response by alliteration: 'Do you see those who are skilful in their work [*bimᵉla'ktô*]? They will serve kings [*mᵉlākîm*]; they will not serve common people' (22.29). The term 'skilled' (*māhîr*) could here refer to an administrator in training, like when *Amenemope*'s similar admonition has in view the career of a successful scribe (ch. 30) (Lichtheim 2006: 162), yet the skill is unspecified, 'skilled' is of wider application, and the saying as a whole is exemplified in Hiram of Tyre, a worker in bronze (1 Kgs 7.14).

Another Diptych of Symbolic Meals (23.1-8; see 9.1-6, 13-18)

The scene now shifts from standing before kings to sitting with a ruler. Within the sustained second-person sequence of admonitions, a sub-structure may be identified at the beginning of ch. 23, namely a meal scene doublet (23.1-3, 6-8), separated by a small block of related admonitions (23.4-5). Here is found the striking imagery of three separated passages in *Amenemope* (in chs. 7, 11, and 23) (Lichtheim 2006: 152, 154-55, 160). What is also notable, however, is the similarity to the meal doublet in Prov. 9.1-18, both in the two-meal structure and in the occurrence of a block of related admonitions placed between them, as also in an emphatic repetition which ties the scenes together (23.3a, 6b, compared with 9.4, 16). The first scene and the intervening passage are as follows.

> When you sit down to eat with a ruler,
> observe carefully [*bîn tābîn*] what is before you,
> and put a knife to your throat
> if you have a big appetite.
> Do not desire the ruler's delicacies,
> for they are deceptive food. (23.1-3)

> Do not wear yourself out to get rich;
> be wise enough to desist.
> When your eyes light upon it, it is gone;
> for suddenly it takes wings [*kᵉnāpayim*] to itself,
> flying like an eagle toward heaven [*haššāmāyim*]. (23.4-5)

The first meal description (23.1-3) is very similar to the *Amene-mope* passage which cautions the future administrator to main-tain an awareness of his inferior social status when dining with his social betters (ch. 23) (Lichtheim 2006: 160). In Proverbs, however, the emphasis is on the deceptive quality of the food. Despite their appetizing appearance, the delicacies of the rich are not a wise one's nourishment, which is wisdom's more substantial banquet (9.2-5). The interpretive centrepiece between the meal scenes (23.4-5) sug-gests that the meal is a symbolic one. The reference to wisdom is explicit, and the young are cautioned about accepting the attractive overtures made by men of power and wealth, which is symbolized in such spurious food (23.4-5). The evanescence of material posses-sions is described in *Amenemope* with similar imagery. 'They made themselves wings like geese, and they fly away to the sky' (ch. 7) (Lichtheim 2006: 152).

The second meal description concerns the deceptive fare of one consumed by greed.

> Do not eat the bread of the stingy;
> do not desire their delicacies;
> for like a hair in the throat, so are they.
> 'Eat and drink!' they say to you; but they do not mean it.
> You will vomit up the little you have eaten,
> and you will waste your pleasant words. (23.6-8)

At this symbolic table, the miser is focused on getting richer, not on the needs of his guest, and his tempting food, like the nobleman's, is sickening, not nourishing. In *Amenemope*, metaphorically eating the property of the poor will make the unjust administrator sick (ch. 11) (Lichtheim 2006: 154-55).

Prudent Reticence and an Example of the Abuse of Power (23.9-11)

Two brief admonitions conclude the first, more *Amenemope*-like sec-tion of 'the words of the wise'. Whereas the Egyptian administrator cautions his son not to 'empty your belly to everyone' (ch. 21) (Lich-theim 2006: 159), the Israelite wise one makes the point in plain language that a youth's choice of wisdom will inform his choice of company, which, in the present context, would be the powerful, and there is very little point in engaging in such conversations, for after all, 'fools despise wisdom' (1.7). 'Do not speak in the hearing of a fool, who will only despise the wisdom of your words' (23.9). A final admonition recalls one blatant abuse of power, adding that the fatherless are victims of the previously mentioned crime of removing property boundary-stones (22.28). 'Do not remove an ancient landmark or encroach on the fields of orphans, for their redeemer is strong; he will plead their cause [*yārîb 'et-rîbām*] against you' (23.10-11). The notion of Yahweh's partiality to the victims of injustice is again expressed in legal imagery, where Yahweh becomes the advocate or redeemer (*gō'ēl*) of the fatherless who have no one else to defend them, taking up their cause in a legal dispute (22.23).

A Concluding Reflection on the First Part of the Words of the Wise (22.17–23.11)

Early in Proverbs the young are warned, through the imagery of a life of wisdom as a journey along a path or way, to avoid unwholesome travel companions (2.12-16). In the first section of 'the words of the wise', meal imagery is used for the same purpose. The company of the rich and powerful must be entered with the utmost circumspection, for their metaphoric, tempting food is spurious or sickening. The wise will live, rather, from Wisdom's nourishing words (9.1-6). Also in this section, one's resources must be used wisely (22.26-27), and appropriating the land of the poor is a pernicious example of greed for wealth (23.10-11). The company of the incorrigible is best avoided altogether (23.9). In the rest of 'the words of the wise', the motif of the quest for wisdom is quite explicit.

A Father's Wisdom-Teaching (23.12–24.22)

The Discipline of Accepting Instruction (23.12-14)

Several of the admonitions in the second part of 'the words of the wise' refer to acquiring wisdom.

> Apply your mind to instruction
> and your ear to words of knowledge.
> Do not withhold discipline from your children;
> if you beat them with a rod, they will not die.
> If you beat them with the rod,
> you will save their lives from Sheol. (23.12-14)

This advice, as does the proverb, 'Grandchildren are the crown of the aged, and the glory of sons is their fathers' (17.6), spans three generations. The ruined profligate's rueful admission about neglecting his teachers' advice (5.13) would substantiate the comment that 'a young person will not die from instructional blows, but from their absence, for (premature) death results from uncorrected folly' (Clifford 1999: 212).

Parental Involvement (23.15-16)
The theme of parental joy re-emerges, when a father hears his son speaking with respect for the rights of others (23.15-16). The totality of a parent's thought and feeling is expressed symbolically in the rejoicing 'heart' (mind) and 'kidneys' (soul, NRSV), the inner source of emotion.

Upright Desire, Not Unholy Envy (23.17-18)
The temptation to become rich and secure by joining the company of the prosperous wicked is countered by a reminder, that the wise live trustfully in Yahweh's protective presence (3.5-8). 'Always continue in the fear of the LORD' (23.17). Only people who do this have a real and secure future. 'Surely there is a future, and your hope will not be cut off' (23.18).

Other Company to be Avoided (23.19-21)
A preventive warning about over-indulgence in both food and drink is presented as a father's wisdom teaching. 'Listen, my son, and be wise' (23.19a), and the saying is again built around the motif of undesirable company: 'Do not be among winebibbers, or among gluttonous eaters of meat'. The dreaded prospect of destitution is opened up as the penalty for the lethargy induced by over-indulgence: 'For the drunkard and the glutton will come to poverty, and drowsiness will clothe them with rags' (23.21). In the Torah, gluttony and drunkenness are the vices of an incorrigible son, and the penalty is public stoning (Deut. 21.18-20).

Interlude: Acquire Wisdom, for your Parents' Sake (23.22-25)
The duty of children to honour their parents (Deut. 5.16) is expressed as wisdom teaching. Children honour their parents by learning their wisdom: 'Listen to your father who begot you, and do not despise your mother when she is old. Buy truth, and do not sell it; buy wisdom, instruction, and understanding' (23.22-23). As the women of Bethlehem exclaimed, children are expected to care for an aged, widowed mother (Ruth 4.15). Finally, the motif of parental joy in wise children (10.1; 23.15-16) rings out over and over: 'The father of the righteous will greatly rejoice; he who begets a wise son

will be glad in him. Let your father and mother be glad; let her who bore you rejoice' (23.24-25).

Female Characters to Avoid (23.26-28)
A wise father who has rejoiced in the wife of his youth (5.15-19) now asks his son to contemplate the happy outcome of his father's fidelity: 'My child, give me your heart, and let your eyes observe my ways'. Associating with a woman outside the marriage bond is described as encountering the three perils awaiting an unwary traveller: a deep, concealed pit, a narrow, inaccessible well (the antithesis of the faithful husband's well of life-giving waters, 5.15), and an ambush. 'For a prostitute is a deep pit; an adulteress is a narrow well. She lies in wait like a robber and increases the number of the faithless' (23.27-28).

Evoking a Drunkard's Experience (23.29-36)
The serious threat of this vice of the rebellious son, namely overindulgence in strong drink, to any young man's life and happiness receives more attention in this section (see above, 23.19-21) than in the previous 'proverbs of Solomon', where intoxication is said poetically to be incompatible with wisdom (20.1), while the topic is not mentioned at all in chs. 1–9. Here a poem is created so as to evoke imaginatively the actual experience of being drunk, to the extent that this is achievable through the rhetoric and poetry. First, the audience's involvement in the learning process is sought, with a series of six rhetorical questions about the effects of intoxication: 'Who has woe? Who has sorrow? Who has strife? Who has complaining? Who has wounds without cause? Who has redness of eyes?' (23.29). A picture of misery is created, of one voicing grief and anguish, and causing disruption. He has bruises and discoloured eyes. The answer is given bluntly in the only third-person couplet in the poem: 'Those who linger late over wine, those who keep trying mixed wines' (23.30). A group of drunkards stays up late, and, in a perversion of a king's wise investigation (*ḥqr*) of matters of state (25.2-3), the revellers try out (*ḥqr*) mixed wine. The rest of the passage continues in the second person. First, the occasion is presented: 'Do not look at wine when it is red, when it sparkles in the cup, and goes down smoothly' (23.31). Then the youth is led to imaginatively suffer the effects: 'At the last it bites like a serpent, and stings like an adder' (23.32). Wine appeals to the sight and taste, but its effects are painful and toxic. These include distorted vision ('your eyes will see strange things'), disordered speech ('your mind utter perverse things'), and the loss of balance ('you

will be like one who lies down in the midst of the sea, like one who lies on the top of a mast') (23.33-34). The drunkard's words are placed on his lips: "'They struck me", you will say, "but I was not hurt; they beat me, but I did not feel it. When shall I awake? I will seek another drink"' (23.35). He is unable to ward off bumps and bruises (23.29), as all feeling is lost, and he has become an incorrigible fool. The Hebrew words evoke the hissing of the biting snake (*kᵉnāḥāš yiššāk*—'bites like a serpent', *kᵉṣip'ōnî yapriš*—'stings like an adder', 23.32).

Avoid the Company of the Subversive (24.1-2)

One who mixes with bad companions for riches' sake will inevitably become like them, a perpetrator of acts of violence. 'Do not envy the wicked, nor desire to be with them; for their minds devise violence, and their lips talk of mischief' (24.1-2, as in 1.10-19).

Interlude: Wisdom Sayings (24.3-9)

a. *Wisdom as the Project of a Lifetime (24.3-4)*. The metaphor of the completion of a house, from design, to construction, to furnishing and adornment, serves to illustrate the role of wisdom throughout the whole course of a successful man's life. The use of synonyms sustains the wisdom imagery: 'By wisdom a house is built, and by understanding it is established; by knowledge the rooms are filled with all precious and pleasant riches' (24.3-4).

b. *Wisdom is Strength, as Wisdom Claimed (24.5-6; cf. 8.14)*. The efficacy of sound practical judgment in the course of constructing one's life is now illustrated with the image of military strategy, where an army of inferior strength can overcome a more powerful opponent through clever strategy. In securing one's future, wisdom, and not the accumulation of material resources, gains the desired result: 'Wise warriors are mightier than strong ones, and those who have knowledge than those who have strength; for by wise guidance you can wage your war, and in abundance of counsellors there is victory' (24.5-6).

c. *Wisdom in the Assembly (24.7-9)*. 'Wisdom is too high for fools; in the gate they do not open their mouths' (24.7). The son who disdains wisdom teaching will have no standing in the public arena, that is, in the gate of the town, where all the community's affairs were openly discussed (de Vaux 1961: 152). A second assembly scene displays the odious reputation of the socially disruptive: 'Whoever plans to do evil will be called a mischief-maker [*ba'al-mᵉzimmôt*]. The

devising [*zimmâ*] of folly is sin, and the scoffer is an abomination
to all' (24.8-9). The sobriquet 'mischief-maker', literally 'master of
intrigue', ripples through the crowd when a certain person appears.
All in all, the gates imagery in 24.7-9 creates an idealistic picture
of the social respect enjoyed by wise citizens. Fools are silent, the
malicious have the reputation they deserve, and the opponents of
wisdom (scoffers) are loathed by all. What actually takes place in
the gates may be otherwise (22.22), as the next advice also suggests.

Courage in a Judge (24.10-12)
The wise one now places on the son's own lips the excuses of a weak
and corrupt judge, and then refutes them: 'If you faint in the day of
adversity (*ṣārâ*), your strength being small (*ṣar*); if you hold back
from rescuing those taken away to death, those who go stagger-
ing to the slaughter; if you say, "Look, we did not know this"—does
not he who weighs the heart perceive it? Does not he who keeps
watch over your soul know it? And will he not repay all according to
their deeds?' (24.10-12). This wisdom teaching illustrates the adage
that wisdom is strength (24.5), for a Yahweh-fearing administrator will not hesitate to speak out for the innocent. God's scrutiny of
the human heart, known in 'the proverbs of Solomon' (15.3), would
render futile all excuses of ignorance.

Doublet: Respecting the Rights of Others, and the Continuation of the Household (24.13-20)
In the introduction, recalling a father's advice is likened to rel-
ishing the sweetness of honey (24.13), and the continuation of the
family is ensured through a life guided by wisdom teaching: 'If you
find it [wisdom], you will find a future, and your hope will not be
cut off' (24.14). This incentive is repeated at the end, along with the
image of the transgressor's extinguished household lamp (24.20).
The deprivation of a future is expressed as the premature death of
the unjust person, and his children's insecurity (13.22), amount-
ing to the cessation of the household. Quite similar advice to the
three admonitions comprising this teaching was given in the warnings in 3.27-31 about disrupting the social *shalom* (3.2) consequent
on living in wisdom and the fear of Yahweh. In the latter case, the
rewards and sanctions are couched simply in terms of Yahweh's
blessing or curse on the household (3.33). The instruction in the
first section of Proverbs forms a doublet with the present one in 'the
words of the wise', the former expressing retribution in terms of
Yahweh's intervention, the latter envisaging what the divine blessing or curse entails for the household's future. The first disruptive

practice, taking advantage of the defenceless in the community, is described metaphorically as plundering: 'Do not lie in wait like an outlaw against the home of the righteous; do no violence to the place where the righteous live' (24.15). The phrase 'the home of the righteous' (*nᵉwēh ṣaddîq*) repeats the expression in 3.33 for the human abode which receives Yahweh's blessing. The image is of a predator waiting outside a dwelling to pounce on the unsuspecting occupants as soon as they emerge. The motivation, 'though they fall seven times, they will rise again; but the wicked are overthrown by calamity' (24.16), repeats the wisdom of the proverb on the survival of the righteous and the eventual downfall of the wicked (10.25).

The second admonition refers to taking malicious joy in another's misfortune: 'Do not rejoice when your enemies fall, and do not let your heart be glad when they stumble' (24.17). The other person is presumed to be at fault, which has provoked Yahweh's anger. 'Or else the LORD will see it and be displeased, and turn away his anger from them' (24.18). Such irreligious gloating is divorced from the humility which, in the prior instruction, alone wins Yahweh's favour (3.34). In the third admonition, a son imbued with his father's wisdom will know how to maintain the fear of Yahweh in situations which seem very difficult to reconcile with Yahweh's wise disposition of the created world: 'Do not fret because of evildoers. Do not envy the wicked' (24.19). As mentioned above, the eventual prevalence of justice is expressed metaphorically: 'For the evil have no future; the lamp of the wicked will go out' (24.20).

Respecting the Whole Social Order (24.21-22)
A final admonition associates Yahweh and the king in the exercise of judgment and retribution: 'My child, fear the LORD and the king, and do not disobey either of them; for disaster comes from them suddenly, and who knows the ruin that both can bring?' (24.21-22). The envisaged disobedience may refer to political rebellion, but it also looks back to the ideal king's intolerance of malice in his associates, and his punitive judgment, as referred to in the royal proverbs (e.g. 20.8, 26), and also anticipates the royal proverbs that begin the following section of 'the proverbs of Solomon' (25.1–29.27).

Additional Words of the Wise (24.23-34)

This appendix to 'the words of the wise' comprises five teachings, some in direct address, some in the third person, and they are all set in the household or at the gates. Agricultural images occur again, both for establishing a successful household (24.27), and, in the final poem in the section, for depicting the demise of a once flourishing household (24.30-34).

Impartial Judgment (24.23b-25)

> Partiality in judging is not good.
> Whoever says to the wicked, 'You are innocent',
> will be cursed by peoples, abhorred by nations;
> but those who rebuke the wicked will have delight,
> and a good blessing will come upon them. (24.23b-25)

Two antithetical cases are proposed, marked out by the repetition of 'good' (24.23b, 25). A proverb has already described a judge's partiality as 'raising the face' of the guilty defendant (18.5), that is, doing that person a favour that violates justice. Here, however, the metaphor is, literally, 'taking note of' the defendant's face, that is, judging out of human respect, in favour of the rich, the powerful, or a person with whom one is personally connected. The penalty is social disparagement, whereas an honest, courageous judge (24.10-12) will be esteemed by the people, a value so prized by the wise (3.4).

Sincere Speaking (24.26)

Making a sincere response is described metaphorically as a gesture of intimacy: 'One who gives an honest answer gives a kiss on the lips'. The Septuagint links this saying to the previous one, and so suggests that the kiss is bestowed on, rather than by, the respondent. 'And men will kiss lips that answer well'.

The Years of Youth (24.27)

'Prepare your work outside, get everything ready for you in the field; and after that build your house'. Through the repetition of 'prepare' and the similarity of *ma'ᵃkālāh* ('her sustenance', 6.8) and *mᵉla'ktekā* ('your work', 24.27), this admonition echoes the description of the diligent harvest ant in 6.8, so making the point that the critique of sloth in Proverbs applies particularly to the young, who are urged not to squander the precious years of early manhood.

On Resentment and Unbridled Revenge (24.28-29)

'Do not be a witness against your neighbour without cause, and do not deceive with your lips' (24.28). Here the audience is not a gullible youth being seduced into a life of violence and oppression, as in the first parental instruction (1.8-19) where the language is partially identical, but the mature perpetrator of an act of injustice. The wise one's advice is, 'Do not be a witness against your neighbour without cause [*ḥinnām*], and do not deceive [*pth*] with your lips,' an echo of the men of violence attempting to 'entice' (*pth*) a youth to join them (1.10): 'let us wantonly [*ḥinnām*] ambush the innocent' (1.11). The saying complements that on venal judges (24.23). The admonition concludes when the culprit's sentiments of revenge are placed on the hearer's lips: 'Do not say, "I will do to others as they have done to me; I will pay them back for what they have done"' (24.28-29). Vengeance belongs to Yahweh (24.18), and in the 'proverbs', 'it is their glory [of those with good sense] to overlook an offence' (19.11).

A Household's Sad Demise (24.30-34)

To conclude the section, the wise one speaks in the first person, as an experienced father advising his son: 'I passed by the field of one who was lazy, by the vineyard of a stupid person; and see, it was all overgrown with thorns; the ground was covered with nettles, and its stone wall was broken down. Then I saw and considered it; I looked and received instruction' (24.30-32). Here the public face of indolence is apparent, and is an occasion of household shame, as in 10.5. There follows a tendentious citation of the householder's words, as in the case of the drunkard (23.35-36), the corrupt judge (24.24), and the false witness (24.29). The rationalization, 'a little sleep, a little slumber, a little folding of the hands to rest', begins with a mocking lilt, *me'aṭ šēnôt me'aṭ tenûmôt*. The concluding lesson is addressed both to the indolent farmer, but equally to any young person of the book's audience: 'And poverty will come upon you like a robber, and want, like an armed warrior' (24.33-34). Again, indolence is criticized as a serious threat to the house-building enterprise of a successful life (24.27). The final two half-verses repeat the conclusion of the instruction on sloth in the first section (6.10-11).

Concluding Comments

The wisdom teaching in 'the words of the wise', in the form of a father's instruction to an inexperienced son on the threshold of public life, maps out a path to success and happiness. The foundations of a successful life are diligence, restraint in matters of food and drink, and of the sexual appetite. There is a repeated concern to address the appeal of unjustly acquired riches, and the desire to be like those who have them. While many points of similarity to the first section of Proverbs (chs. 1–9) have been mentioned in the introduction to this section, and thereafter, it may be noted, after reading 'the words of the wise', that here the disciple of wisdom is in a different situation from the naive youth addressed in chs. 1–9, on matters internal to the household, emphasizing fidelity and prudent management. This son, on the other hand, will be expected to exercise the office of judge and to be a witness, to act with even-handed, at times, courageous fairness, without respect of persons. Enriching himself at the expense of the defenceless of Israel will bring certain retribution, and when required, he should give an honest answer, without duplicity. Unworthy behaviour will not escape a Yahweh-fearing king's attention, and indolence will bring to nought his life's wisdom project. In turn, he will instruct and discipline his own son, and be a model for his imitation. The instructions of 'words of the wise', then, complement the first set of instructions, and, as has been mentioned in the commentary, they also express, in the form of the exhortation, many of the concerns of the preceding 'proverbs of Solomon'. These teachings are brief, and sometimes picturesque, and outcomes are laid down succinctly. The addressee is urged to treasure them as his father's bequest, savouring them for their clarity and euphony. While the motivations are compelling, yet the teacher, too, exercises restraint, delivering short instructions, and respecting his son's ability to choose freely. The following section, entitled 'other proverbs of Solomon that the officials of King Hezekiah of Judah copied' (25.1), will provide many additional observations for a wise son's reflection.

Proverbs 25.1–29.27: Other Proverbs of Solomon that the Officials of King Hezekiah Copied

An Ordered and Beautiful World (25.1-28)

Both stylistically and topically, the proverbs transmitted by King Hezekiah's professional scribes fall into two sections, (a) wisdom through metaphor and simile (chs. 25–27), and (b) living wisely in a turbulent society (chs. 28–29). Rhetorically, the transition from the style of paternal advice in 'the words of the wise' to the second section of 'proverbs' is smoothed through the continuation of second-person admonitions in ch. 25, so that also here, as in the previous section, a wise father teaches his son. In ch. 25 alone, six admonitions are mingled with seventeen third-person sayings. The abstract terms, 'life' and 'death', 'wisdom' and 'folly', 'righteousness' and 'wickedness', so evident in the antithetical parallelism of the opening chapters of the previous collection of proverbs, are absent, and instead, the advice is expressed, through synonymous parallelism, in images of beauty and majesty, or of everyday ordinariness, making ch. 25 one of the most colourful parts of Proverbs. As invited to in the preface (1.6), youths may attain wisdom by reflecting on such figurative language. Thematically, the teachings in this chapter concern kings and courtiers bringing justice to the people, but also the duty of all to exercise restraint, to relate to others in the community in justice and charity, and to respect the social order.

Title (25.1)

'These are other proverbs of Solomon that the officials of King Hezekiah of Judah copied' (25.1). The three most senior ministers of Hezekiah (728–709 BCE) are referred to in 2 Kgs 18.18, however without mention of the royal scribes. Cox sets the scene of the literary activity in Hezekiah's court as follows: 'Hezekiah seems to have been almost a second Solomon, though on a smaller scale. With no political rivals, and no opposing king in the northern kingdom of

Israel, he had the leisure to set about strengthening and centralis-
ing learning in Judah' (Cox 1982: 210).

Proverbs of Glory and Shame (25.2-10)

The collection made by King Hezekiah's scribes begins fittingly with
a block of four royal proverbs, whose keyword is 'king' or 'kings', and
which advise a young courtier how to contribute to the exercise of
wise governance. First, 'It is the glory of God to conceal things, but
the glory of kings is to search things out' (25.2). The only previous
proverb on God and the king depicted a God-fearing king's docil-
ity to Yahweh (21.1). Now a sage has devised an artful antithetical proverb about God and the king in terms of glory, the gaining of
social esteem. In Proverbs, the secret things of God's creation are
the depths of the human heart (15.11), and knowledge of the future
(16.33). In the antithesis, the king's glory is not derived from his
high office, but rather from his ability to make wise and just decisions through diligent enquiry. The second royal proverb repeats
the term 'search out' (*ḥqr*): 'Like the heavens for height, like the
earth for depth, so the mind of kings is unsearchable' (25.3). The
wise one is quick to point out that the king's scrutiny is not reciprocal. Whereas Jonathan could 'sound' (*'eḥqōr*) his father's intentions
about David (1 Sam. 20.12), this king is not subject to such scrutiny. Rather, his profound knowledge is expressed in imagery that
hints of the divine knowledge (15.11). A king's actions are indeed
subject to human scrutiny (29.14; 31.4-9), but, in the thinking that
guides practical policy (21.1), or in the king's knowledge of his subjects (20.8), a courtier cannot expect to be party to everything that
the king, with Yahweh's help (21.1), has investigated. Moreover,
a confidant can betray the 'secret of a king' (see Tob. 12.7). 'Take
away the dross from the silver, and the smith has material for a
vessel; take away the wicked from the presence of the king, and his
throne will be established in righteousness' (25.4-5). In the third
royal proverb, the smelting imagery highlights the need for upright
officials in the royal administration, where the corrupt are likened
to an unwanted impurity in a precious metal, to be removed without hesitation lest the people be denied justice. 'Do not put yourself
forward in the king's presence or stand in the place of the great;
for it is better to be told, "Come up here", than to be put lower in
the presence of a noble' (25.6-7a). This fourth royal proverb, having
the form of an experienced noble's or administrator's advice to a
young, aspiring courtier, illustrates the saying that 'humility goes
before honour' (15.33b). A youth needs to know that he can make
an effective contribution only when invited to do so by his patron,

whose power of discretion is complete, and self-promotion at court can lead to humiliation. The deterrent of shame, or social disapproval, complements the theme of glory, or social esteem, in the previous proverbs. Here moral abstracts, like pride and haughtiness (16.18), are not invoked, but in the 'better than' literary form, there is an appeal to the disciple's practical judgment and enlightened self-interest.

The motif of shame, defining a youth's rejection from society, continues in the next two admonitions (25.8-10), having as keywords the terms 'neighbour' and 'court', or 'dispute' (*rîb*). The court scene in the first of these two proverbs on settling disputes may be the royal court, or before an appointed judge, but also in the gates of the town in the presence of the elders: 'What your eyes have seen do not hastily bring into court (*rîb*); for what will you do in the end, when your neighbour puts you to shame?' (25.7b-8). Such rash litigation and tale-bearing could be motivated by revenge and harbouring grudges (see 25.21-22), and the advice is similar to, 'Do not quarrel with anyone without cause, when no harm has been done to you' (3.30). To summon the elders to the gates, and to become a plaintiff, on superficial, flimsy evidence is a violation of justice, and the resulting shame is the ultimate penalty as regards a person's standing in the community. Secondly, 'Argue your case (*rîbᵉkā rîb*) with your neighbour directly, and do not disclose another's secret; or else someone who hears you will bring shame upon you, and your ill repute will have no end' (25.9-10). The caution is about voicing a grievance in tale-bearing instead of resolving the issue with the other person.

Precious Objects as Metaphors of Wisdom Teaching (25.11-12)

There is no explicit mention of wisdom in ch. 25, but the teacher-pupil relationship is evoked: 'A word fitly spoken is like apples of gold in a setting of silver' (25.11). The beauty of golden, ripened fruits is enhanced by their engraved silver containers. Such precious tableware could adorn the metaphorical house of the wise (24.4). In educational terms, the perfect setting of a wise saying is the ear of an eager disciple (15.31). The next saying reiterates the previous one. 'Like a gold ring or an ornament of gold is a wise rebuke to a listening ear' (25.12). A youth will acquire wisdom through listening to, and heeding firm guidance. As the parents advised in their first recorded words (1.8-9), the jewellery that most enhances the appearance of the young is the ability to learn from teaching and instruction.

Weather Images Recalling Previous Teachings (25.13-14)

'Like the cold of snow in the time of harvest are faithful messengers to those who send them; they refresh the spirit of their masters' (25.13). An important way to earn one's patron's trust is to be a faithful courier or messenger (10.26). The point is illustrated by the way that the refreshing coolness of a snowfall would lift the spirits of heat-exhausted harvesters, abstracting from the reality of any attendant destructive rain. 'Like clouds and wind without rain is one who boasts of a gift never given' (25.14). The young will find that empty promises of financial gain abound (23.6-8), but the only sure way ahead is solid service and industry. 'In an agrarian world, rain is an image of life and abundance, since vegetation and crops depend on it', and the appearance of 'clouds that produce no rain is one of the ultimate disappointments' (see Ryken, 'Rain', *DBI*: 694).

How to Speak to one's Patron or a Ruler (25.15)

It is not the forceful or angry outburst which carries weight (15.1), and patience and gentle words are a client's only recourse with an administrative official: 'With patience a ruler may be persuaded, and a soft tongue will break a bone' (25.15). The broken bone image expresses the power of the gentle word, for the resistant bones give strength and solidity to the whole body (Job 40.18). There are two nasal sounds in each half-verse ('*appayim...qāṣîn / lāšôn...gārem*).

Pleasure in Moderation (25.16-17)

'If you have found honey, eat only enough for you, lest you be sated with it and vomit it. Let your foot be seldom in your neighbour's house, lest he become weary of you [lit. be sated with you] and hate you' (25.16-17). Over-indulgence on the part of the guest produces revulsion in the host.

Other Images of Socially Destructive Behaviour (25.18-20)

'Like a war club, a sword, or a sharp arrow is one who bears false witness against a neighbour' (25.18). False witness could lead to the sentencing of the innocent, whose plight is likened to a civilian being attacked with weapons of war. Like a sharp arrow, a witness's lie comes unexpectedly and penetrates deeply, it can come from close quarters, and cut and thrust like a sword (like rash words, 12.18), or it can inflict a brutal battering. The swish of the weapons is echoed in two 's' sounds in the first half-verse, and with three 'sh' sounds in the whole proverb (*mēpîṣ wᵉḥereb wᵉḥēṣ šānûn 'îš 'ōneh bᵉrē'ēhû 'ēd šāqer*). 'Like a bad tooth or a lame foot is trust in a faithless person in time of trouble' (25.19). Everyone can do without a toothache, while having a lame foot severely restricts movement. Such is the lingering, hurtful aftermath of misplaced trust. 'It's like pouring vinegar on soda to sing songs to a troubled heart' (25.20, Clifford). Vinegar and soda are incompatible. The effects of depression on the human spirit are not exaggerated in this image of aggravation, for, if 'from the least to the greatest, biblical people generally sang and played instruments (1 Sam. 16.18; Job 30.31)' (see Ryken, 'Music', *DBI*: 576), such an antipathy to music would represent a serious disorder. There is no place for thoughtlessness in human communication, and good intentions are no substitute for timeliness.

Turning Hatred to Love (25.21-22)

> If your enemies are hungry, give them bread to eat;
> and if they are thirsty, give them water to drink;
> for you will heap coals of fire on their heads,
> and the LORD will reward you (25.21-22).

Enmity is to be countered with love, not revenge, and love can effect an astonishing transformation in the offender. Live coals on the sensitive head suggests the burning shame of having one's hostility met with love, or could allude to an Egyptian ritual signifying genuine repentance (see Ryken, 'Romans, letter to the', *DBI*: 739). The reward of such magnanimity is the restoration of social harmony (16.7).

Images of Damaging and Uplifting Speech (25.23, 25)

Literally 'the secret tongue' in 25.23 refers to speaking ill of people behind their back, which produces a very perceptible cloud of anger on the victim's face, just as the invisible north wind is revealed by the rain it causes. 'The north wind produces rain, and a backbiting tongue, angry looks' (25.23). Another weather-related image, a refreshing cool drink on a summer's day, captures one of life's joys, receiving a message from a distant loved one. 'Like cold water to a thirsty soul, so is good news from a far country' (25.25).

Courage in an Administrator (25.26)

Righteousness is put to the test in situations where moral courage is needed, for example, in the case of a judge offered a bribe. Everyday imagery makes the point just as effectively as a more extended admonition (24.10-12). 'Like a muddied spring or a polluted fountain are the righteous who give way before the wicked' (25.26).

Restraint in Seeking Advancement (25.27)
The chapter draws to a close, as it began, with a saying on glory: 'It is not good to eat much honey, or to seek honour on top of honour' (25.27). The sickening effect of over-indulgence in honey is an image of the spiritual nausea produced by an intemperate quest for esteem, and the deterrent is in terms of personal disillusionment.

Lack of Self-Control (25.28)
A city whose defences have crumbled, with the enemy pouring in, illustrates the well-known theme of the link between wisdom and self-control (14.29; 18.13): 'Like a city breached, without walls, is one who lacks self-control' (25.28).

Concluding Comments
The proverbs of the 'officials of Hezekiah' are a fitting continuation of the wisdom of 'the words of the wise', when, through the sayings in the form of second-person address, a father engages directly with his youthful audience with a certain intimacy. Some of the colourful images derive from geography and climate: there is snow (25.13), a north wind and rain (25.23), while some clouds bring no rain (25.14). Outdoors there are springs, and a well which can be polluted (25.26), and you could find honey as you walk (25.16). Indoor images include precious jewels and valuable household objects (25.11-12), and perhaps stored weapons of war (25.18). Overall, the world of ch. 25 is ordered and beautiful, and the young are advised to keep it so. The tone of fatherly advice will continue in ch. 26, which will be almost entirely concerned with perverse or incompetent speech.

Malice, Incompetence and Stupidity (26.1-28)
Chapter 26 includes many speech proverbs, which are distributed throughout each of the four topical groups comprising this chapter, namely the proverbs on folly, on sloth, on disruptive speech, and on malicious duplicity, with keywords uniting each topical group. The use of metaphor and comparison, the salient characteristic of ch. 25, continues in ch. 26, but the images now are harsh or incongruous, and they illustrate types of behaviour or character types to be avoided. There is a reminder, though, that there is a class of people incapable of learning through images (26.7). The first twelve proverbs concern the fool (*kᵉsîl*), followed by four proverbs on the 'sluggard' (*ʿāṣēl*), then five proverbs are linked by the keywords of 'strife' (*rîb, mādôn, midyānîm*), with, finally, six proverbs linked by the keyword, 'enemy' (*śônēʾ*).

Images of the Fool (26.1-12)

The characteristics of a fool (*kᵉsîl*) are well known. He has no need
of advice (18.2), and a frequently noted trait is lack of self-control,
notably in speech (12.23). His language damages others (10.18), for
he lacks any moral sensitivity (10.23). It is wise to avoid the fool
(17.12), whose fate is inevitable (19.29). This character type has
already been sketched unsympathetically, with occasional sarcasm
(17.12, 24), and an expression of bewilderment (17.16). The fool in
ch. 26 has few, if any, additional character traits, but these sayings
make a conspicuous addition to the previous proverbs about the
fool by their concentrated use of simile, in keeping with the prevailing synonymous parallelism in chs. 25–27.

'Like snow in summer or rain in harvest, so honour is not fitting for a fool' (26.1). The musical word pair *qayiṣ* ('summer') / *qāṣîr*
('harvest') occurs again (6.8; 10.5). The wise one now changes the
picture of refreshing snow at harvest time (25.13) into an image of
incongruity, adding that of damaging rain during the cereal harvest
(as in 28.3, and 1 Sam. 12.17). The impression gained is of an incompetent person in high office who is paid respect solely in view of his
position. This saying is a negative complement to 25.2, on the true
glory of the capable king. The image of a bird aimlessly flying about
conveys a consoling message to one innocent of breaching seriously
the divine-human relationship, yet being the subject of a rashly
uttered curse: 'Like a sparrow in its flitting, like a swallow in its
flying, an undeserved curse goes nowhere' (26.2). Though threatening in the first instance (12.18), such an implicitly foolish utterance
lacks the power of God to inflict harm on its intended victim. The
first half-verse has the sound appeal of a repeated long 'o' and long
'u' vowel: *kaṣṣippôr lānûd kaddᵉrôr lā'ûp*. The next saying suggests
the fittingness of a disciplinary beating for fools (19.29): 'A whip for
the horse, a bridle for the donkey, and a rod for the back of fools'
(26.3). The expression is terse: 'a whip for…a bridle for…and a rod
for'. While righteousness includes the humane treatment of domestic animals (12.10), yet the animal aspect singled out now is the
need to be controlled by physical means, because, unlike the wise,
self-motivated ant (6.6-8), they lack intelligence (see Ps. 32.9). The
next two proverbs claim attention by an apparent contradiction,
which the wise one does little to resolve. A riddle contains an element of contradiction (Judg. 14.18), and so the two following contra-
dictory admonitions may be considered a figure of speech, which the
wise one leaves the reader to interpret: 'Do not answer fools according to their folly, or you will be a fool yourself' (26.4), and 'Answer
fools according to their folly, or they will be wise in their own eyes'

(26.5). Each admonition contains the word 'like' (k^e), attached to the abstract 'folly', and not to a concrete image of comparison. In life, the wise will encounter the dull and irrational, and it is very difficult to know how to respond to a person who has no interest in understanding (18.2). All the wise one can suggest is not to be drawn into adopting the fool's perspective (26.4), and yet to avoid confirming the fool in his self-conceit, by one's silence (26.5).

An image of almost unimaginable self-mutilation makes the point to officials that it is worse than useless to ask a person who delights in expressing his own opinion to be one's representative: 'It is like cutting off one's foot and drinking down violence, to send a message by a fool' (26.6). The wise ones take pride in teaching by figurative language (1.6), and the next proverb expresses frustration with the dullard's inability to learn by this means: 'The legs of a disabled person hang limp; so does a proverb in the mouth of a fool' (26.7). A second caution (after 26.1) is given a future patron about advancing an unworthy person, and expecting to receive faithful service: 'It is like binding a stone in a sling to give honour to a fool' (26.8), which is to disarm a weapon, and then trying to use it. Next, one can easily imagine a reeling drunkard getting a thorn in his hand, which only adds to his misery and the disorder he creates, but the saying concerns the figurative thorn in a fool's mouth: 'Like a thorn entering the hand of a drunkard is a proverb in the mouth of a fool' (26.9). The misuse of figurative language inflicts hurt on the stupid and all who hear. This comparison illustrates the saying about another type of fool ($^e w\hat{\imath}l$), 'the mouth of fools is impending destruction' (10.14). The picture of an archer turning his weapon on everyone within range suggests the damage done, not only to the sender (26.6), but to all concerned, by entrusting a message to one filled with irrationality and self-conceit. 'Like an archer who wounds everybody is one who hires a passing fool or drunkard' (26.10).

The wise one does not extend the respect due to domestic animals to the unclean dog (Exod. 22.31), and the dog imagery in the next saying is more demeaning than the above horse and donkey comparison (26.3). 'Like a dog that returns to its vomit is a fool who reverts to his folly' (26.11). A fool's enslavement to his opinions reminds the poet of a dog returning to its filth. The final saying in this group presents a rhetorical ray of hope, even to the dull and socially irresponsible, for even worse is the state of those who are 'wise in their own eyes', that is, closed to the programme of education to wisdom and the fear of God (1.7, and 3.7; 12.15): 'Do you see persons wise in their own eyes? There is more hope for fools than for them' (26.12). This expression of a teacher's frustration (compare 26.7) is made in confidence to docile disciples.

Four Proverbs on the Sluggard (26.13-16)

The sayings on sloth reflect a concern for the education of desire. Early in the book, there is an appeal to earnestly desire wisdom (2.1-4; 3.15), and the fulfilment of desire is a significant aspect of emotional satisfaction (13.12). While sloth, as the absence of all desire, is not seen as wickedness, sloth has the capacity to place wisdom beyond a young person's reach. Not only will a sluggard's life-project fail, through inability to support oneself and to maintain a household (6.6-11; 24.30-34), but laziness will inflict shame on parents and family (10.5). If a provocative taunting (6.6-11) has failed, and threats of the gravity of the situation (20.4; 21.25) are ineffective, a final recourse is had to bemused satire, expressed in a concentrated use of figurative language, with two of the four proverbs in this block repeated from 'the proverbs of Solomon' (10.1–22.16). Each of the sayings will be cited, with a comment. 'The lazy person says, "There is a lion in the road! There is a lion in the streets!"' (26.13; see 22.13). Lions need food and cover, and they did not mingle with the human population (Fowler, 'Lion', *EDB*: 824), which suggests how exaggerated and ridiculous is the rationalization placed on the sluggard's lips. 'As a door turns on its hinges, so does a lazy person in bed' (26.14). Such lethargy is especially evident when the time comes to rise in the morning, illustrated by a humorous comparison with the movement of a turning door. 'The lazy person buries a hand in the dish, and is too tired to bring it back to the mouth' (26.15, repeated from 19.24). He is even too lazy to keep himself alive. Finally, and sadly, in its root cause, sloth is equated with the arrogant rejection of learning: 'The lazy person is wiser in self-esteem [in his own eyes] than seven who can answer discreetly' (26.16). Sound repetition (*miššibʿâ mᵉšîbê*) links the first two words in the second half-verse, and there is a rhyme in the first and last words (*ḥākām*, 'wise' / *ṭāʿam*, 'discretion'). This numerical proverb cites a case where the one exceeds the seven, that is, the lazy pupil's confidence in his blind rationalizations is greater than the combined wisdom of all those (the seven) who speak with good judgment.

Four Proverbs on Creating Strife (26.17-22)

'Strife' (*rîb*, 26.17, 21) and 'quarrelling' (*mādôn*, 26.20-21) are key-words in this unit on four social disrupters. The reader is left to imagine the nasty, unexpected reaction of a passing, scavenging

dog to a well-intentioned attempt to fondle it. Such is one 'who med-
dles in the quarrel of another' (26.17). A more alarming image is of
a maniac discharging lethal weapons on everyone in sight. This picture is intended to discourage telling lies as a senseless joke: 'so is
one who deceives his neighbour and says, "I am only joking"' (26.18-
19). A normally soothing domestic image captures the diminish-
ing glow of a fire dying out: 'For lack of wood the fire goes out, and
where there is no whisperer, quarrelling ceases' (26.20). This fire,
however, is destructive quarrelling, and negative comments are the
fuel. Next, charcoal is placed on the hot embers, and the flames
are fuelled with wood: 'As charcoal is to hot embers and wood to
fire, so is a quarrelsome person for kindling strife' (26.21). Finally,
metaphorical dainties are not the food of the wise: 'The words of a
whisperer are like delicious morsels; they go down into the inner
parts of the body' (26.22). On this occasion, they are not vomited up
(23.8), but they lodge in the stomach, and are very slow to digest
(26.22 = 18.8).

Five Warnings about Smooth-talking, Violent Men (26.23-28)

In this group, the keyword is enemy (*śn'*) in its noun or verbal
forms (26.24-25, 26, 28), and the warnings are not about behaviour to avoid, but rather the wise father cautions his son about
being the unwitting victim of malice, like the robbers' victims in
the first parental instruction (1.11-12). The point of the warnings
is that such 'enemies' speak fine-sounding words, and the inexperienced could be deceived. The first saying is introductory: 'Like
the glaze covering an earthen vessel are smooth lips with an evil
heart' (26.23). The NRSV 'glaze' translates a reconstructed, difficult Hebrew text, and as well, 'smooth lips' replaces the Hebrew
expression, 'fervent lips'. The ceramics image, together with the
lips and heart antithesis, clearly pictures a gracious exterior over-
laying interior baseness. In the following first 'enemy' proverb,
gracious words are not what they appear to be, but are the expression of an intention to deceive: 'An enemy dissembles in speaking [lit. with his lips] while harbouring deceit within' (26.24).
There is a thought and expression contrast, accentuated by the
use of *qereb* ('inmost being'), where deceit resides, in parallel with
'lips', where the deceiver pretends to be well-intentioned: 'When
an enemy speaks graciously [*yᵉḥannēn qôlô*], do not believe it ['*al-
taʾᵃmen-bô*], for there are seven abominations concealed within'
(26.25). Here, the warning implicit in the two previous proverbs
is made clear through the second-person address. As in Ps. 25.19,

the enmity pictured in these sayings is, in the end, considered life-threatening, rather than being a matter of sentiments of aversion or antipathy. The gravity of the contemplated evil is revealed in the seven abominations image, reminiscent of Yahweh's abominations in 6.16-19. The latter list includes bloodshed and false witness, and in the present saying such crimes are said to reside in the deceiver's heart. The gravity of the enemy's intentions is borne out in the next saying. 'Though hatred is covered with guile, the enemy's wickedness will be exposed in the assembly' (26.26). If the assembly refers to the gathering of elders and people at the city gates for the administration of justice (24.7-8), concealed hatred would have led to serious, public offences, like cursing the innocent (26.2), giving false witness, or even bloodshed. The wise one is convinced, however, that in the gates, justice will eventually prevail, and evildoers will get the reputation they deserve. This conviction is expressed metaphorically in the next proverb: 'Whoever digs a pit will fall into it, and a stone will come back on the one who starts it rolling' (26.27). Falling into a pit is an image of evildoers falling victim to the harm they plot for others, as in Ps. 7.15. After the labour of digging a cistern as an animal trap, to fall into it oneself would be a bitter result. In a second, parallel image, a huge stone uncontrollably crushes the person who sets it in motion. In the experience of the wise ones, evil-doing will be self-destructive. That is, unjust gain (1.11-19, sexual incontinence (2.16-19), and collaboration with smooth-talking evildoers (2.12-15), may be attractive options in the short term, but they are not the way to wisdom, happiness and success. The 'enemy' group is completed with another saying on damaging speech, in particular, lies and flattery: 'A lying tongue hates its victims, and a flattering mouth works ruin' (26.28). The 'lying tongue' is an expression known from 12.19. The liar wounds his victim, and though pleasant to hear, flattery finally ruins the gullible, and it is well to be warned.

Concluding Comments

In this chapter, the picture of order and beauty in the world and society in ch. 25 is realistically complemented by images of malice, incompetence and stupidity. Laziness is easily observed, but the social fabric can be torn by imprudence (26.17), irresponsible jokes (26.18), and, more insidiously, by snide remarks and backbiting (26.20-22). It is also important to be warned about the presence of evil concealed with charm and flattery (26.23-28). The use of comparisons and synthetic parallelism continues in ch. 27.

Household Wisdom (27.1-27)

The literary form of father–son instruction continues in ch. 27 with five admonitions (27.1-2, 10, 11, 13, 23-27), one of which is an encouragement to acquire wisdom (27.11), following which there is a reference to the simple (*peṭā'yim*, 27.12), who have yet to do that (1.4). In keeping with the literary form of parental advice, the imagery in ch. 27 evokes life in the household (27.13, 14, 15-16), and the topics of a person's emotional states (27.4, 7, 9), friendship (27.5-6, 10), and character formation (27.19, 21). We see pictures of household objects (27.9, 22), of house-construction (27.3), and of the household environs (27.18). Following the block of fool (*keṣîl*) proverbs (26.1-12), there are two, here non-sequential proverbs, on another type of fool, the *'ewîl* (27.3, 22).

Empty Praise (27.1-2)
A first pair of admonitions concern praising and boasting (27.1-2), terms which translate forms of the same Hebrew verb (*hll*): 'Do not boast about tomorrow, for you do not know what a day may bring' (27.1) and, 'Let another praise you, and not your own mouth—a stranger, and not your own lips' (27.2). In the light of a saying on Yahweh's disposition of events (16.9), a God-fearing youth will respect his own limits. Boasting about tomorrow's accomplishments is premature (18.12), and childish.

When One is Heavier than Two (27.3-4)
'A stone is heavy, and sand is weighty, but a fool's provocation [*ka'as*] is heavier than both' (27.3). The grief (*ka'as*) inflicted on a father by a foolish son (17.25) is an example of such insupportable provocation. Next, a proverb of relative value and a rhetorical question illustrate the crushing momentum of a betrayed husband's fury (6.34): 'Wrath is cruel, anger is overwhelming, but who is able to stand before jealousy?' (27.4).

Softening Salutary Pain (27.5-6)
Another proverb of relative value plays on the hidden/revealed antithesis: 'Better is open rebuke than hidden love' (27.5). In Proverbs, a father's rebuke is such an expression of love (3.12). In the following antithetical saying, the three Hebrew terms in the second half are the opposite of the three terms in the first half: 'Well meant are the wounds a friend inflicts, but profuse are the kisses of an enemy' (27.6). The saying could answer the question, 'When is a wound better than a kiss?' All the rebukes offered in friendship

should not destroy the friendship, for at the best they are expressions of loyalty, and can cleanse away evil (20.30), but even one hypocritical kiss is too much (from the NRSV) or to be prayed against (NAB). A proverb of antithetical appetites illustrates the paradox of the bitter being sweet: 'The sated appetite spurns honey, but to a ravenous appetite even the bitter is sweet' (27.7). This saying has an educational application in Proverbs, where the learner who hungers and thirsts for wisdom (as in 2.4, equivalently) will digest quite unpalatable truths (19.20). The self-satisfied fool, wise in his own eyes, however, shows contempt for wise guidance (15.5), even when it is sweet as honey (24.13).

A Man's Place (27.8)

'Like a bird that strays from its nest is one who strays from home' (27.8). It would be pleasing to repeat this proverb of similarity, with the term 'straying' being repeated, and 'from its nest' (*min-qinnāh*) sounding like 'from his place' (*mimmᵉqômô*). The unnatural behaviour of a restless, vulnerable bird, separated from where a bird should be, captures the sense of how inappropriate it is for a man to be without links to his own 'place', that is, family, community, and friends.

A Friend in Need (27.9-10)

Friendship is prized by the wise, and has been the subject of a number of reflections, where the loyalty of a true friend has been singled out (18.24; 19.4, 6-7). Now images of sensual delight evoke the healing sweetness of a friend's counsel in time of trouble: 'Oil and perfume gladden the heart, and the sweetness of friendship rather than self-reliance' (so NJB for the difficult Hebrew second half-verse, whereas the NRSV follows the Septuagint: 'but the soul is torn by trouble'). Pursuing the topic of loyalty, the father now addresses his son, counselling him, first, to remain loyal to friends, including an old family friend. The second parallel admonition builds on the first, by advising not to count on blood ties for support when that is really needed, and the advice is clinched by a concluding proverb of relative value; what counts in distress is the availability of help, and a blood-relative may be absent, or choose to remain aloof: 'Do not forsake your friend or the friend of your parent; do not go to the house of your kindred in the day of your calamity. Better is a neighbour who is nearby than kindred who are far away' (27.10).

A Father's Wisdom Teaching (27.11-13)

The second-person addresses in chs. 25–27 provide a teaching context for the third-person adages, and at this point, which, by design or by chance, marks the midpoint of chs. 25–29, the motif of paternal wisdom instruction is explicit: 'Be wise, my child, and make my heart glad, so that I may answer whoever reproaches me' (27.11). In Proverbs, the expression 'my son' ('my child', NRSV), is always used in relation to instruction, a father's greatest responsibility to his child. By way of motivation, the father appeals, uniquely in the two sections of 'the proverbs of Solomon', to his own experience, namely to the honour or shame he will experience on account of his son's behaviour. The grief and bitterness experienced by parents on their child's failure (17.25) has the context of social approval or rejection. Two previous proverbs are now brought in to illustrate the peril of ignoring a father's summons. First an antithesis depicts the one who defers leaving behind innate, uncommitted simplicity as a naive traveller destined for trouble: 'The clever see danger and hide, but the simple go on, and suffer for it' (27.12 = 22.3). This is illustrated in the following warning about the ruin entailed in being liable for another's debt: 'Take the garment of one who has given surety for a stranger; seize the pledge given as surety for foreigners' (27.13 = 20.16). The stranger is someone to whom one is not obligated by bonds of loyalty. In an exercise of the imagination, the wise one summons his son to exact the pledge, that is, the person or property of the imprudent guarantor, here symbolized in the garment of the poor given in pledge, and needed back to survive the night (Exod. 22.26).

Two Examples of Domestic Annoyance (27.14-16)
The first example is structured on the 'blessing-curse' word-pair (11.26), and is a reminder that words of wisdom are timely (25.20), and loud, early morning greetings and well-wishing will get a hostile reception: 'Whoever blesses a neighbour with a loud voice, rising early in the morning, will be counted as cursing' (27.14). A second source of domestic annoyance is unfortunately not confined to the early morning. Not only is the point made with one image, but two additional images suggest a husband's inability to do anything about it: 'A continual dripping on a rainy day and a contentious wife are alike; to restrain her is to restrain the wind or to grasp oil in the right hand' (27.15-16).

Proverbs of Character Formation (27.17-21)
The image of a smith, or the householder, using an iron hammer to pound out a sharp edge on blunt iron, illustrates the need of tough human interaction for growth to wisdom and maturity: 'Iron sharpens iron, and one person sharpens the wits of another' (27.17). 'The

wits of another' is literally 'the face of another', and 'face' in Hebrew may represent the very person (2 Sam. 17.11), but also the edge of a weapon (Jer. 21.7). The domesticated fig tree, like water in one's own cistern (5.15), is an image of prosperous self-sufficiency in the time of Solomon and Hezekiah (1 Kgs 4.25; Isa. 36.16). 'Anyone who tends a fig tree will eat its fruit, and anyone who takes care of a master will be honoured' (27.18). The cultivation of the fig tree, and enjoyment of the fruit suggests diligent service and its rewards. 'Just as water reflects the face, so one human heart reflects another' (27.19). In another household image, the reflected face illustrates the ability of a friend's counsel to clearly reflect back one's own state of mind. The wise are aware that sight is a precious gift of God (20.12); however, the restless, covetous gaze is compared with the abode of the dead's insatiable appetite for corpses (1.12). 'Sheol and Abaddon are never satisfied, and human eyes are never satisfied' (27.20). The greedy eye of the stingy man (23.6; 28.22) is brought to mind (compare the generous man with the 'good eye', 22.9). Praise would not normally be compared with a purifying fire, an image that that is more understandably linked to God's discriminating judgment (17.3), yet one's reaction to praise can also reveal true character. 'The crucible is for silver, and the furnace is for gold, so a person is tested by being praised' (27.21). The subject's reception of the praise referred to in 27.2 is here explored. Finally, in an expression of frustration, the wise one bluntly depicts the resistance of the fool (*ewil*) to the process of education to wisdom: 'Crush a fool in a mortar with a pestle along with crushed grain, but the folly will not be driven out' (27.22).

A Paradigm of Wisdom (27.23-27)
The poem has the appearance of an exhortation to take up the life of the sheep-rearing farmer. Livestock require attention (12.10), and 'sheep were totally dependent on shepherds for protection, grazing, watering, shelter and tending to injuries' (see Ryken, 'Sheep, shepherd', *DBI*: 782). 'Know well the condition of your flocks, and give attention to your herds' (27.23). Here the grazier is proposed as a model of the wisdom, diligence and foresight needed to establish a flourishing household. The story of the varied, unstable fortunes of the monarchy in Israel and Judah would argue for choosing a way of life within one's grasp, and with a guaranteed income. 'For riches do not last forever, nor a crown for all generations' (27.24). The successful shepherd works in harmony with the seasons (10.5), and the phases of the shepherd's year are noted: the new growth of pasture after the early rains, the withering of the grass in long,

late summer, and the reaping of upland fodder for storage. 'When the grass is gone, and new growth appears, and the herbage of the mountains is gathered'; all this guarantees the bountiful satisfaction of a householder's needs and obligations.

> the lambs will provide your clothing,
> and the goats the price of a field;
> there will be enough goats' milk for your food,
> for the food of your household
> and nourishment for your servant-girls. (27.26-27)

This poem is an encouragement to all to meet the great challenge to establish a successful household through diligence and foresight. Coming at the end of chs. 24–27, the picture of the successful sheep-farmer's stable household presents a striking contrast with the dismal picture of the ruined vineyard that concludes 'the words of the wise' (24.30-34).

Concluding Comments

The abundant comparisons that characterize the first section of the officials of Hezekiah's collection (chs. 25–27) have an instructional aim. In ch. 25, a stable, ordered world of wisdom is depicted, and ch. 26 contains warnings about the social damage that words can inflict. In ch. 27 the household and a son's character-formation are in focus. The next two chapters will be discussed together, because of their antithetical and more abstract style, and the recurring picture of the state of the envisaged society.

Personal Responsibility in a Lawless Society (28.1–29.27)

Almost all the sayings in the two final chapters of the second section of Solomon's proverbs (chs. 25–29) are in the third-person style, yet the wise father twice addresses his son directly (29.17, 20). After the abundant images of comparison in chs. 25–27, with their capacity to evoke in the audience an experience of good or ill, we find in chs. 28–29 a return to the poetry of antithesis that prevailed in chs. 10–15, where the advantages of goodness are highlighted through contrast with the disadvantages of evil, and there is frequent use of abstract terms, such as the wicked and the righteous, justice, integrity, and calamity. Imaginative comparisons are found, however (e.g. 28.3, 15). The theme of parental wisdom re-emerges with a certain emphasis. Other proverbs concern self-control and household management. Wisdom and a good conscience are a young person's most precious possession, and the attraction of quick and easy gain is to be resisted. Society is in disorder; the whole people, and particularly the poor, are oppressed. As was the case with 'the proverbs of Solomon' (10.1–22.16), the sayings in chs. 28–29 will be discussed in topical groups.

Keeping a Good Conscience (28.1, 4, 5, 6, 13, 14, 17, 25)

When wickedness prevails, having a good conscience is the key to happiness, and without it, wealth is of little value. The guilty see a threat at every turn, and they are portrayed with humorous contempt, whereas the proudly walking lion images the social poise bestowed by a blameless conscience: 'The wicked flee when no one pursues, but the righteous are as bold as a lion' (28.1). Next, people whose consciences are formed by wise teaching can expect to struggle with those who know no norms but greed, and collusion with men of power: 'Those who forsake the law praise the wicked, but those who keep the law struggle against them' (28.4). Another antithetical proverb brings together the three interrelated components of the life of the wise, namely, a correct understanding, righteous conduct, and religious reverence: 'The evil do not understand justice, but those who seek the LORD understand it completely' (28.5). The next antithesis sums up succinctly the theme of many proverbs in chs. 28–29, and at the same time, offers a word of encouragement: 'Better to be poor and walk in integrity than to be crooked in one's ways even though rich' (28.6). A youth whose conscience resists the appeal of easy gain through collaboration in corrupt practice, remains better off, even if confined to relative poverty. A proverb concerns the hiding of individual guilt: 'No one who conceals transgressions will prosper, but one who confesses and forsakes them will obtain mercy' (28.13). The term 'transgression' (*peša'*) is used elsewhere in Proverbs in reference to speech (10.19; 12.13), or, in the verbal form, to official corruption (28.21), or shameful treatment of parents (28.24). While overlooking another's offence has been praised (17.9), in the present proverb concealing one's own offence is detrimental, and the proverb refers to the restoration of the offender's broken relationship with the community through public confession of the transgression (as in Ps. 32.1-4). In Isa. 51.13, the phrase 'fearing continually' describes discouragement in the presence of oppression, but in the next proverb fearing continually is desirable: 'Happy is the one who is never without fear, but one who is hard-hearted will fall into calamity' (28.14). In the light of the antithesis, this type of fear could refer to being always aware of the inevitable consequences of evil, while the hard-hearted choose to live brazenly with a bad conscience. On the theme of the individual conscience, there is a guilt that cannot be removed: 'If someone is burdened with the blood of another, let that killer be a fugitive until death; let no one offer assistance' (28.17). This more lengthy proverb of three clauses, while composed in the casuistic style of legislation (see the case proposed in Exod. 21.12, 'whoever strikes a person mortally shall be put to death'), is a pedagogical warning, illustrating the terrible plight of one guilty of murder or manslaughter. He carries forever the burden of guilt, and is destined to suffer alone. In this case, acknowledging the transgression and restoration to the community (28.13) is not an option. In the metaphor of life as a journey along a dangerous road, harbouring guilt and fear of exposure is likened to setting a trap for one's own feet: 'The fear of others lays a snare, but one who trusts in the LORD is secure' (29.25). In the antithesis, an attitude of trust in Yahweh offers a sense of walking safely amidst danger.

The Impact of Rulers on Society (28.2, 12, 28; 29.2, 8, 16)

In these chapters the scene often changes from the state of the individual to that of society as a whole, and to its leaders: 'When a land rebels it has many rulers; but with an intelligent ruler there is lasting order' (28.2). 'Transgression' [*peša'*, 'rebellion' in the NRSV] may pervade the whole of society (29.16), and lead to a succession of rulers, none of whom is better than the society out of which they came, as in the translation, 'a country which transgresses gets one statesman after another' (McKane). In the second half-verse, a wise one attributes good government to the ruler's wisdom, reiterating Wisdom's claim that wise kings and rulers create a just and stable society (8.15-16). The impact of rulers on the emotional tone of society is the topic of four antithetical proverbs in chs. 28–29 (28.12, 28; 29.2, 16). Whereas prophetic oracles also target social injustice and the corruption of leaders (e.g. Mic. 2.1-11; Zeph. 3.1-13), these proverbs show how rulers can affect their subjects' emotional states, and the presence or absence of the social *shalom* which is wisdom's gift (3.2). In the first such proverb, people who feel stalked by corrupt administrators keep out of the way. How different is their sense of jubilation and even public celebration when just rule is restored: 'When the righteous triumph, there is great glory; but when the wicked prevail, people go into hiding' (28.12). (For public celebration on the occasion of a change of ruler, see 2 Kgs 11.14.) The second such proverb begins with the conclusion of the previous one (28.12): 'When the wicked prevail, people go into hiding; but when they perish, the righteous increase' (28.28).

In the new antithesis, the bad ruler inevitably falls, and righteous people appear again in great numbers. From an educational perspective, if the young are to live wisely in a corrupt world, they need the long-term vision, that goodness will eventually triumph, and that siding with injustice provides no lasting gain. A third proverb on the people and their rulers begins with the prevalence of the righteous, which is how 28.28 concluded: 'When the righteous are in authority, the people rejoice; but when the wicked rule, the people groan' (29.2). This saying, like 28.12, contrasts the lot of the people under both righteous and wicked rulers, and here the word 'people' (*'am*) emphatically concludes each half-verse. Rejoicing is frequent in Proverbs, and in most of the twenty occurrences, joy is associated with the human heart (e.g. 12.25; 15.13), and sometimes as well with the pleasure experienced by parents when their children are wise (e.g. 10.1; 23.25). The vitality of a well-governed society, too, breaks out into surges of popular joy, just as universal groaning is an image of oppression (Exod. 2.23). The fourth proverb on the lot of citizens under wicked rulers almost envisages their oppressed victims coming out of hiding, as in 28.12, and delighting in the demise of their oppressors: 'When the wicked are in authority, transgression increases, but the righteous will look upon their downfall' (29.16). Experience has demonstrated that it will eventually go badly with oppressors, and the immature need to be warned that collaborators will share the fate of their associates (see 1.14). A related proverb (29.8) concerns the capacity of the arrogant, or scoffers, to metaphorically inflame the city, literally 'set a city panting', as the verb concerns exhalation: 'Scoffers set a city aflame, but the wise turn away wrath' ('calm the fury', NAB). This picture of destructive unrest is more alarming than that of the citizens hiding in fear (28.12). The scene is set for the antithesis. It is implied that the wicked are overthrown, and the just restore order and stability. 'Turning away' (*yāšîbû*) in 29.8b rhymes with 'set aflame' (*yāpîḥû*) in 29.8a.

Beware of Greed (28.3, 20-22, 25, 27)

Many social ills stem from greed: 'A poor man who oppresses the poor is a beating rain that leaves no food' (28.3 RSV). This saying could refer to an official of lowly status oppressing the class from which he came, so that the poor are at the mercy, not only of the corrupt ruling class, but even more so, of those from whom understanding might have been expected (see Clifford 1999: 243). Chapter 28 concludes with a number of sayings about the social impact of personal greed, and they suggest that such unrighteous desire is a major threat to a youth's personal integrity. The first enunciates the general principle that one's responsibilities to others, in various spheres, will be dishonoured through the desire to get rich, which brings long-term consequences: 'The faithful [i.e. trustworthy person, NJB] will abound with blessings, but one who is in a hurry to be rich will not go unpunished' (28.20). Specifically, partiality in a judge, for even a trifling emolument, is an example of unbridled greed (28.21). Just as the judge's favouritism is expressed in a bodily gesture ('acknowledging the face' of the guilty), so, the covetous character is depicted as one with, literally, an 'evil eye', that is, a greedy eye, which stops him seeing that ill-gotten gain is short-lived: 'The miser is in a hurry to get rich and does not know that loss is sure to come' (28.22). The next greedy character is sketched as, literally, 'one who has enlarged his appetite'. Not he, but one who trusts in Yahweh, will be filled to satisfaction (28.25). Finally, no one is worse off through generosity to the poor, whereas turning a blind eye will merit the poor man's curses, and the stingy one will bear the consequences (28.27).

Family Upbringing (28.7, 24; 29.1, 3, 15, 17)

A previous caution about self-indulgence in food and drink advised the sons of the well-to-do that poverty was its consequence (23.20-21). A proverb now appeals to a youth's sense of family solidarity: 'Those who keep the law are wise children, but companions of gluttons shame their parents' (28.7). In the light of this proverb, the parents in the Torah who denounce their dissolute son (Deut. 21.20-21) may be motivated by a sense of deep shame, and the desire to regain their honour. A proverb concerns the breach of the fundamental child-to-parent relationship. One who gets rich at the expense of his parents is labelled a member of a gang of brigands (like those in 1.11): 'Anyone who robs father or mother and says, "That is no crime", is partner to a thug' (28.24). Such a son sees no offence (*pěša'*) in ignoring his obligations to his parents. In his rationalizing comment, he is an outrageous example of the fool wise in his own eyes (see 26.12). As was the case in the first collection of the proverbs (10.1–22.16), so, as chs. 25–29 draw to a close, the theme of parental training in wisdom receives rhetorical emphasis (see also 19.18): 'One who is often reproved, yet remains stubborn, will suddenly be broken beyond healing' (29.1). People become wiser by learning from reproof (13.18), but this character remains literally 'stiff-necked', and never learns, as in 10.17. The second half-verse allots to the recalcitrant the penalty awaiting the scoundrel (6.15). The term 'broken' (*šbr*) can refer to a maimed or injured animal (Exod. 22.10), so that stiff-necked resistance to education does not indicate strength, but rather fragility, and when the fall comes, the fracture is irreparable. The topic soon changes to joy in the household (10.1; 27.11): 'A child who loves wisdom makes a parent glad, but to keep company with prostitutes is to squander one's substance' (29.3). A youth's sexual incontinence ruptures family bonds, and the patrimonial inheritance is frittered away. Whatever the state of society at large, the foundations of wisdom and righteousness are laid in the household, and at an early age, when the mother was especially involved (see 4.3-4). All this is evoked in rapidly sketched, strong antitheses, depicting a child who has been trained in wisdom, then one whose education has been neglected, and the complementary roles of father and mother: 'The rod and reproof give wisdom, but a mother is disgraced by a neglected child' (29.15). A woman's standing in society is here at stake, not only, as elsewhere (17.25), her personal satisfaction. 'Discipline your children, and they will give you rest; they will give delight to your heart' (29.17). This direct appeal, with three references to 'you', suggests that imparting discipline is not always easy for parents (13.24), but the long-term rewards are great.

Reflections on the Lot of the Poor (28.8, 11; 29.7, 13-14)

A saying about usury has a place in the context of greed and the plight of the poor: 'One who augments wealth by exorbitant interest gathers it for another who is kind to the poor' (28.8). The proverbs on usury do not emulate the extensive teaching of the Torah on the topic (Exod. 22.25; Lev. 25.35-37), legislation that rests on a sense of solidarity with the poor of the people of Israel. Rather, the conviction that the wealth of the wicked is worthless (11.18), and that Yahweh repays the one who makes a loan to the poor (19.17), is expressed in memorable aphorisms, in this case (28.8) in an ironic variation of the metaphor of the substitution of the worthy for the unworthy (see 13.22). There is an attempt to alleviate the plight of the poor by extolling wisdom over wealth: 'The rich is wise in self-esteem [lit. wise in his own eyes], but an intelligent poor person sees through the pose' (28.11). One may recall the expression 'intelligent son' *(bēn mēbîn)* in 28.7. The intelligent poor person would be a person whose conscience has been formed according to the norms of wise teaching, and who is able to discern the moral poverty that can go with material wealth. The mistake which the rich often make is to equate their wealth with wisdom and true success. Another proverb on care of the poor dwells on the righteous one's ability to make practical decisions in their favour, referred to as knowledge, a term in the emphatic beginning and end positions in the Hebrew proverb: 'The righteous know the rights of the poor; the wicked have no such understanding' (lit. 'do not understand knowledge') (29.7). As has been well illustrated in the first 'proverbs of Solomon', amongst the right relationships nurtured by the righteous citizen is care for the poor. Next, 'the poor and the oppressor have this in common: the LORD gives light to the eyes of both' (29.13). In the context of injustice and oppression, the juxtaposition of oppressors and their victims would be less serene than suggested in the first half-verse, and could have the backdrop of a city's disintegration (compare 29.8, and the scene depicted in Ps. 55.10-11). Yet the God-fearing wise one seizes on a stabilizing consideration, namely the presence of the unseen maker of both the powerful and the defenceless. Three 'sh' sounds carry the first half-verse along (*rāš weʾîš teḳāḳîm nipgāšû*). 'If a king judges the poor with equity, his throne will be established forever' (29.14). This proverb, with the only other royal proverb in chs. 28–29 (29.4), upholds the ideal of a monarch ruling with justice and care for the defenceless, complementing the royal proverbs in ch. 25. In the previously discussed group of proverbs referring to unjust and oppressive rulers, there is no explicit reference to the king. In the present saying, the throne, symbol of royal power, is envisaged as a structure stably erected on a firm foundation, namely justice for the poor. The wise authors and collectors of the sayings in 'the proverbs of Solomon' show a consistent appreciation of the benefits of royal rule. In their view, the poor and their oppressors are fundamentally equal (29.13), and the king, when judging, will demonstrate Yahweh's regard for the poor (22.22-23). The rhythmical first half-verse has three 'm' sounds (*melek šôpēṭ beʾemet dallîm*).

Indiscipline on the Personal and Household Levels, and Lack of Restraint in the House of the State (29.18-22)

'Where there is no prophecy, the people cast off restraint, but happy are those who keep the law' (29.18). If the term 'vision' here refers to prophecy (NRSV), as in prophetic texts (e.g. Isa. 1.1; Ezek. 7.26), this would be the only reference in Proverbs to prophecy. Prophecy provides necessary leadership in society, without which people 'get out of control' (see Exod. 32.25 for the same expression). 'Law' (*tôrâ*), in the antithesis, is usually priestly teaching (Ezek. 7.26), but in Proverbs this term refers to wisdom teaching (1.8; 3.1; 4.2). The point of the saying is that whatever the sad condition of society, happiness can be achieved through the disciplined practice of wisdom, which includes righteousness, and the fear of God. After the proverb on disciplining a son (29.17), the wise one has a word of advice for one who would be a successful householder: 'By mere words servants are not disciplined, for though they understand, they will not give heed' (29.19). While in Israel 'a domestic slave really formed part of the family' (de Vaux 1961: 85), yet slaves needed to obey and to work. The form which firm treatment could take is known to the audience and not stated. In the next proverb (29.20), the rhetorical question, 'do you see someone who is hasty in speech?' is followed by a sarcastic indictment (as in 26.12): 'There is more hope for a fool than for anyone like that'. Using again the accepted institution of slavery, the wise one can cite another example of the need for discipline: 'If a man pampers his servant from childhood, he will turn out to be stubborn' (29.21 NAB). Household slaves included the children born to a slave (Exod. 23.12), and such slaves could receive better treatment than those that were bought. The first half-verse refers to the householder, who, in his own childhood, or in the childhood of a domestic slave, treats the slave indulgently. The ambiguous second half-verse refers either to such a slave growing up stubborn, or to his being a cause of grief to his master, just when his services are required to ensure his master's happiness. Next, a proverb depicting in parallel two synonymous character types illustrates the social disruption that anger provokes: 'One given to anger stirs up strife [= 15.18a], and the hothead causes much transgression' (29.22). Literally a 'man of anger' and 'possessor of wrath' (Toy), is a variation of 'man of wrath' and 'possessor of anger' (22.24). The habitually angry person goes about shattering relationships on all sides (as in 6.14b). Anger is incompatible with wisdom, and wisdom education includes training in restraint.

Knowing one's Place, and the Peril of Human Respect (29.23-24, 27)

Once again honour is the reward of faithful service (see 25.6-7), and may not be prematurely snatched: 'A person's pride will bring humiliation, but one who is lowly in spirit will obtain honour' (29.23). This antithetical proverb works through the use of paradox in each half-verse. A stern warning concerns failure to testify against a thief through human respect: 'To be a partner of a thief is to hate one's own life; one hears the victim's curse, but discloses nothing' (29.24). The situation envisaged is the curse pronounced in court against a witness who will not speak out (Lev. 5.1). One who saw the crime, but says nothing, is the thief's actual or virtual accomplice. The final proverb in the officials of Hezekiah's collection is coined out of generations of experience: 'The unjust are an abomination to the righteous, but the upright are an abomination to the wicked' (29.27). In the state of Israelite society depicted in chs. 28–29, the choice placed before the young is not easy. The way of life of the righteous is incompatible with that of the wicked, and the practice of justice and care for the poor will provoke opposition. In the proverbs of these final chapters of King Hezekiah's collection, the wise ones offer a youth the long-term view they need, if they are to resist the attraction of ill-gotten wealth, cultivate prudence and restraint, and act with integrity. Justice, however, will eventually prevail, and only the upright will be able to hold their heads high in the restored city.

Concluding Comments

At this point, the reader of the book of Proverbs has completed a survey of the central core of the book, comprising the two sections of 'the proverbs of Solomon' (10.1–22.16; 25.1–29.27), by which the whole book can fairly be named, and the enclosed section of paternal wisdom instructions in 'the words of the wise' (22.17–24.34). The latter teachings, at the centre of the book, express in the form of paternal instruction much of the wisdom of the previous and the following proverb sayings. Chapters 1–9, containing a limited number of more artistically elaborated paternal teachings, and poems of personified Wisdom, are a preface to the central core, promising a feast of learning for the one committed to the quest for wisdom. The concluding section of longer poems in chs. 30–31 nicely balances the first section, so as to complete a symmetrically structured book of wisdom teaching.

Proverbs 30.1–31.31: Three Concluding Portraits

Introductory Comments

The imagery in the final three poems is reminiscent of chs. 1–9. In ch. 31 a mother appears as teacher (31.1-9), indeed as a wisdom teacher (31.26), and a mother's teaching is also referred to in chs. 1–9 (1.8; 6.20). Both the first and last sections contain differing descriptions of the housewife (5.18-19; 31.10-31), while the adulteress, depicted in 7.10-20, is also a subject in Agur's reflections (30.20). The numerical sayings in Proverbs are found in the first and last sections (6.16-19; 30.15-16, 18-19, 21-23, 24-28, 29-31). The abundant use of animal imagery in ch. 30 is anticipated by the images of gazelle, bird, ant, ox, stag, hind and doe in chs. 5–7, while a listing by the bodily members in 30.11-14 occurs in 6.12-19. Thematically, three exemplary wise ones appear in the final chapters. Agur utters a mature reflection on his life-time experience as a wise one, King Lemuel's mother delivers a pithy lesson on the essence of governance, providing an important supplement to the proverbs on kingship in 10.1–22.16, while the wise housewife in 31.10-31 personifies many aspects of the wisdom the book extols.

The Words of Agur (30.1-33)

A God-fearer's Experience of the Quest for Wisdom (30.1-9)

> The words of Agur son of Jakeh. An oracle.
> Thus says the man: I am weary, O God,
> I am weary, O God. How can I prevail?
> Surely I am too stupid to be human;
> I do not have human understanding.
> I have not learned wisdom,
> nor have I knowledge of the holy ones (30.1-3).

The title 'the words of Agur' evokes 'the words of the wise' (22.17), the title of the previous section of wisdom instructions (22.17–24.34). Agur, the speaker, is either a proper name (NRSV), or a common noun, that is, the assembler, or gatherer. The term *hammaśśā'* ('oracle',

NRSV) could be read as an Arabian place or clan name, Massa (RSV), the eponymous son of Ishmael (Gen. 25.14), so that Agur's words would represent the wisdom of the east (Jer. 49.7; 1 Kgs 4.30). Agur's father, Jakeh, is otherwise unknown.

This 'oracle' is a poetic reflection on personal experience, which, unlike the first-person reflection that concludes 'the words of the wise' (24.30-34), is deeply religious, and includes an earnest prayer to God. The introductory 'thus says the man' evokes the introduction to the words of another foreigner, Balaam (Num. 24.3). Agur's expression of weariness in the quest for wisdom (30.2) rests on one of a number of possible adaptations of a difficult Hebrew text, which reads, literally, 'to Ithiel, to Ithiel and Ucal' (RSV), and his sentiments are comparable with the psalmist's admission of the 'wearisome task' of comprehending the prosperity of the wicked whilst maintaining his own integrity (Ps. 73.16). In the light of the confidence of all previous wisdom teachers in Proverbs, a sage's admission of failure to acquire wisdom is surprising. His claim to lack human understanding likens him to the fool (12.1), or the domestic animals (26.3), a sentiment also shared by the psalmist (Ps. 73.22). In the context of Agur's piety (30.5-6), this is a genuine expression of humility, depicting him as one who is not wise in his own eyes (3.7). The wisdom that he has failed to learn is the knowledge of the ways of God, as communicated to his heavenly council of holy ones (Ps. 89.5-7).

> Who has ascended to heaven and come down?
> Who has gathered the wind in the hollow of the hand?
> Who has wrapped up the waters in a garment?
> Who has established all the ends of the earth?
> What is the person's name?
> And what is the name of the person's child?
> Surely you know! (30.4-6).

Agur uses terms echoing God's refutation of Job's claims to have a case against God (Job 38.4-7). All the rhetorical questions require a negative answer: as if any human beings have transcended their earthly limits, or exercised power over the basic elements of air, water, and earth. No human name can be attached to the non-existent one with such knowledge and power, or to anyone who has been taught to act like that.

> Every word of God proves true;
> he is a shield to those who take refuge in him.
> Do not add to his words,
> or else he will rebuke you,
> and you will be found a liar (30.5-6).

Agur now speaks like a truly god-fearing wise one, who has learned that wisdom proceeds from God, not unassisted human effort (2.6-7). His trust rests on a personal experience of God's closeness, and of God's word, throughout all his doubts and difficulties. He speaks like David: 'This God—his way is perfect; the promise of the LORD proves true; he is a shield for all who take refuge in him' (2 Sam. 22.31). God's word has indeed been 'proved true', that is, refined, tested like gold in a crucible, although it is Agur himself who has had the refining experience. The advice not to add to God's word is similar to Moses' advice to the people of Israel to keep the divine commands, which are the people of Israel's wisdom (Deut. 4.2, 6). Agur, however, describes God as a wisdom teacher who asks for retention of his words, and who issues rebuke (2.1; 3.11-12). All told, Agur is portrayed as a God-fearing sage, conversant with, and adapting the language of David and Moses to his experience of an initially failed quest for wisdom, and of the bestowal of a wisdom proceeding from the mouth of God. The notion of adding (30.6) is a hint announcing the various numerical lists, of which the first, a 'two', follows immediately.

Agur then humbly prays for what he most values, to continue in the fear of God for the rest of his days. This desire is couched in terms of a plea for a modest sufficiency of material goods, lest either abundance or deprivation drive him to faithlessness and blasphemy.

> Two things I ask of you;
> do not deny them to me before I die:
> Remove far from me falsehood and lying;
> give me neither poverty nor riches;
> feed me with the food that I need,
> or I shall be full, and deny [*kḥš*] you,
> and say, 'Who is the LORD?'
> or I shall be poor ['*iwwārēš*], and steal,
> and profane [*tpś*] the name of my God (30.7-9).

While Agur's requests are invested with solemnity by the mention of his death, like Elijah's final words in 2 Kgs 2.9, yet he seems to be envisaging a normal life-span. First, he prays to maintain his good name through loyalty and reliability in his social dealings. His second request, to be free from both affluence and deprivation, relates to the first. If a judge can take a bribe for a paltry gain (28.21), a hungry man will give false evidence in order to stay alive. Agur then explains why all he needs is a modest sufficiency. He links having a full stomach (30.9a) with a denial of the divine providence and the divine ordering of the world, which would include scoffing at the notion of the retribution that will befall the wicked. He would become like the intolerable fool sated with bread (30.22b). The term for the denial of God that could flow from satisfaction (*khš*, 30.9a) is also used in prophecy in the context of denial of the retribution of the wicked (Jer. 5.12). After mentioning the danger of having too many possessions, Agur goes on to explain his fear of falling into penury. The restitution for theft could be exacting (6.30-31), but his concern is not so much for the pain of deprivation, as for the loss of his sense of reverence for God. By laying hands on another's property, he might be led eventually to lay hands on (*tpś*, also in 30.28) the name of God. He is referring to blasphemy, and even cursing God when struck with affliction (Job 2.9).

Further Reflections on Enough and Too Much (30.10-33)

In discussions of the redaction of ch. 30, Agur's words are considered to end, in their greatest extent, at 30.14, with other and earlier cut-off points being commonly discerned. They are followed by another section, the collection of numerical verses about creatures arousing a poet's wonder (30.15-33). The entire chapter, however, up to the next editorial superscription (31.1), may be read as Agur's words, which include different types of expression, namely a second-person admonition (30.10), a list of character types without numerical mention (30.11-14), and the numerical sayings (30.15-33). These different types of expression are unified, however, and linked to the preceding personal testimony, through an unfolding thematic bond. Having chosen to live in the fear of Yahweh, and with few material possessions, Agur proceeds to reflect on human behaviour in the light of the harmony of all the components of creation, including the human, plant, and animal worlds, and even the basic elements of fire, water, and earth. He makes frequent use of numerical listings to suggest the connectedness of both inanimate creation and the behaviour of animals and humans. The smallest creatures can demonstrate how to be effective with few resources (30.24-28). He observes humans transgressing by excess, whether by interference (30.10), or by arrogance and oppression (30.11-14). Yet the desire to possess more is pervasive (30.15-16). A reckless pursuit of power and wealth strikes at the heart of the household, and shreds the fabric of society (30.11-14, 17). Some aspects of creation cannot be reduced to more or less, and seem to defy any categorization (30.18-19). A sated appetite smothers any sense of right and wrong (30.20), and self-assertion is appropriate only when made in harmony with the rest of creation (30.29-31). Throughout, Agur is intrigued by the notion of being sated (30.9, 15, 16, 22).

a. *An Admonition (30.10)*. The reflections begin with an admonition: 'Do not slander [lit. 'tongue'] a servant to his master, lest he curse you, and you be held guilty' (NAB: and you have to pay the penalty) (30.10). Undue interference in the affairs of another person's household is the first example of indiscretion by excess. The defenceless slave will retaliate with his or her own tongue, invoking the divine power against the informant, and God, the defender of the poor (22.23), will not condone this mean degradation of a slave's lowly status. A deserved curse is a potent vehicle of woe (3.33, and compare 26.2), which the young and inexperienced would need to avoid.

b. *A List of Four Generations (30.11-14)*. This is structured as an anaphora (like 30.4), with the repeated keyword, 'generation', or 'those who' (*dôr*), introducing the successive (four) sayings. (i) 'There are those (*dôr*) who curse their fathers and do not (*lō'*) bless their mothers (*'immô*)' (30.11). The term 'curse' from the previous proverb is repeated in a saying about the relationship of children and parents. As the power of the blessing and curse derives from God, one who curses parents invokes the divinity in a breach of a basic, divinely established human relationship (Exod. 20.12), and commits an act of unspeakable impiety, both to one's parents and to God. In the words of another wise one, neglecting and demeaning one's needy parents is just as much an affront to God as is cursing them (Sir. 3.16; see Di Lella 1986: 157). (ii) 'There are those [*dôr*] who are pure [*ṭāhôr*] in their own eyes yet are not cleansed of their filthiness [*dôr ṭāhôr bᵉ'ênāyw ûmiṣṣō'ātô lō' ruḥāṣ*]' (30.12). The notion of cultic purity is used metaphorically for ethical integrity (15.26). Agur observes how some people think they are pleasing to God, while being actually unfit for the divine presence. The saying highlights the contrast between a deceptive self-appraisal and one's real worth before the creator God. The four 'o' sounds make a melodious saying. (iii) 'There are those [*dôr*]—how lofty [*mâ-rāmû*] are their eyes, how high their eyelids lift [*yinnāśē'û*]' (30.13). This saying is also built on the symbolism of the eyes, with arrogance demonstrated in the lifted-up eyes, or face (21.4). Each half-verse contains a long 'u' vowel. (iv) 'There are those [*dôr*] whose teeth are swords, whose teeth are knives, to devour the poor from off the earth, the needy from among mortals' (30.14). In this saying the two parallel Hebrew terms for teeth may refer respectively to the front and back teeth of this group of predators. They are depicted as devouring monsters, first biting into their prey with sword-like incisors, and then their molars are as sharp as shredding knives.

Their victims are the most helpless, whom it will devolve on the king to defend (31.9).

c. *A Two-Three Saying (30.15-16)*

> The leech has two daughters;
> 'Give, give,' they cry.
> Three things are never satisfied;
> four never say, 'Enough':
> Sheol, the barren womb,
> the earth ever thirsty for water,
> and the fire that never says, 'Enough.'

Agur wonders that the desire for more, which he has renounced (30.8), is yet so pervasive, to be found not only in rapacious animals, of which the leech is another example, but even in the fundamental elements of earth and fire, and right down to subterranean Sheol. The empty, literally closed womb, is an image of 'the desire of a childless wife for children' (Toy), as expressed in Rachel's anguished plea (Gen. 30.1). The two, three, and four device builds up the list to a climax. Sound repetition is notable in the second line, containing 'o' twice in each half-verse (*šālôš hēnnâ lōʾ tiśbaʿnâ ʿarbaʿ lōʾ-ʾāmᵉrû hôn*).

d. *The Fate of the Rebellious Son (30.17)*

> The eye that mocks a father
> and scorns to obey a mother
> will be pecked out by the ravens of the valley
> and eaten by the vultures.

By metonymy, the scornful, defiant eye represents the rebellious child who severs relationship with his parents. He will not live long (20.20), and no child of his will close his defiant eyes (unlike Jacob, Gen. 46.4). Thrown into a trench, like a condemned criminal (Jer. 26.23), he becomes the prey of scavenging animals. Such imagery has a foundation in the legislation about a rebellious son (Deut. 21.18-21), and well expresses the link between disrespect and the social death that inevitably follows.

e. *A Pair of Three-Four Sayings (30.18-23)*

> Three things are too wonderful for me;
> four I do not understand:
> the way of an eagle in the sky,
> the way of a snake on a rock,

the way of a ship on the high seas,
and the way of a man with a girl (30.18-19).

The three-four numerical proverb highlights the mystery of the four 'ways', especially the climactic fourth. The first way is the eagle's, repeating the term signifying 'vulture' in 30.17. The mystery of its path or movement perhaps refers to the eagle's ability to suddenly swoop down on its prey (Job 9.26) (McCullough, 'Eagle', *IDB* II: 1), or conversely, to sweep the prey suddenly upward out of sight (23.5). The mysterious 'way' of the serpent could refer to a snake's elusive, gliding movement (Jer. 46.22), while the sight of an incoming ship would arouse wonder in the observer standing on the shore, perhaps on account of its unknown provenance and itinerary (see Ryken, 'Ship, shipwreck', *DBI*: 786, on the mystery of shipping for the 'biblical landsman'). The first three ways serve to awaken in the reader a sense of the mystery in creation. The metaphorical fourth way is the climax to which the first three were leading. The way of a man with a girl refers to the 'perpetual enigma' of relationship between the sexes (Alonso Schökel 2000: 98). The 'way' of an adulteress is an addendum to the four previous mysterious ways. 'This is the way of an adulteress: she eats, and wipes her mouth, and says, "I have done no wrong"' (30.20). The wonder lies in the contradiction between the defilement of the marriage relationship, symbolized in eating to satisfaction, and the adulteress's untroubled return to its external observances.

Under three things the earth trembles;
under four it cannot bear up:
a slave when he becomes king,
and a fool when glutted with food;
an unloved woman when she gets a husband,
and a maid when she succeeds her mistress (30.21-23).

A second list of four is grouped as a three-four sequence (as in 30.15b). Agur, who is content with little, is either amused by, or intolerant of the seizure of honours, and he expresses his discomfort in an image of the tottering earth, which we see giving way under a weight it was never created to support. The earth here does not have a human voice, but if it could speak, it would complain, like God, when carrying the burden of Israel's meaningless feasts (Isa. 1.14). As elsewhere in the Bible, the poet links the behaviour of humans to the earth from which they came (Gen. 6.11; Hos. 4.1-3). He says no more of the slave's rise to power than the proverb (19.10). Historically, it is inconceivable that a slave, who was not his own master, and could be bought and sold, should become a king in

Israel, though Toy refers to Zimri (1 Kgs 16.9), an officer (servant/slave) of King Elah of Israel, who reigned for a week after assassinating his royal master. A fool glutted with food is the second of earth's intolerable burdens, a possibility which Agur has prayed to avoid. Like the psalmist who has overcome the crisis of trust occasioned by the prosperity of the arrogant (Ps. 73.17-20), Agur is critical of the scoffers whose 'bodies are sound and sleek' (Ps. 73.4). The third intolerable change in social status concerns a woman who has long remained unmarried, so being kept under the authority of her father, but is at last under the authority of her husband, the notion signified in the Hebrew term for a woman getting married. We are left to imagine the details of her arrogant behaviour. As for the maid when she succeeds (lit. is made the heir of) her mistress, there is no biblical parallel for a woman, the mistress, owning the property and being able to bequeath it (Toy). Gaining the inheritance may be understood metaphorically as gaining her master's favour, and so becoming the real mistress of the house.

f. *Four Small but Wise Ones (30.24-28)*

> Four things on earth are small,
> yet they are exceedingly wise:
> the ants are a people without strength,
> yet they provide their food in the summer;
> the badgers are a people without power,
> yet they make their homes in the rocks;
> the locusts have no king,
> yet all of them march in rank;
> the lizard can be grasped in the hand,
> yet it is found in kings' palaces.

These four small creatures lack the very quality that would seem necessary for them, but they succeed with the little with which they are naturally endowed because they are wise. Harvest ants are apparently without strength, because they seem to struggle to carry the individual grains to and from their ant-bed, yet, through diligence and foresight, they lay up provisions for winter when the fields are non-productive (as in 6.6-8). Badgers 'without power' can yet build nests in inaccessible places, having wisdom in the sense of technological skill (Isa. 40.20). There is something to respect even in an invading army of swarming, destructive locusts (as in Joel 2.1-11), namely, their ability to hold formation and systematically devour large areas, while a human host needs to be led by a king (1 Sam. 8.20). Finally, to continue the royal imagery, only the great ones of the land are admitted to the royal palace to appear before the king enthroned, yet small and vulnerable lizards, having no power or influence, can come and go as they please.

g. *A Final Three-Four Saying (30.29-31)*

> Three things are stately in their stride;
> four are stately in their gait:
> the lion, which is mightiest among wild animals
> and does not turn back before any;
> the strutting rooster, the he-goat,
> and a king striding before his people.

In the light of the proverbs, the confident self-assurance of the righteous (28.1b) is now depicted in the image of a righteous king walking proudly at the head of a grateful people. It is clear that this king's throne is secure, and that the people appreciate the benefits he brings (29.14). The majestic stride is the focus of the image, which is the climactic fourth example in this list of graded numbers (see Ryken, 'Numbers in the Bible', *DBI*: 599), and Agur has found three analogies in the animal kingdom that heighten appreciation of a king's royal bearing. As for the lion, while also the biblical horse may be fearless in the face of danger (see Job 39.22 for the horse), the lion is the most majestic in its stride. Then the sturdy loins of the strutting rooster impart strength to his tread, and the he-goat, the third example of a majestic stride, is to be imagined as confidently leading the flock (Jer. 50.8).

h. *Restraining Anger (30.32-33)*

> If you have been foolish, exalting yourself,
> or if you have been devising evil,
> put your hand on your mouth.
> For as pressing milk produces curds,
> and pressing the nose produces blood,
> so pressing anger produces strife.

However the ambiguous Hebrew terms in the two clauses of the hypothesis are understood, the situation envisaged seems to be one of a potentially explosive confrontation with another person. This is the time for restraint, described typically in terms of body members (13.3). The advice is then reinforced by a metaphorical argument. First, a household image illustrates how a process of pressing produces a change in substances, followed by a personal image of a pressure-induced bleeding. The two illustrations of pressing make the point that anger and disputes are not inevitable, but anger is an emotion for which humans must take responsibility, and anger and strife can be avoided by the exercise of timely restraint, especially in speech (see 26.20-21). The moralizing conclusion not only repeats the term 'pressing', but the Hebrew word for 'anger' (*'appayim*), literally 'nostrils', is now used, which occurred, in its singular form, as 'nose' (*'ap*) in the previous example, in accordance with Hebrew usage, where the emotion of anger is named in terms of the appearance of the nose.

Agur's pensive reflections on moderation and excess throughout all creation are now followed by the words of another foreign wise one, which are, stylistically, the most imperious of the book's instructions.

Lemuel's Mother's Instruction (31.1-9)

Superscription (31.1)
'The words of King Lemuel. An oracle that his mother taught him' (31.1). The first notable point is that Lemuel is not the name of any Israelite king, which is reinforced when the Hebrew term *maśśā'*, a prophetic oracle (e.g. Hab. 1.1), repeated from 30.1, is read as a proper noun, referring to the Arabian place name, as in the RSV ('The words of Lemuel, king of Massa, which his mother taught him'). The advice of this foreign queen to her son would be recognized by an Israelite audience as consistent with the ideals of Torah, the prophets, and the psalms, in regard to the behaviour of kings and leaders. It also complements the image of kingship in the royal proverbs. This is the only specific example of a mother's teaching, though the mother's teaching is mentioned in parallel with the father's teaching in chs. 1–9 (1.8; 6.20). There the youngest children were entrusted to the mother's care (4.3), but Lemuel's mother's words, as indeed the mother's teaching referred to in 1.8-19 and 6.20-35, concern serious matters of ethical behaviour, so that a mother would have continued to advise her children as they approach adulthood, or, in the case of Lemuel, as he was about to assume the kingship. This maternal instruction, moreover, is best understood in the light of the special mother-son relationship that unfolds in the opening words.

Introduction: The Mother Claims her Son's Attention (31.2)
'No, my son! No, son of my womb! No, son of my vows!' (31.2). The queen addresses her child in tones of endearment and maternal love (Isa. 49.15), and with some urgency. As son of her womb, Lemuel is her own child, not one adopted by a childless woman (Gen. 16.2),

and the expression 'son of her vows' recalls the birth of Samuel (1 Sam. 1.11). The promise of Lemuel's mother's vows and prayers may well have been to dedicate the child to God in view of his eventually meeting the divine expectations of kingship. This teaching, then, carries forward her initial dedication up to the time when the prince is preparing to assume office, and, without mentioning God, she counsels him about how a king in God's service can be expected to behave, that is, first and foremost, to exercise the royal office of judgment on behalf of the helpless and the oppressed of his subjects. The instruction comprises four admonitions.

The First Word of Advice (31.3)

'Do not give your strength to women, your ways to those who destroy kings.' The queen-mother first points out that a king can be undone by sexual indulgence (1 Kings 11), no less than any man, in terms of the parental instructions in chs. 1–9 (see, for example, 5.1-23; 6.20-35; 7.1-27). The term 'ways', in parallel with 'strength', suggests in this context a whole way of life, including the royal projects (Alonso Schökel and Vílchez Líndez 1984: 523), while 'destroy' is the strong term previously referring to the blotting out, or wiping away of shame (6.33). The king is being cautioned not to become consumed in the affairs of the royal harem, so as to have little energy left for governance.

The Second Word of Advice (31.4-5)

> It is not for kings, O Lemuel,
> it is not for kings to drink wine,
> or for rulers to desire strong drink;
> or else they will drink and forget what has been decreed,
> and will pervert the rights of all the afflicted.

The first line is kept in suspense by repetition of the subject before the point is made. If strong drink is a peril for every youth (23.20-21, 29-35), it is also a trap for the future king. The motivation is that wine induces complacency, dissipating a ruler's sense of responsibility (Isa. 28.7). The unspecified decree evidently concerns the king's duty to uphold the rights of the needy, a duty referred to in the proverb (29.14). When the cause of the afflicted comes before the king for judgment, he, no less than the elders assembled in the gates (22.22), is bound to uphold the humanitarian legislation protecting them. In the Israelite context, the king had no legislative power, being himself subject to the law (Deut. 17.19), but, on the other hand, the king was a judge, and held judicial power (de Vaux 1961: 151). De Vaux also writes that Israelite legislation is distinguished from other Eastern codes by the humaneness of its sentences, with the codes protecting the stranger, the poor, the oppressed, the widow and the orphan (see Deut. 24.5–25.4). The mother's concern is that the poor and afflicted are the first victims of the abuse of judicial power (22.22).

The Third Word of Advice (31.6-7)

> Give strong drink to one who is perishing,
> and wine to those in bitter distress;
> let them drink and forget their poverty,
> and remember their misery no more.

The third admonition forms a bridge between the second and the fourth, being tied into the preceding by the repetition of 'give' (31.3) and the wine/strong drink parallel (31.4), and anticipating the following plea for the poor and needy. The term 'forget' is repeated from 31.5, but now in a positive sense. While kings can abuse the gift of wine, Lemuel's mother concedes that wine has a use, and she thinks spontaneously of the subjects who are her greatest concern, those same poor and oppressed, without her necessarily referring to any particular custom or occasion of offering relief.

The Fourth Word of Advice (31.8-9)

> Speak out for those who cannot speak,
> for the rights of all the destitute.
> Speak out, judge righteously,
> defend the rights of the poor and needy (31.8-9).

She now urges the prince to carry out the king's duty to pass just judgment. The voiceless in society are named the destitute, literally people in the process of passing away, through having no defenders or supports. In the words of the wise, their redeemer, though, is God (23.11), or, in Lemuel's mother's view, her son, as a king dedicated to God. In short, sexual incontinence and intemperance are seen as the principal threats to the responsible discharge of this duty. To ward off complacency and heedlessness, this brief poem rings out with the phrases, 'the rights of the destitute', 'all the afflicted', and 'all the destitute', and the concluding word pair, 'the poor and needy'. Unlike Hannah, Lemuel's mother does not make an explicit reference to the God of her vows, who, however, would not be very different from the one who 'raises the poor from the dust, and lifts the needy from the ash-heap' (1 Sam. 2.8), and who, moreover, looked on the affliction of his maidservant (1 Sam. 1.11). Neither does she exhort her son to the practice of piety. Rather in a few, tightly orchestrated lines, she highlights the character-trait of a king who is in life, as at his birth, truly dedicated to God: he upholds the cause of the helpless in distress.

The idea of kingship in this foreign queen-mother's wisdom teaching makes a notable contribution to the notion of kingship in Proverbs. Lemuel's mother says nothing about the king's rapport with God (21.1), or his penetrating judgment (20.8), or his awesome presence (16.14-15), but her teaching is heralded by one proverb in chs. 28–29, where the corruption of rulers is a recurring theme, and where the king's concern for the poor is the condition of the stability of his reign (29.14).

The Woman of Excellence: A Model of Wisdom (31.10-31)

> A capable wife who can find?
> She is far more precious than jewels.
> The heart of her husband trusts in her,
> and he will have no lack of gain.
> She does him good, and not harm,
> all the days of her life.
> She seeks wool and flax,
> and works with willing hands.
> She is like the ships of the merchant,
> she brings her food from far away.
> She rises while it is still night
> and provides food for her household
> and tasks for her servant-girls.
> She considers a field and buys it;
> with the fruit of her hands she plants a vineyard.
> She girds herself with strength,
> and makes her arms strong.
> She perceives that her merchandise is profitable.
> Her lamp does not go out at night.
> She puts her hands to the distaff,
> and her hands hold the spindle.
> She opens her hand to the poor,
> and reaches out her hands to the needy.
> She is not afraid for her household when it snows,
> for all her household are clothed in crimson.
> She makes herself coverings;
> her clothing is fine linen and purple.
> Her husband is known in the city gates,

taking his seat among the elders of the land.
She makes linen garments and sells them;
she supplies the merchant with sashes.
Strength and dignity are her clothing,
and she laughs at the time to come.
She opens her mouth with wisdom,
and the teaching of kindness is on her tongue.
She looks well to the ways of her household,
and does not eat the bread of idleness.
Her children rise up and call her happy;
her husband too, and he praises her:
'Many women have done excellently,
but you surpass them all.'
Charm is deceitful, and beauty is vain,
but a woman who fears the LORD is to be praised.
Give her a share in the fruit of her hands,
and let her works praise her in the city gates

The poem concluding the book of Proverbs is the only one in Proverbs having the acrostic form. Every line begins with a successive letter of the Hebrew alphabet, a device that gives the poem, and the book, a sense of completion. The echoes of the beginning of the poem at its end also confer a structural unity. This remarkable woman, depicted with bold and rapid brush-strokes, receives the sage's unqualified praise. Her importance is acknowledged when she is referred to as 'a capable wife' (*'ēšet-ḥayil*, 31.10), a complimentary phrase by which Boaz refers to Ruth ('a worthy woman', Ruth 3.11, NRSV). She is like Wisdom in person, in that happy is the man who can find her (3.13), and her value, like Wisdom's value, is suggested with the image of jewellery (31.10; 3.15). Such praise would echo the sentiments of her husband, a prominent citizen in the town, who realizes that in her he has 'an unfailing prize' (31.11 NAB). The portrait is composed with clothing imagery more than any other. Her physical strength and dignified bearing are described metaphorically as clothing (31.17, 25), and many hours of her day and night must have been devoted to cloth and garment manufacture. She is skilled in spinning the wool and flax fibres she selects in the market-place (31.13, 19), makes her own bed-covers (31.22), and the finished garments are, in turn, sold to a merchant, literally Canaanite, a term for a Phoenician trader (see Rainey, 'Canaan, Canaanites', *EDB*: 214), perhaps also in the market-place (31.24). She is herself a very well-dressed woman (31.22), who also sees that the servants are well-clothed: even the rare snowfall would not find them unprepared (31.21). The provision of food for the household (31.15) is another sign of her practical care, and an important component of her portrait. In this regard, the poet compares her with Solomon's ships, laden with cargo from afar (31.14; 1 Kgs 9.27-28). The productive vineyard is on land which she chose herself, and purchased with her earnings, and in daylight it would surely stand as an external sign of the household's prosperity and of the industry of the mistress (in contrast to the neglected vineyard in 24.30-31), as does the undimmed household lamp at night-time (31.18). Her efficiency and success is coupled with generosity to the poor (31.20), a trait we would expect of a paradigm of wisdom, in view of the attention to generosity and compassion in the second half of the first section of proverbs (10.1–22.16), and now of the responsibilities of kings towards the afflicted (31.1-9). Her contribution to her family's welfare and happiness extends beyond material provision. A wise woman, she is sought after for the good advice she faithfully gives (31.26). Like every mother, she would train her younger children (4.3), and teach her older children (1.8-9), and she counsels her husband (31.11-12) and governs the household (31.27). The poem celebrates her achievements, and the few feelings attributed to her flow from the performance of tasks of household management. While imbued with a reverential fear of Yahweh (31.30), she seems to be otherwise without concerns. Her generous and timely provision for all contingencies enables her to 'laugh at', that is, not to fear for, the future (31.25). She also enjoys the success of her undertakings (31.18).

This woman's achievements are anchored in her household, but she would be well known in the city gates, where she helps the poor and needy (31.20), and where her husband enjoys the standing achieved through her support (31.23). A tone of praise suffuses this description, beginning in the introduction (31.10), and given implicitly by the sage-poet throughout, while the poem concludes with her husband and children singing her praises (31.28-31). Having cited her husband's tribute (31.29), 'many women have done excellently' (*'āśû ḥāyil*), which repeats a term in 'a capable wife' (*'ēšet-ḥayil*, 31.10), the poet even encourages the town community in the gates to join in this chorus of praise (31.31), in appreciation of her exceptional worth and achievements.

The Excellent Woman in the Context of the Book of Proverbs

This idealized portrait is symbolic in that she models for male youths under instruction and training the character traits considered desirable in a woman, wife, and mother. She is the crown of her husband (12.4), the crown on his head imaging the blessings of guidance, of the capable management of his household and his children, the enhancing of his standing in the community, and the gaining of his trust and praise. This final poem makes an important precision to the basic house-building metaphor for wisdom. Proverbs has aimed to teach an Israelite boy to build the house of his life in wisdom, and the poem of womanly wisdom provides a living demonstration of the place a wise woman might have in that project. This wife and mother shows how the concept of wise house-building (14.1) goes far beyond material construction, and includes the creation of a thriving household economy, orderly governance, and especially fostering the growth and development of her husband and children.

The Excellent Woman Compared with Personified Wisdom

This woman is a living person, who can be easily visualized in her wise and tireless activity. True, we are not told that she is beautiful and lovely (Gen. 29.17), indeed physical beauty is discounted in favour of the inner quality of fear of Yahweh (31.30). We can, however, imagine her tirelessly going about her tasks, selecting her threads, assessing a field, offering kindly counsel, teaching her children, and smiling in satisfaction with tangible achievement. In her humanity, she can be understood as personifying practical, womanly wisdom. On the other hand, Personified Wisdom can be visualized as a woman only to some extent. She is seen mingling with the crowd in the market place and in the gates, where she competes with vendors for attention (1.20-21), she makes a threatening gesture (1.24), and bears gifts in both hands (3.16). We can see her freshly constructed house, and imagine her banquet preparations (9.1-3). The focus however is on her thoughts and words, and she is humanized only to the extent required to let us hear them. The excellent woman, while no more a rounded character than any other in the book of Proverbs, demonstrates before our eyes the contribution that a wise woman was considered to make to Israelite society at a certain point of time. This chaste, loyal, and industrious woman can also be compared by way of contrast with the adulteress in chs. 1–9, who is presented as a rival to Personified Wisdom for the affections of the youth under instruction. The ideal woman is home-centred, the adulteress is always on the move (7.11); she bears herself with dignity, whereas the adulteress prowls at dusk, and lurks in the streets and squares (7.12). She is faithful, and her bed-coverings, like her own and her household's clothing, are manufactured at home through productive diligence, while the adulteress uses exotic coverings to allure her victim and betray her husband (7.16). The portrait of the practical wife whose chief adornment is the fear of Yahweh complements the more sensuous and romantic description of the ideal wife in an early instruction (5.18-19). If a youth is to succeed in his life's vocation to construct his house in wisdom, as the excellent woman's husband apparently has (31.23), then he would be advised to find a Yahweh-fearing woman who can gain his trust and admiration (31.11, 28-29).

Appendix: Solomon as the Author of Proverbs

Introduction

While the authors of Proverbs commentaries who wrote before the era of historical-critical scholarship accepted that Solomon was the author of Proverbs in the literal and historical sense, each author creates a somewhat different depiction of Solomon. I will first examine how Solomon, as assumed author of Proverbs, has been portrayed in a number of significant pre-historical-critical Proverbs commentaries. Then, scholars writing on the authorship of Proverbs from a historical-critical perspective have somewhat different understandings of Solomon's role in the production of the book, as will appear when I examine how Solomon's authorship is understood in a number of twentieth-century commentaries. The latter survey opens up a wider topic than that of Solomon as author, namely the very historical and literary foundations of the biblical depiction of Solomon himself.

Solomon as the Author of Proverbs in Pre-Historical-Critical Christian Commentaries

(Note: In this section, I use—with the permission of John Wiley & Sons—an abridged version of part of an article which I have previously published [Moss 2002: 199-211]. My citations of Bede are from Hurst 1983: 21-163; those of Grotius are from Grotius 1775; and those of Calmet are from Calmet 1792, with my own translations.)

Introductory Remarks

The west wall fresco in the chapter hall of St Maria Novella in Florence illustrates the place once held by Solomon in the religious imagination of the Christian West (see Offner and Steinweg 1979, vol. 6: 22). The title of the painting is the 'Triumph of St Thomas Aquinas'. Seated on the left and right of the enthroned saint are ten figures of the Old and New Testament representing the Holy Scriptures from which St Thomas' teaching received its inspiration. The

Old Testament figures—Job, David, Moses, Isaiah, and Solomon—complete the row at either end, and the text displayed in Solomon's open book is Prov. 1.1-2. Andrea Bonaiuti's fresco and the pre-Enlightenment commentaries on the book of Proverbs share the assumption that Solomon and his proverbs are inseparable. However, Solomon in the fresco is an ambiguous figure, being the only one of both Testaments without a halo and without the 'S' (Sanctus) in the inscription. In this way, too, the fresco corresponds with the early commentaries, where the author of Proverbs shares both the wisdom and the failings of Solomon in 1 Kings.

While the early commentaries on the book of Proverbs share a common assumption of the historicity of the superscriptions, Solomon has been depicted in quite different ways. This point will be made in my discussion of Proverbs in Origen's commentary on the Song of Songs, and the Proverbs commentaries of Bede, Hugo Grotius, and Augustin Calmet.

Origen

Because of the influence of Origen on the subsequent Christian interpretation (see O'Keefe 2006: 197), I preface this study of Christian commentaries with a brief consideration of Origen's references to Solomon's proverbs in his interpretation of the Song of Songs, since only fragments of his works on Proverbs have survived (Alonso Schökel and Vílchez Líndez 1984: 110). In the Song of Songs commentary, Proverbs has a place alongside Ecclesiastes and the Song of Songs in the trio of Solomon's interrelated works. Origen asks why the Church, in accepting 'three books from Solomon's pen', places Proverbs first, Ecclesiastes second, and the Song of Songs third. He finds that the relationship between these books may be understood in the light of the classification of the Greek philosophic books. Whereas the Greeks had three branches of learning—moral, natural and inspective (Origen, ed. Lawson 1956: 40)—so too, 'for his part, Solomon, in order to differentiate between the branches of learning, issued them in three books, arranged in their proper order' (p. 41). The Greek science to which the book of Proverbs corresponds is moral science, 'which inculcates a seemly manner of life and gives grounding in habits that incline to virtue' (p. 40). Again, 'first in Proverbs, he taught the moral science, putting rules for living into the form of short and pithy maxims, as was fitting' (p. 41). He adds later, 'It behoves him who desires to know wisdom to begin with moral instruction' (p. 43). For Origen, the similarity of Solomon's works to works of Greek philosophy is no accident. He employs the motif of 'the theft of the Greeks' (p. 40 n. 67) and writes that the wisdom of the Greeks actually derives from Solomon, who received his wisdom directly from God (1 Kgs 4.29-30 [Eng.]).

> It seems to me, then, that all the sages of the Greeks borrowed these ideas from Solomon, who had learnt them by the Spirit of God in an age and time long before their own; and that they put them forward as their own inventions, and, by including them in the books of their teachings, left them to be handed down also to those that came after (Prologue to the Song of Songs, p. 40).

Having related Solomon's works to Greek learning, Origen proceeds to interpret them from a Christian perspective, thanks to his perception of the spiritual sense. While recognizing the literal meaning, in terms of the literary forms in which the books are cast, he develops the spiritual meaning at much greater length. In Proverbs Solomon teaches the moral discipline which is the foundation of the higher stages of the spiritual life. As for Ecclesiastes and the Canticle, he writes:

> If, then, a man has completed his course in the first subject, as taught in Proverbs, by amending his behaviour and keeping the commandments, and thereafter, having seen how empty is the world and realised the brittleness of transitory things, and has come to renounce the world and all that is therein [Ecclesiastes]...he will follow on to desire the things that are not seen, and that are eternal. (pp. 45-46)

Origen's Solomon, then, was inspired to write a 'divine philosophy' having a threefold structure, in which the moral instruction in Proverbs is the first stage, and which culminates in the teaching of the Song of Songs.

Origen relates Solomon to Christ and the New Testament by understanding him as a type of Christ. In his comments on Solomon's titles in Prov. 1.1, he notes that in Hebrew the name 'Solomon' (*shelomoh*) relates to the word 'peace' (*shalom*). He continues: 'It is, I think, unquestionable that Solomon is in many respects a type of Christ, first in that he is called the Peaceable' (p. 51). Typologically 'Solomon the peaceable one, anticipates the divine bringer of peace' (Norris 2006: 211). In their spiritual sense Solomon's titles in Prov. 1.1 refer to Christ, and 'Israel' designates the Christian people, both in the intermediary stage of the church on earth, and in its perfected state in Heaven. 'Therefore in the first book, where he grounds us in ethical teaching, Solomon is called king in Israel— not Jerusalem as yet; because, although we be called Israel by reason of faith, we have not yet got so far as to reach the heavenly Jerusalem' (Origen, ed. Lawson 1956: 52). In the spiritual sense of Proverbs, the addressees are the Christian faithful, and faith cannot exist without moral reform (Crouzel, in Brésard, Crouzel and Borret 1991: 42). In conclusion, Origen understands Solomon as a type of Christ, and the moral instructor both of the church and of the faith-filled Christian soul.

Bede

The description of Solomon that we find in Bede's commentary on the book of Proverbs is shaped by Bede's attention to both the literal sense and the spiritual sense. Bede's method is to comment progressively on the text in terms of both the literal and the spiritual meaning. For example, Bede writes on Prov. 1.1 that Solomon attached the name 'proverbs' (*parabolae*) to the book. He adds, however, that his reason for selecting this title was 'so that we would understand what he says not according to the letter, but "more highly", signifying that the Lord would speak to the crowds in parables'. (For the senses of Scripture in Bede, see de Lubac 1998, vol. 1: 90-93, and Holder 1990: 404-407.) Whereas in expounding the literal meaning of the text, Bede portrays the historical king of Israel as the author of the book of Proverbs and a teacher of wisdom, in the spiritual meaning, which he finds equally in the text, Bede transforms the historical king and wisdom teacher into a Christian teacher.

In the literal meaning, Solomon is the author of the entire book of Proverbs. He affixed the title (1.1) and repeated it at 10.1. The proper names Agur (30.1) and Lemuel (31.1) are read as common nouns designating Solomon. Bede uses 1 Kings to gloss the Proverbs commentary with additional biographical details. For example, when Solomon refers to himself as an only son in 4.3, he disregards Bathsheba's first child by David (Bede on 4.3). Again, given the opportunity to choose, Solomon preferred the love of wisdom to all other things (on 4.7). Lemuel's (i.e. Solomon's) mother is, in the literal sense, Bathsheba 'who could correctly be understood to have taught him these things as a child' (on 31.1). While in the literal meaning Solomon is a teacher of Israel, his words have Christian significance as well. From Prov. 1.1 onwards, Bede devotes as much space or more to the spiritual meaning. 'By his own name and the peaceful condition of his kingdom he (Solomon) denotes the perennial kingdom of Christ and the church' (on 1.1). Arthur Holder writes:

> In all his works Bede was striving more to edify his readers than to investigate unknown theological territory. And he was convinced (no doubt rightly) that what would edify most was a spiritual interpretation of Scripture centring on Christ, the Church, and the sacramental life (Holder 1990: 407).

According to the spiritual sense, personified Wisdom in Proverbs 8 is understood to be 'the Lord who spoke openly to the world and spoke nothing in secret' (on 8.1). Wisdom's house of seven columns 'is certainly the church of Christ, and the columns are the doctors of holy church full of sevenfold spirit, as were James, Cephas, John' (on 9.2). When Bede reads the praises of the good wife (31.10-31), he hears 'the wisest of kings, Solomon, repeating the praises of holy church, in verses few but full of truth' (on 31.10).

Again, Bede's Solomon addresses the Christian faithful, in particular the people who listened to Bede himself and his fellow preachers. Commenting on 'Hear, my son, your father's instruction and do not spurn your mother's teaching' (1.8), Bede writes: 'He (Solomon) begins to admonish carefully each of the faithful to prefer the discipline of the divine law to the allurements of the wicked. In truth a crown follows the observance of the former, and eternal death the crimes of the latter.' Solomon admonishes his hearers not to associate with adulteresses. 'By the foreign woman can be understood the perversity of heretics: they are strangers to Christ and members of the church. They deceive the innocent with enticing speech' (on 2.16). 'The light on the king's face' is the joyful face of Christ seen by those given to live with him in eternity (on 16.15). Solomon's audience reaches to the contemporaries of Christ and the apostles. 'Do not walk in the way with them' (1.15) is addressed to the Jews who believed in Christ, telling them not to deal with the Jews who were persecuting Christ. The 'afflicted righteous' (11.8) are the Christian martyrs, and the impious one destroying his neighbour with his speech is the heretic. The wise one in the book of Proverbs is the Christian pastor of souls.

In conclusion, Bede comments on Proverbs in the literal sense to find its author to be the historical Solomon of 1 Kings. In the literal sense of Proverbs, Solomon is, moreover, not only the wise king, but also and especially a wisdom teacher. Again, in the spiritual sense, Solomon is a Christian teacher because he intended the spiritual meaning that Bede expounds. Solomon's audience are all Christians from the time of Christ to the Northumbrian faithful. The wise and foolish characters of Proverbs are the saints and martyrs and heretics of Christian history. If Bede's exegesis is nothing less than an attentive listening to the voice of God for the sake of the Church and its ministry, then his portrait of Solomon as a doctor of the Anglo-Saxon church is one clear expression of his pastoral concern. Thanks to a spiritual interpretation, Solomon emerges as an image of Bede himself, doctor of the Church, the disciple of Origen, Augustine and Gregory (see Holder, 1990:

404-10; for Bede's own list of church doctors, see de Lubac 1998, vol. 1: 273 n. 20).

Hugo Grotius

Hugo Grotius (1583–1645), lawyer, politician and statesman, has been considered the last representative of the humanist movement, which flourished in Holland in the first half of the seventeenth century (for this and the following comments, see Reventlow 1988: 175-91). His scriptural commentaries lend support to the view that humanistic exegesis was primarily a philological enterprise. Grotius' commentary on Vulgate Proverbs contains abundant references to classical literature and philological comments on the Hebrew text and early Greek versions. However, it is Grotius' concern to insert the Bible into its times, to explain the historical background of names and events, that most shapes his picture of Solomon. When Grotius inserted the Bible into history, however, he did not intend to question the Scriptures' authority, and in principle he accepted the tradition that the biblical books are the product of the authors whose names are attached (for Grotius' scepticism in certain cases, see Reventlow 1988: 183).

Grotius writes that the book of Proverbs includes wisdom sayings of numerous wise persons besides Solomon himself. Even Solomon is a compiler as well as an original author. 'This book seems to be a selection of the best sayings from the very many authors before Solomon. The emperors of Constantinople had such collections drawn up for their own use' (Grotius 1775: 415). Grotius recognizes that Agur (30.1) is not a translation of Solomon, as Jerome had written, but the name of a sage whose words compare with two of the Greek poets (p. 432). Neither is Lemuel (31.1) to be understood as Solomon, but as Hezekiah (p. 433. See 2 Kgs 18.2).

Grotius relates Solomon's sayings to oriental history, to the extent that the latter was known before the dawn of ancient Near Eastern archaeology, but especially classical antiquity. The components of Hebrew wisdom correspond to the Greeks' division of knowledge (on 22.20). Moreover, time and again, he parallels one of Solomon's proverbs with a saying from the classical authors to supplement the information in the biblical text. For example, he comments on the public standing of the husband in 31.23, writing that this 'was owing no doubt to the senatorial dignity of his attire', and then he cites Homer and Plautus for the wifely manufacture of such garments.

Whereas in Bede's conception of theology, Solomon teaches a revelation from God for the pilgrim's journey to God, Grotius' Solomon is involved in the humanist's task of reviving the classics for the betterment of society, Church, education and government (for a comparison of Grotius with the Fathers in general see Hagen 1990: 26-27). This is his most distinctive feature, and as an author whose Proverbs was a collection of extant works, he may even be likened to a Byzantine emperor.

Augustine Calmet

The fourth and last pre-historical-critical portrait of Solomon to be examined is the work of one recognized by his contemporaries as the greatest Bible scholar of the eighteenth century. In his complete Bible commentary Augustine Calmet OSB (1672-1757) sought to give the simple, literal meaning of obscure scriptural passages. To this end he summoned all the erudition which he possessed in ancient history, lexicography and philology (Ages 1965: 340). In some respects Calmet pens a traditional portrait of Solomon. He maintains that Solomon is the speaker of all the poems that the book contains. Like those before him, Calmet introduces details about Solomon from the historical books (see Calmet's comments on the adulteress in 7.26). Nonetheless, Calmet's portrait of Solomon is distinctive in two respects. First, he places himself in a community of readers of Proverbs and notes how the reader's attention may be maintained.

> The mention of the name and rank of the wisest king served assuredly to commend the work to readers and to gain a fair hearing. For by nature we are prone to listen to famous men, sublime in name and knowledge... The brief parabolic style also elicits a favourable hearing. Precepts expressed parabolically gently delight the soul. Jesus Christ taught not otherwise (Calmet 1792: 452-53).

To stimulate the attention of the reader of Proverbs, Calmet cites the example of the Queen of Sheba 'who made a long journey to be present to learn Solomon's wisdom and test him in riddles' (on Prov. 1.6, p. 454 n. 6). He highlights Solomon's rhetorical skill in avoiding monotony by introducing a 'pleasing variety of argument. Now God speaks, now Wisdom, often Solomon for himself.' Calmet's readers are reminded that the wise one calls the disciple 'my son' out of love (on 3.1, p. 466). Secondly, Calmet refers to the family context of Solomon's teachings. 'Solomon notes that parents are to be as wise and learned as they need to be, for he admonishes children to report everything to their parents, and not to depart in the least from their rules, commands and admonitions, nor from the religion

and rules the parents follow' (on 1.8, p. 455). Solomon is an example
of the love and devotion children owe their parents. He refers all his
education and the glory of his wisdom to the instruction he received
from both his parents (on 1.8, p. 455). Solomon showed his parents
a lasting deference and tender affection, especially his mother (as
is evident from the rest of Proverbs) who it is right to believe was
showered with as many graces as David after their adultery (on 4.1,
p. 475). Solomon devotes almost all of ch. 31 to the praises of his
mother, whom he commemorates under the title of the good wife.
'He wrote the most magnificent and gracious tribute of all those to
be read in the Old Testament about women. He proposed her an
outstanding example to other women and to souls who seek sanc-
tification through the exercise of Christian virtues' (on 31.10-31,
abbreviated).

Calmet's Solomon, then, is a devoted son, a wise father, and a
considerate instructor, writing a reader-friendly book. Retaining
the traditional conservative assumption of Solomon's authorship,
Calmet pens a benign portrait of Solomon.

Solomon as the Author of Proverbs in Recent Commentaries

André Barucq: Solomon as Author by Attribution, the Wise Ones of Israel being the Real Authors of Proverbs

André Barucq begins his discussion of Solomon's authorship of
Proverbs noting that Israel's wisdom literature has links with the
intellectual life and literature of the ancient Near East. Egyptian
wisdom literature preserved the names of authors or compilers of
teachings, and this practice is found in works coming from ancient
Semitic culture as well. In the Bible, Barucq writes, only the names
of Solomon in Prov. 25.1 and of Ben Sira have been preserved in this
sense. Otherwise the names attached to wisdom literature are fictional names under which the books present their wisdom, as in the
case of the Solomon attribution in Prov. 1.1. There is perhaps an
indirect reference to the grounds of the attribution of Proverbs to
Solomon when Barucq refers to Solomon's skill in expressing himself in songs and proverbs, as well as to his judgments and science (1
Kgs 3.16-28; 5.9-14 [Eng. 4.29-34]; 10.1, 8-9, 23). He wants to make
the point that such an understanding of royal wisdom has prece-
dents in documents of the ancient Near East (Barucq 1964: 11-15).

All told, the topic of Solomon's authorship is a minor aspect of
Barucq's 'Introduction' to the book of Proverbs. Proverbs is, in fact,
a synthesis of Israelite wisdom, comprising nine booklets differing

in date and origin, whose wisdom observations date from pre-
Solomonic times to the fifth century (pp. 20-26). The wise ones
responsible for Proverbs were a Yahweh-fearing group, distinct
from the wise who incurred prophetic reproof. They were moralists
and pedagogues, they were in contact with the people and popular
wisdom, and they developed the ability to express their teaching in
a variety of literary forms.

Dermot Cox: The Age of Solomon and Solomon in the Wisdom Tradition

In the 'Introduction to Sapiential Literature' (1982: 2-79) which pre-
cedes his Proverbs commentary, Cox refers to the authors of Proverbs and the other wisdom literature as the sages or the wisdom
writers (see pp. 2-12). The different sections of the book of Proverbs
illustrate the development of Wisdom from a very early oral tradition to the final version of the book, probably in the fifth century
BCE (pp. 30-31). Cox sets the attribution of Proverbs to Solomon
(1.1; 10.1) within an ongoing literary tradition, in which Solomon
is regarded as the 'founder' of wisdom (p. 3). This tradition was
strengthened on theological grounds late in its development, when
wisdom was perceived to be attained as a gift of God, rather than
acquired through human discipline (pp. 56-57). It was then considered that God created the world by his wisdom. Cox suggests that
such thinking probably lies behind the story of Solomon and his gift
of wisdom (1 Kgs 3.4) 'which left an indelible mark on the wisdom
writers' (p. 57). In a comment on Prov. 1.1, Cox looks at the attribution from the perspective of an ongoing readership. He writes that
'the superscription "Proverbs of Solomon" is not meant to indicate
authorship, but to remind the reader of the richness of the wisdom
heritage now placed before him' (p. 97).

Cox discusses the historical setting of the attribution in the light
of the circumstances of the 'age of Solomon' (pp. 38-42). With the
establishment of a monarchic administration in the Canaanite-
Egyptian style around the tenth century BCE, there was a need to
apply wisdom to government, and to teach the technique of government to a class of aspiring officials and administrators (p. 39).
Cox writes that 'education was very much an education in the lib-
eral arts, and not merely in administration' (p. 40). He continues
that

> it is in this context that Solomon is seen as the 'pattern of let-
> ters' and of the sapiential tradition. Whatever his actual contri-
> bution, and this is lost in the mists of obscurity, he established
> the social circumstances in which the career of letters became

possible, and even honourable. It can be no cause for wonder
that many of the more polished literary works in the wisdom
corpus are artificially attributed to him (p. 40).

There would be a close relationship between the portrait of Solomon in 1 Kgs 4.29-34 and the educated elite of his day. This portrait 'is also a description of a particular *kind* of person and a particular society that could produce such: a society of cultivated people, given to letters and the arts, with a particular international cast of mind' (pp. 21-22).

Cox's discussion of the attribution of the sapiential literature to Solomon highlights the particular social and political context in which the foundations of the attribution were laid, and also envisages the tradition of the attribution.

José Vílchez Líndez: A Survey of Research on Solomon and the Origins of Wisdom

In his 'Introduction' to the book of Proverbs (Alonso Schökel and Vílchez Líndez 1984: 95-107), José Vílchez Líndez brings together the scholarship on the composition and dating of the materials. It is not Solomon but the wise ones who have centre stage in Proverbs research. Their activity dates from the time of Solomon, and was intensified towards the end of the eighth century. They assembled the oral traditions which form the substratum of the great Solomon collections, and also of the other lesser collections which were gradually formed. Vílchez Líndez writes that in view of his discussion of the role of Israel's wise ones in research, the question of Solomon's real authorship of Proverbs is superfluous. Here we have an instance of an attribution or a pseudonym. The wisdom books were attributed to Solomon, as were the legal writings to Moses, and the psalms to David. There was, however, an historical time of Solomon, and the earliest strata of Proverbs may go back to that era, or even before it, some authors attributing more of the material to the time of Solomon, some less (pp. 105-106). Compiling the sayings in Proverbs is the achievement of 'that anonymous chain of sages who patiently gathered, as precious stones, the proverbs and maxims which were repeated amongst the people and in the schools, and to which they contributed their more or less original creations' (p. 106). As for the contribution of Solomon to the composition of the book of Proverbs, historically speaking, Vílchez Líndez's findings seem to infer that Solomon was a king who may have encouraged the gathering of existing proverbs, and perhaps also the composition of new proverbs.

Arndt Meinhold: Solomon as Posthumous Author by Attribution

Arndt Meinhold notes that the book of Proverbs as a whole and two of the sections are ascribed to Solomon, king of Jerusalem, who is considered in the Old Testament as the wisest of the wise. 'His superlative wisdom (1 Kgs 3.28; 5.9) overshadows anything comparable in the wisdom of the East and Egypt' (1 Kgs 5.10-11 [4.30-31 Eng.]; 10.1-3, 13-25) (Meinhold 1991, vol. 1: 21). In reality, however, no verse in Proverbs can be named that has Solomon even as probable author, though the tradition of Solomon's authorship cannot be entirely discounted, for the origins of proverbial speech, numerical sayings, and even exhortations can reach far back into the past. The threefold mention of Solomon's authorship is not to be understood in the literal historical sense, but as an attribution. Meinhold reiterates the point made by Cox that Proverbs' wisdom teaching is presented as equivalent to the wisdom of the wisest of kings. The attribution to Solomon was made in stages in the case of Proverbs, and was effectively put in place in the first century BCE, when both the Psalms of Solomon and Wisdom were attributed to him. Septuagint Proverbs enhances Solomon's authorship by omitting the superscriptions within the book, and by dropping the names of Agur and Lemuel. Meinhold concludes his discussion of the authorship of Proverbs (pp. 21-23) by identifying the collectors and composers of the Proverbs material as the group of upper-class wise ones, who exercised important administrative and educational roles in the Jerusalem royal court.

Richard Clifford: Solomon, Littérateur and Royal Author

Richard J. Clifford accepts the view that 'wisdom literature was conventionally ascribed to Solomon, as psalms were ascribed to David and laws to Moses' (Clifford 1999: 3), and that the real authors of this anthology of collections of sayings were scribes of the royal court who were responsible for the production of literature for temple and court (p. 8). Nonetheless, Clifford offers a clearer view of Solomon's literary activity than the scholars discussed above. He writes that 'there is no reason, however, to doubt that some of the book is "by Solomon", for as king he would have collected, sponsored, or possibly even written, various kinds of writing, including literature (*belles lettres*), as 1 Kgs 4.29-31 recognises' (p. 3).

Bruce Waltke: The Historical Solomon of 1 Kings

Bruce K. Waltke's view of Solomon's authorship of Proverbs is in striking contrast to that of the previously mentioned scholars, and will be discussed at greater length. In his 'historico-grammatical commentary' (Waltke 2004, vol. 1: xxii), Waltke distinguishes the authorship of the sayings and of the completed book (see vol. 1: 36-37). Solomon's authorship of the sayings is not a fictional attribution, but an historical datum, and to regard the attributions in the titles as pseudepigrapha is the real fiction (vol. 1: 31). Chapters 1–24 are to be ascribed to Solomon directly, while chs. 25–29 are a select number of Solomon's three thousand proverbs, transmitted and arranged by the officials of Hezekiah. Solomon, then, is the principal author of the sayings in chs. 1–29, while chs. 30–31 were authored by Agur and Lemuel. The Solomonic authorship of Septuagint Proverbs is named 'fiction' by Waltke, so as to highlight the historical veracity of the Solomon attributions in Hebrew Proverbs (vol. 1: 4). The real author of the book, but not of the sayings, is an anonymous editor who appended chs. 25–31 to the original Solomon collection of chs. 1–24 (vol. 1: 36-37). He lived during the Persian or Hellenistic era, and he allowed 1.1, the original heading of 1.1–24.34, to stand as the title of his final composition (vol. 1: 36-37).

Waltke argues that the case for accepting the Solomonic authorship of chs. 1–24 is based on the data of the biblical narrative (1 Kgs 1–11), and on similarities with ancient Near Eastern wisdom literature. Solomon would have familiarized himself with the collections of proverbs and the sayings that circulated around the Fertile Crescent. Linguistic evidence, too, supports Solomon's authorship (vol. 1: 31-36).

Waltke's commentary makes the historical Solomon present to readers. In the preamble (1.2-7), for example, Solomon invites his addressees 'to feast on his holy food' (vol. 1: 178). He goes on to put ten lectures into the mouth of the father and addressed to 'my son'. Solomon also composes two addresses of woman wisdom, who is a personification of Solomon's inspired wisdom as expressed in his teachings (vol. 1: 10-11). Numerous Proverbs texts are illustrated through a reference to the behaviour of Solomon in 1 Kings.

Concluding Remarks

In five out of the six commentators reviewed, Solomon is an author by attribution, the book of Proverbs as a whole being the work of the wise ones, and not of Solomon himself. The attribution rests on the depiction of Solomon in 1 Kings. Cox and Meinhold add the precision that in attributing Proverbs to Solomon, the author(s) of the titles intended that their readers should accept the wisdom in Proverbs as equivalent to that of Solomon in 1 Kings. This observation may be helpful to the modern reader too, and implies that the narrative of Solomon in 1 Kings is so familiar as to enhance the status of what is about to be read. When Waltke presents Solomon as the real author of Proverbs, he reduces the scope of the tradition history of Solomon's authorship of Proverbs to Solomon as author of Septuagint Proverbs. The ambiguities arising from the historical approach to Solomon's authorship of Proverbs are brought into a broader focus in the light of contemporary Solomon studies.

Studies in the Biblical Solomon

Introductory Remarks

In contemporary research, the topic of Solomon's authorship of Proverbs is overshadowed by the numerous studies on the biblical figure of Solomon in 1 Kings 1–11. A discussion of this broader and yet more fundamental question provides a context in which the research on Solomon as author of Proverbs, as above, can receive appropriate attention. Here I present an overview of the work of six scholars who study Solomon in 1 Kings 1–11 and 2 Chronicles from different perspectives.

Maxwell Miller, Alan Millard and Ernst Axel Knauf: The Historicity of 1 Kings 1–11

J. Maxwell Miller favours a middle course between two extreme positions on the historicity of the biblical account of Solomon (Miller 1997: 1-24 [here p. 24]). The option of Alan Millard and Kenneth Kitchen, he writes, is 'to take the Hebrew Bible essentially at face value'. These scholars argue that 'Solomon is all that the most extravagant biblical passages claim him to be' (Miller 1997: 23). Thomas Thompson, on the other hand, dismisses the Hebrew Bible as a source for historical information, and declares as nonhistorical everything it says about Israelite history (including Solomon) before the mid-ninth century BCE, when Israel begins to turn up for certain in epigraphical sources (p. 23). Miller's view is that 1 Kings 3–11 and 2 Chronicles 1–9 give the impression of a legendary figure, larger than life, and they represent 'the Solomonic legend at two stages of its growth', each being completed approximately five centuries after the time in which Solomon would have lived (p. 2). He considers that 'the historical Solomon probably was a local ruler, whose territorial domain would have been limited to

Palestine west of the Jordan (excluding the coastal zone) and some of northern Transjordan' (p. 11).

Miller shows how, in late twentieth-century scholarship, the existence of a Solomonic Age of Enlightenment, during which Solomon's court would have been a centre of international learning and literary activity, was being called into question through a critical examination of the texts, and of the archaeological supports for a 'golden age' (pp. 3-9). In the heyday of the promotion of a Solomonic Age of Enlightenment, biblical scholars claimed to discover passages in 1 Kings that could date back to Solomon's time, and archaeologists proceeded to uncover remains of Solomonic architecture. By the 1980s, however, serious reservations were being made about attributing any biblical passage, or any of the archaeological findings, to the time of Solomon. Miller argues that 'a tenth-century, Palestine-based empire of the territorial extent, opulence, and international influence envisioned by the biblical writers would have been out of keeping with the general circumstances of the times', which he describes as the 'dark age' of the opening centuries of the Iron Age (pp. 13-14).

Alan Millard argues for the historical veracity of the biblical account of Solomon's reign on the grounds of comparative evidence from ancient Near Eastern literature, archaeology and epigraphy (Millard 1997: 30-53). He finds that the account of Solomon's use of gold in the temple and temple furnishings, and in the royal palace, is supported by texts and physical remains of temples from New Kingdom Egypt, Assyria and Babylon of the seventh-sixth centuries down to the Parthenon of Athens. Likewise the regional organization for feeding the royal court would compare with evidence from Egyptian and Assyrian sources. For Millard, the absence of the remains of any Solomonic building, and the absence of references to Solomon in inscriptions, is not an unsurmountable problem, given the history of the city of Jerusalem's destruction and rebuilding, and the renovations necessitated by the limited space within the city. Millard continues by stating that the lack of any extra-biblical references to Solomon can also be accounted for. The Assyrian and Babylonian kingdoms were in decline in the tenth century BCE, and Egypt was generally weak from the eleventh century onwards. The narrative of 1 Kings 1–11, completed in or after the Exile, can still be a satisfactory source for the time four hundred years before. Other parts of Kings compare well with records of other states, and are seen to be reliable records, so why, he asks, should the Solomon Narrative be treated differently from the remainder? In the name of biblical veracity, he argues against the claims that aspects of the biblical text, for example the name of Hiram of Tyre and the reports of 'the troublesome trio' (Hadad of Edom, Rezon of Damascus, and Jeroboam of Ephraim) (1 Kgs 11.14-40), would call into question the extent of Solomon's empire. In conclusion, Millard writes that 'in every ascertainable way Solomon acted in the manner of the kings around him' (p. 53). There is no external or objective evidence negating the Hebrew reports. 'The possibility that those reports do reflect reliably the reign of king Solomon has to be admitted, even if, at present, there is nothing to prove that they do' (p. 53).

Ernst Axel Knauf proposes that a number of discrepancies within 1 Kings 1–11 'hint at a perception of Solomon quite different from the image intended by the text in its final form' (Knauf 1997: 81-95). The first and most indicative of these texts is 1 Kgs 8.12b-13. When v. 12b is expanded and corrected in the light of the Septuagint, and is read in its original context, it referred to El, the supreme god of creation, and to Yahweh who had managed to withdraw from the bright light of the creation domain of El. In 8.13 Yahweh is brought by Solomon as a god subordinate to El, the creator god, to be the chief god of the Jerusalem pantheon. In this symbolic text, Solomon as king of Jerusalem integrated the tribe of Judah into the political and ideological framework of the State of Jerusalem.

Secondly, Knauf claims that certain features of the story of Solomon's accession to the throne (1 Kings 1–2) point to the tension between the Davidic tribe Judah and the State of Jerusalem. He writes that, having gained the kingship in Jerusalem by a *coup d'état*, 'Solomon presented himself (or was presented by his entourage) as David's legitimate successor' (p. 89). He would then have proceeded to extend Jerusalem's power over the highlands of Judah. He suggests that historically there seems to have been a double foundation of biblical Israelite kingship, one by David, one by Solomon.

A third text, providing the weakest case for 'Solomon the Historical' (p. 91), is the record of Solomon's building activities, including the building of the temple, and a number of fortresses (see 1 Kgs 9.15-19). Here Knauf discerns two lists. The shorter list (9.17-18), referring to the cities rebuilt by Solomon following Pharaoh Shoshenq's campaign, would be the earliest. The omission of Jerusalem and Samaria in this list signifies that Shoshenq would have spared them, but ravaged Gezer and cities of the Negev, 'the very power-base of David'. This is another indication of the cleavage between Solomon's kingdom of Jerusalem and David's chiefdom of Judah (p. 95). The longer lists (9.16, 19), which include the Jerusalem temple and multiple fortresses, reflect the Solomon of legend.

In summary, Knauf argues that when these three texts are examined critically, they suggest that the historical Solomon was a usurper who introduced Yahweh, the Judean tribal deity, into the Jerusalem pantheon, and began to subjugate Judah to the State of Jerusalem. He ruled over a relatively small area in Israel's south, at the most from Gezer to Thamar, rather than from the Euphrates to the Brook of Egypt.

Thomas Römer: Solomon in 1 Kings 1–11 from the Perspective of the Development of the Deuteronomistic History

Thomas Römer aims to explain the ambiguities in the description of Solomon in 1 Kings 1–11 through a 'diachronic reconstruction of the formation of 1 Kings 1–11' (Römer 2008: 98-130 [here p. 102]). He attributes the text to three successive groups of Deuteronomistic editors. In the first or Josianic edition of 1 Kings 1–11, Solomon is in the image of the Assyrian kings (pp. 116-23). For example, the account of Solomon's accession to the throne of David his father (1 Kings 1–2) is shaped in parallel with Sennacherib's contested successor, Esarhaddon's coming to power with the help of his mother, Naqia. The history of Solomon's reign, whose centre-point is the building of the temple, begins with the account of Solomon's vision at Gibeon (3.1-15), which functions as 'Solomon's divine legitimation as "wise king" and temple-builder' (p. 119). Solomon's prayer to obtain from Yahweh 'a wise heart' (p. 120) is a recurrent motif in ancient Near Eastern royal ideology: Asshurbanipal claimed to have received wisdom from Nabu, and to have been ordered to care for the sanctuaries of the gods who had brought about the defeat of his enemies and given him matchless strength. In 1 Kings 3 these things are affirmed of Solomon. 'The insistence on Solomon's extraordinary character establishes a parallel with the great Assyrian kings, and, within the context of the books of Kings, with Hezekiah (2 Kgs 18.5) and Josiah (2 Kgs 23.25)' (p. 120). In 4.29-33 [Eng.], Solomon seems, like Asshurbanipal, to have founded a library (p. 121). According to the Josianic scribes, the grandeur of Solomon's kingdom is the result of the construction of the temple (p. 123). This ideology, writes Römer, is found in the account of the reign of Josiah. 'The renovation of the temple is there presented as the prelude to the re-establishment of the "former" greatness of the Davidic monarchy' (p. 123). Solomon's prayer at the temple inauguration is a turning point. Up to this, he is an ideal wise king, and temple-builder. The account of Yahweh's second appearance to Solomon (9.1-9; cf. 3.4-14), however, contains ominous threats, which are plausible in the light of the negative aspects of Solomon's reign and his infidelity in ch. 11.

During the exile the contemporary Deuteronomists inserted additions throughout the first edition. The collapse of Judah would have been the outcome of the abandonment of the law of the centralization of worship on the part of almost all the kings of Judah, beginning with Solomon (ch. 11). It also became necessary at this time to qualify the former promise of an eternal Davidic dynasty by making this promise conditional on fidelity to Yahweh's commands.

A third edition of the Deuteronomistic History would have been produced at the beginning of the Persian era. The editors and their immediate successors (Ezra–Nehemiah) were concerned to define the specific status of the people of Israel, who are now identified through observance of the Mosaic Torah, to which Solomon's success is attributed (2.3). Israel's special status required separation from the other peoples, whom we now find to have remained in the land after the conquest (9.20-22). It was then that mixed marriages were prohibited (Ezra 9.10; Nehemiah 13), and so Solomon's numerous wives become 'foreign women', who were the cause of his undoing (1 Kgs 11.1-8). Finally, Römer suggests that in a post-Deuteronomistic redaction of 1 Kings 1–11, Solomon is depicted as a king taken out of a fairy-tale, in response to the Persian kings, whom he again surpasses in wisdom and wealth. The visit of the Queen of Sheba presents Solomon in their likeness, and the story of Solomon's judgment (3.16-28) may also have been inserted at this time (pp. 128-29). Römer concludes by noting the changes in Solomon's character throughout the course of the Deuteronomistic History, from the ambiguities of the last chapters of 1 Kings 1–11, up to his presentation as a legendary king in the last texts to be added to those chapters. 'Doubtless this last image of Solomon has stamped the reception of his character in Judaism and Christianity, but these ambiguous aspects have never totally disappeared' (p. 130).

Pauline Viviano: Solomon in the Completed Text of 1 Kings

Pauline A. Viviano considers that the conclusions based on an identification of the Deuteronomistic historians' sources, and on numbering the Deuteronomistic editions, remain 'highly speculative' (Viviano 1997: 336-47 [here pp. 336-37]). She undertakes a study of the portrait of Solomon in the Deuteronomistic History as a whole. There every king is evaluated in terms of the Deuteronomistic standard of what constitutes authentic worship of Yahweh.

She writes that by and large 1 Kings 1–10 presents Solomon and his reign in a favourable light. The accumulation of detail about his marriage to Pharaoh's daughter, his wisdom, his wealth, his fame, and his building projects, in which construction of the temple is particularly noted and described, creates the impression of an era of unparalleled peace and prosperity under the reign of a wise king. All this is lost in 1 Kings 11 because of Solomon's idolatry. Solomon is the first of Israel's kings to be accused of idolatry, and his kingship is a failure (p. 345).

'Beyond the Books of Kings,' continues Viviano, 'Solomon will be remembered for his wisdom (Prov. 1.1; 10.1; 25.1), or his wealth and splendour (Cant. 3.7, 9, 11; 8.11, 12), but for the Deuteronomistic historian he is remembered as the one who built the Temple (2 Kgs 21.7; 24.13; 25.15) *and* as the one who built high places to the gods of his foreign wives (2 Kgs 23.13), and so strayed in fidelity to the God who loved him' (p. 347). Finally, the presentation of Solomon in 1 Kings 1–11 as a whole is compared with the depiction of Solomon in 2 Chronicles, where he is presented 'as one who, from first to last, was completely faithful to Yahweh' (p. 346). His role as temple-builder is highlighted, and even Solomon's wisdom has its referent in temple-building.

Philippe Abadie: The Beginning of the Reception of Solomon (Solomon in 2 Chronicles)

In his study of Solomon in Chronicles (Abadie 2008: 338-55), Philippe Abadie notes that a full quarter of 2 Chronicles is dedicated to the reign of Solomon. This account centres on the temple, whose construction was prepared by David, then entrusted to and accomplished by Solomon. Solomon's future role is already suggested in the David story (1 Chron. 18.8). David, a man of war (1 Chron. 28.3), is contrasted with Solomon, the man of peace (1 Chron. 22.9), who was destined to construct the house of God's rest (1 Chron. 28.2). Abadie argues that the parallels drawn between David and Solomon in Chronicles do not lessen the stature of Solomon as temple-founder. The temple plan which David gave his son was not his own, but it was received in writing from the hand of Yahweh (1 Chron. 28.19). In this regard David is paralleled with Moses, who received the tablets of the law written by the hand of God (Exod. 31.28 [*sic*]; see Exod. 31.18). Neither David nor Moses, however, could bring the institution of Israel's worship to conclusion. This was accomplished by Solomon, the king chosen by God to build the temple, not a king merely by right of succession (1 Chron. 22.7-10; 28.5-7; 29.1). Accordingly, the Chronicler omits from his source in 1 Kings all the intrigues in 1 Kings 1–2. The infidelity and its consequences in 1 Kings 11 become transformed into an account of a serene old age, as peaceful as the time of his youth (2 Chron. 9.23-26). Abadie also discusses the apparent minimizing of Solomon's wisdom in Chronicles through the omission of passages of 1 Kings 1–11 which do not seem to be negative in regard to Solomon. These would include his just judgment (1 Kgs 3.16-28), and the account of his wise administration (1 Kgs 4.1–5.14 [Eng. 4.1-34]). Abadie argues that Solomon's wisdom is not diminished in 2 Chronicles, but given a different orientation in the service of the main theme, the king chosen by God to build the temple. He is seen in his cultic activity rather than in the exercise of kingly justice. The wisdom of government becomes wisdom in temple construction, while other aspects of his wisdom are minimized. Such a shift in the concept of wisdom is understandable in view of the Chronicler's audience. The Judean kingship belonged to the postexilic community's distant past, whereas the people now identify themselves through association with their temple.

Concluding Remarks
The historicity of the portrait of Solomon in 1 Kings 1–11 has been a significant topic in research, where a number of different approaches lead to widely different understandings of the historical Solomon. Miller goes behind the text to argue that Solomon's empire as described in the biblical account is out of keeping with the general circumstances of the times. Millard's historical criticism of the biblical text leads him to the opposite conclusion: the biblical account of Solomon has historical credibility. Knauf arrives at a radical reconstruction of the historical Solomon by identifying, through literary criticism, the historical core embedded in the text. Römer identifies three different portraits of Solomon in 1 Kings 1–11, located in successive stages in the development of the Deuteronomistic History. Viviano sets aside the historical question altogether in her study of the completed text of 1 Kings 1–11, in the light of the Deuteronomistic standard for evaluating a kingship. Abadie argues that the portrait of Solomon in 1–2 Chronicles is shaped to highlight the construction of the temple, so that those texts depicting Solomon's wisdom in 1 Kings 1–11 interest the Chronicler to the extent that they support his image of Solomon as temple-builder. Abadie's study of Solomon in 1–2 Chronicles introduces the topic of the reception of Solomon in tradition.

Conclusion

In the historical-critical commentaries on the book of Proverbs, much more attention is given to the role of Israel's wise ones in the production of Proverbs than to Solomon. In the majority consensus of scholarship, Solomon is the author of Proverbs and other works of wisdom literature by attribution. While the literary basis of the attribution is Solomon's portrait in 1 Kings 1–11, the historical foundation of his fame has been found located in times from the era of Solomon himself to as late as the early Persian period.

Throughout the history of the reception of Solomon up to modern times, one aspect of the biblical narrative, the visit of the Queen of Sheba, has been singled out and given romantic and fanciful interpretations (for representations of Solomon the lover, see Kunz-Lübcke 2004: 256-96, and for the many guises of Solomon throughout the course of English literature, see LaBossiere and Gladson 1992: 721-23). The depictions of Solomon as the author of Proverbs in the pre-historical-critical Christian commentaries on Proverbs, however varied and historically-conditioned, are based on an entire biblical text, and they merit their place in studies of the reception of Solomon.

References

Abadie, Philippe, 'Du roi sage au roi bâtisseur du Temple: un autre visage de Salomon dans le Livre des Chroniques', in Claude Lichtert and Dany Nocquet (eds.), *Le Roi Salomon: un héritage en question. Hommage à Jacques Vermeylen* (Brussels: Lessius, 2008), pp. 339-55.

Adams, Samuel L., *Wisdom in Transition: Act and Consequence in Second Temple Instructions* (Leiden: Brill, 2008).

Ages, Arnold, 'Calmet and the Rabbis', *The Jewish Quarterly Review* 55 (1965), pp. 340-49.

Alonso Schökel, Luis, *A Manual of Hebrew Poetics* (Subsidia biblica, 11; Rome: Pontifical Biblical Institute Press, 2000).

Alonso Schökel, Luis, and José Vílchez Líndez, *Proverbios* (Nueva Biblia Española: Sapienciales, I; Madrid: Ediciones Cristiandad, 1984).

Anderson, A.A., *The Book of Psalms* (2 vols.; NCB; London: Oliphants, 1972).

Barucq, André, *Le Livre des Proverbes* (SB; Paris: Gabalda, 1964).

Bede, *Proverbia Salomonis*, in D. Hurst (ed.), *Bedae Venerabilis opera. Pars II: Opera exegetica; 2B* (Corpus christianorum, series latina, 119; Turnhout: Brepols, 1983), pp. 21-163.

Bidmead, Julye, 'Lots', in David Noel Freedman (ed.), *Eerdmans Dictionary of the Bible* (Grand Rapids: Eerdmans, 2000), p. 825.

Brésard, Luc, Henri Crouzel and Marcel Borret, *Origène, Commentaire sur le Cantique des Cantiques* (SC, 375; 2 vols.; Paris: Cerf, 1991).

Bridges, Charles, *Proverbs* (Crossway Classic Commentaries; Wheaton, IL: Crossway Books, 2001).

Calmet, Augustine, *Commentarius literalis in Proverbia Salomonis* (Würzburg: Franc. Xaver Rienner, 1792).

Clifford, Richard J., *Proverbs: A Commentary* (OTL; Louisville, KY: Westminster/John Knox Press, 1999).

Cohen, A., *Proverbs: Hebrew Text and English Translation with an Introduction and Commentary* (London: Soncino, rev. edn, 1985).

Cox, D., *Proverbs, with an Introduction to Sapiential Books* (OTM, 17; Wilmington, DE: Michael Glazier, 1982).

Craigie, P.C., 'Biblical Wisdom in the Modern World. I. Proverbs', *Crux* 15.4 (1979), pp. 7-9.

Di Lella, Alexander A., *The Wisdom of Ben Sira: A New Translation and Notes by Patrick W. Skehan; Introduction and Commentary by Alexander A. Di Lella OFM* (AB; New York, Doubleday, 1986).

Fowler, Donald, 'Lion', in David Noel Freedman (ed.), *Eerdmans Dictionary of the Bible* (Grand Rapids: Eerdmans, 2000), p. 811.

Fox, Michael V., 'The Pedagogy of Proverbs 2', *JBL* 113 (1994), pp. 233-43.

—*Proverbs 1–9: A New Translation with Introduction and Commentary* (AB; New York: Doubleday, 2000).

Gilbert, Maurice, and Jean-Noël Aletti, *La sapienza e Gesù Cristo* (Turin: Gribaudi, 1981).

Grotius, Hugo, *; Annotationes in Vetus Testamentum. I. Ad Librum* Proverbia orum (Halle: J.J. Curtius, 1775), pp. 131-57.

Hagen, K., 'What Did the Term *Commentarius* Mean to Sixteenth-Century Theologians?', in Irena Backus and Francis Higman (eds.), *Théorie et pratique de l'exégèse biblique au XVIe siècle: Actes du troisième colloque international sur l'histoire de l'exégèse biblique au XVIe siecle* (Geneva: Droz, 1990), pp. 13-38.

Holder, Arthur G., 'Bede and the Tradition of Patristic Exegesis', *Anglican Theological Review* 72 (1990), pp. 399-411.

Holladay, John S., Jr, 'House, Israelite', in David Noel Freedman (ed.), *The Anchor Bible Dictionary* (6 vols.; New York: Doubleday, 1992), vol. 3, pp. 308-18.

Hurst 1983: see above under Bede.

Knauf, Ernst Axel, 'Le roi est mort, vivre le roi! A Biblical Argument for the Historicity of Solomon', in Lowell K. Handy (ed.), *The Age of Solomon: Scholarship at the Turn of the Millennium* (Leiden: Brill, 1997), pp. 81-95.

Kunz-Lübcke, Andreas, *Salomo: Von der Weisheit eines Frauenliebhabers* (Leipzig: Evangelische Verlagsanstalt, 2004).

Lang, Bernhard, *Wisdom and the Book of Proverbs: A Hebrew Goddess Redefined* (New York: Pilgrim Press, 1986).

LaBossiere, Camille R., and Jerrey A. Gladson, 'Solomon', in David Lyle Jeffrey (ed.), *A Dictionary of Biblical Tradition in English Literature* (Grand Rapids: Eerdmans, 1992).

Lichtheim, Mariam, *Ancient Egyptian Literature: A Book of Readings. II. The New Kingdom* (Berkeley: University of California Press, 2006).

Lubac, Henri de, *Medieval Exegesis* (2 vols.; vol. 1 trans. Mark Sebanc; Grand Rapids: Eerdmans and Edinburgh: T. & T. Clark, 1998).

McCullough, W.S., 'Eagle', in George Authur Buttrick (ed.), *The Interpreter's Dictionary of the Bible* (4 vols.; Nashville: Abingdon Press, 1962), II, p. 1.

McKane, W., *Proverbs: A New Approach* (London: SCM Press, 1970).

Meinhold, Arndt, *Die Sprüche* (2 vols.; Zürcher Bibelkommentare; Zürich: Theologischer Verlag, 1991).

Millard, Alan, 'King Solomon in his Ancient Context', in Lowell K. Handy (ed.), *The Age of Solomon: Scholarship at the Turn of the Millennium* (Leiden: Brill, 1997), pp. 30-53.

Miller, J. Maxwell, 'Separating the Solomon of History from the Solomon of Legend', in Lowell K. Handy (ed.), *The Age of Solomon: Scholarship at the Turn of the Millennium* (Leiden: Brill, 1997), pp. 1-24.

Moss, Alan, 'Proverbs with Solomon: A Critical Revision of the Pre-Critical

Commentary Tradition in the Light of a Biblical Intertextual Study',
HeyJ 43 (2002), pp. 199-211.

Norris, Richard A., 'Typology', in John A. McGuckin (ed.), *The SCM Press
A–Z of Origen* (London: SCM Press, 2006), pp. 209-11.

Offner, Richard, and Klara S. Steinweg, *A Critical and Historical Corpus
of Florentine Painting*. III/6. *The Fourteenth Century* (Locust Valley,
NY: J.J. Augustine, 1979).

O'Keefe, John J., 'Scriptural Interpretation', in John A. McGuckin (ed.),
The SCM Press A–Z of Origen (London: SCM Press, 2006), pp. 193-97.

Origen, *The Song of Songs: Commentary and Homilies* (ed. R.P. Lawson;
ACW, 26; New York: Newman Press, 1956).

Rainey, Anson F., 'Canaan, Canaanites', in David Noel Freedman (ed.),
Eerdmans Dictionary of the Bible (Grand Rapids: Eerdmans, 2000),
pp. 213-15.

Römer, Thomas, 'Salomon d'après les Deuteronomistes: Un roi ambigu', in
Claude Lichtert and Dany Nocquet (eds.), *Le Roi Salomon: un héritage en question. Hommage à Jacques Vermeylen* (Brussels: Lessius,
2008), pp. 98-130.

Reventlow, Henning Graf, 'Humanistic Exegesis: The Famous Hugo Grotius', in Henning Graf Reventlow and Benjamin Uffenheimer (eds.),
*Creative Biblical Exegesis: Christian and Jewish Hermeneutics through
the Centuries* (JSOTSup, 59; Sheffield: Sheffield Academic Press, 1988),
pp. 175-91.

Ryken, Leland, James C. Wilhoit and Tremper Longman III (eds.), *Dictionary of Biblical Imagery* (Downers Grove, IL: InterVarsity Press, 1998).

Schroer, Silvia, and Thomas Staubli, *Body Symbolism in the Bible* (trans.
Linda M. Maloney; Collegeville, MN: Liturgical Press, 2001).

Strola, Germana, 'Il desiderio autentico descritto attraverso un antonimo
ovvero: [e massime sul pigro nel libro dei Proverbi', *RivistB* 53 (2005),
pp. 3-30.

Toy, Crawford H., *A Critical and Exegetical Commentary on the Book of
Proverbs* (ICC; Edinburgh: T. & T. Clark, 1904).

Vaux, Roland de, *Ancient Israel: Its Life and Institutions* (trans. John
McHugh; London: Darton, Longman & Todd, 1961).

Viviano, Pauline A., 'Glory Lost: The Reign of Solomon in the Deuteronomistic History', in Lowell K. Handy (ed.), *The Age of Solomon: Scholarship at the Turn of the Millennium* (Leiden: Brill, 1997), pp. 336-47.

Waltke, Bruce K., *The Book of Proverbs: Chapters 1–15* (NICOT; Grand
Rapids: Eerdmans, 2004).

Weinfeld, Moshe, *Deuteronomy and the Deuteronomic School* (Oxford:
Oxford University Press, 1972).

Complementary Readings

Aletti, J.-N., 'Séduction et parole en Proverbes i–ix', *VT* 27 (1977), pp. 129-
44.

Alter, Robert, *The Art of Biblical Poetry* (New York: Basic Books, 1985).

Blenkinsopp, Joseph, 'The Social Context of the "Outsider Woman" in Proverbs 1–9', *Bib* 72 (1991), pp. 457-73.

Camp, Claudia V., *Wisdom and the Feminine in the Book of Proverbs* (Bible and Literature Series, 11; Sheffield: Almond Press, 1985).

Clements, Ronald E., 'The Good Neighbour in the Book of Proverbs', in Heather A. McKay and David J.A. Clines (eds.), *Of Prophets' Visions and the Wisdom of Sages: Essays in Honour of R. Norman Whybray on his Seventieth Birthday* (JSOTSup, 162; Sheffield: Sheffield Academic Press, 1993), pp. 209-28.

Crenshaw, James L., *Education in Ancient Israel: Across the Deadening Silence* (New York: Doubleday, 1998).

Estes, Daniel J., *Hear, my Son: Teaching and Learning in Proverbs 1–9* (New Studies in Biblical Theology, 4; Leicester: Inter-Varsity Press, 1997).

Gammie, John J., and Leo G. Perdue (eds.), *The Sage in Israel and the Ancient Near East* (Winona Lake, IN: Eisenbrauns, 1990).

Habel, Norman C., 'The Symbolism of Wisdom in Proverbs 1–9', *Int* 26 (1972), pp. 131-57.

McCreesh, Thomas P., 'Wisdom as Wife: Proverbs 31:10-31', *RB* 92 (1985), pp. 25-46.

Moss, Alan, 'Wisdom as Parental Teaching in Proverbs 1–9', *HeyJ* 38 (1997), pp. 426-39.

Perdue, Leo G., *Wisdom and Creation* (Nashville: Abingdon Press, 1994).

—*Wisdom Literature: A Theological History* (Louisville, KY: Westminster/ John Knox Press, 2007).

Van Leeuwen, Raymond C., 'Liminality and Worldview in Proverbs 1–9', *Semeia* 50 (1990), pp. 111-44.

Waltke, Bruce K., *The Book of Proverbs: Chapters 15–31* (NICOT; Grand Rapids: Eerdmans, 2005).

Washington, Harold C., 'The Strange Woman (נכרי/זרה אשה) of Proverbs 1–9 and Post-Exilic Judaean Society', in Tamara C. Eskenazi and Kent H. Richards (eds.), *Second Temple Studies*. II. *Temple and Community in the Persian Period* (Sheffield: Sheffield Academic Press, 1994), pp. 217-42.

Whybray, Roger Norman, 'City Life in Proverbs 1–9', in Anja A. Diesel, Eckart Otto and Reinhard G. Lehmann (eds.), *'Jedes Ding hat seine Zeit…': Diethelm Michel zum 65. Geburtstag* (BZAW, 241; Berlin: W. de Gruyter, 1996), pp. 243-50.

Index of Biblical References

Old Testament

Index of Authors

Lightning Source UK Ltd.
Milton Keynes UK
UKOW05f2215280118
316864UK00016BA/184/P